ROMAN
ITALY

ROMAN
ITALY
T. W. Potter

British Museum Publications Limited

FOR
SANDRA AND SIMON

© 1987 Timothy Potter

Published by British Museum Publications
46 Bloomsbury Street, London WC1B 3QQ

British Library Cataloguing in Publication Data
Potter, T. W.
Roman Italy.—(Exploring the Roman World)
1. Excavations (Archaeology)—Italy
2. Italy—Antiquities, Roman
I. Title   II. Series
937   DG77

ISBN 0-7141-2042-1

Designed by Harry Green

Set in Palatino by Southern Positives
and Negatives (SPAN), Lingfield, Surrey
and printed in Great Britain by
Butler & Tanner Ltd, Frome, Somerset.

Half-title page Sestertius of Nerva, issued in
AD 97, commemorating the abolition of the
tax levied on Italian towns to pay for the
Imperial post.

Title page View down the west side of the Piazzale
delle Corporazioni at Ostia, with the mosaic
emblems of the shippers.

CONTENTS

ACKNOWLEDGEMENTS

This book has been shaped over many years of excavation, fieldwork and travel in Italy, and also in other parts of the Mediterranean, especially Algeria. I am fortunate that this has brought me into contact with a great number of archaeologists and historians, so that many of the themes discussed here have been issues raised in debate, formal and informal, on all sorts of occasions. My debt to these scholars is therefore huge, and particularly to successive directors, the staff and generations of students and visitors at the British School at Rome. The influence of the late John Ward-Perkins will, in particular, be apparent on very many pages, for it was under his wise tutelage that I was introduced to the fascinations of Italian archaeology. I also owe a considerable debt to his successor, David Whitehouse, a pioneer in the rise of medieval archaeology in the Mediterranean; and to the present director, Graeme Barker, who is no less an innovator in the study of the peninsula's prehistoric landscapes.

I am particularly fortunate to have received the help and encouragement of very many fine Italian scholars. Not the least have been the numerous Superintendents of Antiquities, and their inspectors, who have in one way or another aided the archaeological ventures with which I have been concerned; and, amongst many, Andrea Carandini and his colleagues, who are doing so much to change the face of Roman archaeology in Italy. Practical considerations preclude the individual acknowledgement of this great host of Italian scholars; or, indeed, of those in Britain, France and elsewhere who have, at one time or another, interested themselves in, and advised upon, my projects. But they are all most warmly remembered. Equally, it is a pleasure to recall my former colleagues and students at the University of Lancaster, where much of my early work was debated and written up (and the source of a first-class digging team); the Open

University, for whom I made a short television film on Augustan Italy; and now the lively and informed forum that my present illustrious institution, the British Museum, provides, to the benefit of resident and visiting scholars alike. I am particularly grateful to the British Museum for supporting my various Mediterranean ventures in innumerable ways.

While I must couch most of my debts of gratitude only in general terms, I owe specific and very warm thanks to Catherine Johns, both for advising me on my text and for a huge amount of help with this series as a whole; and to Roger Wilson, for a minute scrutiny of a draft, to the book's great advantage. Naturally, what appears here is my responsibility, but I profoundly appreciate their good counsel and wise learning. My thanks are due also to Tony King and Simon Keay (with Catherine Johns and Roger Wilson, authors of future volumes in the series) for their most helpful comments; and to several individuals, listed elsewhere, for providing photographic illustrations. Finally, I would like to make clear my warmest appreciation of the efforts of those at British Museum Publications, and especially the hard work, steadfast support and sheer good cheer of Celia Clear and Jenny Chattington.

But my greatest debt of gratitude of all goes to my wife, Sandra, for her patience, remarkable fortitude, constructive criticism and, above all, for her encouragement. It is wholly fitting that this book is dedicated to her – and to our very small son, Simon, who arrived in the world almost as the last words were being written – with all my love.

TIM POTTER

INTRODUCTION

When I once asked a colleague why there had been no general survey of Roman Italy, he shrugged his shoulders and replied, 'syntheses are dangerous!' He was, of course, right and this could well explain why no-one has hitherto attempted the task. Syntheses are never easy and, for Italy, the wealth of evidence — from literary sources, inscriptions and archaeology — is such that the task of welding it all together is, to say the least, daunting.

So, we must ask, 'why attempt it?', a question to which there are several answers. At the root of it is the fact that the story of Roman Italy is totally fascinating, especially when seen not just as a part (for example, the period of the Republic), but as a whole. Many volumes have the legitimate but irritating habit of stopping or starting in the middle, usually with the reign of the first emperor, Augustus. This was, it is true, a watershed, but equally it does seem to leave the story firmly in mid-stream. Secondly, the more archaeological accounts have tended to view Roman Italy very much through the sites of Pompeii, Herculaneum, Ostia and Rome; all, to be sure, immensely important and interesting sites, but hardly to be regarded as typical of the country as a whole. I well remember, a long time ago, stumbling across the delightful Roman theatre in the charming town of Lecce, in the far south-east of Italy; its very existence had passed me by, and I felt then that there should have been a book to hand that would help me pursue my favourite Romans. Then, thirdly, there has been the recent renaissance in Roman studies in Italy, currently symbolised by new exploration in the very heart of Rome itself, on the site of the Roman Forum.

This current fashion for Roman archaeology in Italy is an interesting phenomenon. To many eyes the Roman achievement has always been vastly inferior to that of the Greeks, and a much less worthy area of investigation.

This view is still strongly defended, although with less resolution than before. Moreover, in the days of fascism Roman studies had been sadly manipulated to modern political ends. As D. H. Lawrence observed in his evocative book, *Etruscan Places*, published in 1932: 'The Fascists . . . consider themselves in all things Roman, Roman of the Caesars, heirs of Empire and world power.' Lawrence had little time for things Roman, and we can hardly doubt that his views were highly coloured by the prevailing political climate of the time.[1]

In the intermediate post-war years Roman archaeology to some extent waned, arguably the influence of changed political circumstances. A precisely similar circumstance can today be seen in the North African countries which were, until recently, under foreign sway. In the late nineteenth century, for instance, the French consciously thought of themselves as the heirs to Roman colonial power; as J. Toutain wrote: 'the better that is understood the work that the Romans accomplished in their African provinces, then the better we can direct our efforts and more rapidly ensure success'.[2] No wonder that 'native' and Islamic archaeology are now so much in vogue, at the expense of Roman studies.

The revival of Roman archaeology in Italy has come about for many reasons. One of them must be the growth of so-called 'landscape archaeology', which attempts to study not just individual sites but the entire landscape in which they are set. Aerial photography, particularly from the war-years, has here played an important role, but still more influential have been programmes of field-survey: the systemic walking over the ground, recording whatever is apparent, whether standing monuments or buried sites disclosed by ploughing. The first major programme was in southern Etruria, a project prompted by schemes of land reform which at once revealed, but at the same time destroyed, huge numbers of archaeological sites. This was the logical extention of the on-going *Forma Italiae* series (which have as their aim the systematic and detailed archaeological record of the country's different regions), and presaged a host of similar projects up and down the peninsula, many of them still in progress.[3]

'Rescue archaeology' — the investigation of sites being obliterated by modern development — is now well established in Italy; but it has been a series of influential excavations, conducted primarily for reasons of research, that has most promoted the cause of Roman archaeology. Not the least of these was the meticulous examination of two adjacent villas at Francolise, in Campania, between 1962 and 1965, an investigation which set entirely new standards of scientific excavation of this sort of site in Italy.[4] Still more significant was the great programme, launched in 1975, to explore the finely preserved villa at Settefinestre, near the small Roman town of Cosa, about 160 kilometres to the north-west of Rome.[5]

The Settefinestre project was to prove a landmark in innumerable ways. Apart from the excavation itself, which yielded spectacular results, there was also a follow-up campaign of field-survey and smaller-scale excavation. This had the initial aim of setting the site in its broader context, but soon developed wider objectives. All this was explained in a fine exhibition held at nearby Orbetello in 1985 on 'The Romanisation of Etruria' – just one of a series of regional displays devoted to the Etruscans and their land and culture.[6] The interpretation of the villa's history has proved more controversial, not least because of the way that it has been linked to a 'Marxist' view of the decline of 'capitalist' enterprises. Explanations of this sort, closely linked with the concept of 'social evolution', are currently much in vogue in Italian studies – in contrast to Britain, where economies and economics are all the rage.[7] It all makes for a fascinating *pot-pourri* of views: a debate that is never still and never dull, and is constantly heightened as new evidence floods forth.[8]

We shall have much to say about the history of the countryside in Italy, and of the many recent archaeological projects that have served to cast light upon its development. But what of the towns? Urban archaeology is an area of investigation that has now been greatly refined and extended, and not least in Italy. In the early post-war years several highly important excavations were initiated: from 1949 at Alba Fucens, a beautiful, now deserted site of a Roman town, high in the central Apennine Mountains; from 1962 at the site of Ordona, in Apulia; and from 1948 at the picturesque Roman colony of Cosa, not far from the Settefinestre villa – to name but a few. The work at Cosa, by the American Academy in Rome, has been particularly influential, since it opened a window upon a fairly ordinary urban community, created in 273 BC in what was then frontier country.[9] Hand-in-hand with continued investigation of Pompeii and Herculaneum, with their astonishing insight into life in the ancient world, we can now begin to say much more about the layout of Roman towns.

Two other urban investigations should be singled out. One is the Baths of the Swimmer at Ostia where work in the 1960s concentrated upon a meticulous examination of successive layers and their contents (by the same Italian team that investigated the Settefinestre villa). Particular attention was paid to the pottery, in terms both of quantity and of its country of origin. This led to some interesting propositions about the growth and, later, the decline of the Italian economy in Roman times. Such views did not always command consensus, for it was rightly pointed out that the sample came from one small part of just one town – which, as Rome's harbour, was probably not very typical of Italy as a whole anyway.[10] That debate continues fiercely; but it has contributed to the growth of highly important work on artefacts. As our understanding increases about their date, area of manufacture and, in the case of containers, what their contents may have been, so archaeologists are more and more using this information to attempt to reconstruct the patterns of ancient trade. The study of the cargoes of shipwrecks all over the Mediterranean has here proved crucial: a difficult and dangerous task, but one that is continually coming up with new and highly significant information.[11]

Rescue excavation in progress in the Via A. Milano, in the heart of Roman and medieval Brescia. Archaeological work in historic centres of Italian towns is becoming increasingly commonplace.

Rigorous study of the artefacts from another major urban excavation, that of Luni, in north-western Italy, has also provided a wealth of precious data. But the site has proved significant for quite different reasons. Carefully conducted work on the late Roman and early medieval levels has begun to tell us much about the decline of what was once a highly prosperous city, where its burghers made fortunes out of the nearby marble deposits of Carrara. 'Interfaces' in history, where one epoch gives way to another, have always had a particular fascination, and indeed an importance for one's own age: the investigations at Luni have yielded much of relevance and it is both telling and proper that study of the transition from the late Roman to the medieval world has now become the target of many other excavations.[12]

The principal theme of this book, therefore, is to attempt to set some of this new archaeological knowledge against the backdrop evolved over a long period of time by historians of the ancient world. History plays a bigger part than I had first intended, but I found that to deny my narrative a historical framework robbed it of a cohesion that is essential to the story. Equally, I discovered that my limits, both geographical and chronological, had to be wide. Sicily, Sardinia, Corsica and the other islands close to Italy I have excluded; but I have otherwise treated Roman Italy as being much the same as modern Italy, and have ventured further afield whenever it has seemed necessary. Similarly, I have found it helpful on occasion to stray as far back as the Bronze Age and as far forward as the tenth century AD in pursuing my theme, given that so many sites originated well before Roman times and very often remain in occupation down to the present day.

Names have provided something of a problem. I find it a rather exasperating feature of some books that they use only the Roman name for a place that is today large and well known: consequently, I have tended to use place-names in current usage, referring only to the ancient name if it has seemed desirable. I cannot claim total consistency, but I have given both in a list of sites that, I suggest, well merit a visit (see the Gazetteer).

Indeed, in writing this book I have had various sorts of reader in mind. Many, I hope, will have visited the British Museum as interested lay-people, and I have deliberately chosen a considerable number of the illustrations from our own collections, rather than from those of Italian museums. Largely assembled in the later eighteenth and nineteenth centuries, they provide a taste of Roman culture, a preparation for the feast that lies within Italy itself. Moreover, I have assumed little prior knowledge of Italian history, geography or archaeology, in the belief that a book of this sort should be comprehensible in its own right. At the same time, I know from some of my colleagues who have been kind enough to peruse the typescript that a good deal of what I say is unfamiliar, and opens the way for a still more extended dialogue between the Roman archaeology of Italy and that of the northern provinces of the Empire. For that reason I have provided a quite considerable bibliography and a system of references which will help both the student and the specialist to find their way around the literature. Here I have tended to favour works in English, although by no means exclusively.

Twenty years' involvement in Italian archaeology have taught me a good deal but, even so, I found that some of my conclusions advanced here surprised me. For instance, the Imperial period turned out to be a much more exciting episode, both archaeologically and historically, than I had previously believed. Something of all this will, I hope, emerge from these pages. Too much is happening in Roman archaeology in Italy for it to be anything more than an interim statement; but it may help point the way. Syntheses *are* dangerous, but at times they must be attempted.

It remains to add an important postscript. As these words are being written, three other companion volumes are in preparation: *Roman Gaul and Germany*, *Roman Spain* and *Roman North Africa*. Other books are planned. A diversity of authors will ensure a variety of approaches to these very different regions of the Roman world; but in prospect is a novel look at this critical period of history, as it appears to scholars brought up upon a fresh mix of archaeology and history. It seems fitting that the British Museum, one of the early international institutions of the modern age, should take this task under its umbrella: for lay-person and scholar alike there should be an archaeological feast in store.

−1−

THE LAND

After the foothills of the Alps comes the beginning of what is now Italy...
One might guess that it was because of their prosperity that the people who were the first to be named Italians imparted their name to the neighbouring peoples.[1]

These words of Strabo, introducing his readers to the country of Italy, were written around the time of the emperor Augustus (27 BC–AD 14). Today Italy is still a highly prosperous country, a point that is readily borne out by the magnificent network of motorways which carry one with almost effortless ease to nearly every part of the long peninsula. Roman Italy was also a country of fine roads, a triumph of engineering and planning which inspire as much admiration as their modern counterparts. Yet once off the beaten track, whether today or in antiquity, matters are rather different. Anyone who has travelled the long overland miles from Naples to Reggio di Calabria, opposite Sicily, in the days before the opening of the present *autostrada*, will recall the wearing and never-ending sequence of hair-pin bends through the mountains. Getting round the remoter parts of Italy can still be a slow and difficult business, even in good weather. Once winter conditions prevail, it can become dangerous or impossible, splitting Italy off into distinct regions, which constitute one of the country's most indelible characteristics.

Strabo takes his readers on a geographical tour of Italy in the age of the first emperor, Augustus, and we shall do the same. One of his purposes was to identify the many different tribal and ethnic groups that made up the peninsula's cosmopolitan population. Today everyone speaks Italian (although there are some remarkable variations in dialect), but the regional differences are nevertheless still very apparent. In large part they are due to geography, a point that we must stress more fully than Strabo. Anyone entering Italy from the north, whence so many of her invaders have come,[2]

Map showing the Augustan regional divisions, together with the sites and areas mentioned in chapter 1.

will retain a vivid memory of the great barrier of the Alps. They form a seemingly impassable obstacle, particularly when seen from the south, where the mountain slopes are steeper and apparently unbroken. In fact, passage along corridors like the Brenner and the Great St Bernard is easier than might at first appear, especially during the summer months, and transalpine travel extends back into deepest prehistory.[3] Even so, the perils of Alpine journeys made a vivid impression upon some ancient travellers; thus Strabo describing part of the St Bernard crossing: 'If one made even a slight mis-step out of the road, the danger was one from which there was no escape, since the fall reached to chasms abysmal. And at some places the road there is so narrow that it brings dizziness to all who travel it afoot – not only to men, but also to all beasts of burden that are unfamiliar with it.'[4]

Nevertheless, of greater consequence in Italy's history is the massive belt of the Apennine Mountains. Beginning in the far north-west, and rising steeply behind coastal cities like the port of Genoa, the Apennines stretch down the peninsula for a distance of nearly one thousand kilometres. Gaunt and limestone-white, they can rise to a great height: nearly 3,000 metres in the Gran Sasso, to the north of L'Aquila; 2,793 metres in the Maiella, the great massif which forms a backdrop to Ovid's home town of Sulmona. They are also broad: fifty kilometres across in places, elsewhere closer to one hundred kilometres. Straightaway, then, we must distinguish between a mountain culture, bred in rugged terrain where life can be far from easy, and settlement on the lowlands and plains, Italy's most prosperous regions.

Passage across the Apennine Mountains is seldom without difficulties even today. For example, the traveller who drives westwards from the celebrated upland town of Urbino across to the Tiber Valley at Sansepolcro, and thence to Arezzo, has to negotiate long stretches of steep climbs, long descents and innumerable tortuous bends. In winter the road can be impassable, like many routes across the Apennines. Even the determined Hannibal had to give up crossing the mountains in 218 BC, because of the heavy snow.[5] But the Apennines not only impede traffic: they also isolate districts and communities, creating a tension between hill-dwellers and peoples of the plains and separating off different regions. One of the themes that is most prevalent throughout Italian history (and, no doubt, prehistory too) is the antagonism between mountain-folk and their lowland counter-parts. Whether it was a full-scale war, as between the Romans and the Samnites, or just interference by one side or another, the divide is the same. This must be the story behind an inscription put up over the north gate of the hill-town of Saepinum, near Altilia, high in the Abruzzi, about AD 170. The townsfolk had evidently been interferring with the passage of flocks of sheep moving from one area of pasture to another which, no doubt very inconveniently, meant that huge numbers of animals passed right through the civic centre. On the inscription the magistrates are firmly instructed to 'abstain from committing outrages on the contractors for the sheep flocks . . . lest it may be necessary that there should be a judicial investigation about this'.[6]

Many mountain communities still remain very isolated. One has only to visit some of the long, enclosed valleys which cut their way to the Adriatic Sea down the eastern flank of the Apennines in central Italy to appreciate the point. Moreover, here the mountains stretch almost to the sea, leaving only small strips and pockets of flatter land along the coast and at the mouths of the rivers. Despite the emergence of some large towns, like Ancona and Pescara, this region was never destined to play much of a formative role in Italy's history.

The Boiano Gate, built in AD 4, at the town of Saepinium, high in the Apennine Mountains. The streets lead to the forum, at the centre of the town.

Within the Apennines, however, the topography does vary very considerably. There are upland lakes and basins which, once drained, can provide fertile land. One such is the former Fucine Lake, a great flat plain with the town of Avezzano at one end; 700 metres up, and surrounded by mountains that rise another 1,000 metres or more, one stumbles upon it with some surprise while driving eastwards from Rome. We shall see later how in Claudius' day the Romans tried to drain it, just as they worked hard to manage the rich, hill-girt flatlands that stretch northwards from Rieti. Nevertheless, most of the mountains, except for some of the valleys, are not suited to arable cultivation; above all, once the woodland is cleared, they provide pasture for grazing, an economic fact of life which, in Italy, is as old as farming itself.[7] Even the high Gran Sasso and the Maiella play their part. Since time immemorial, once the winter snows have melted in May, the shepherds have taken their flocks up to the mountains to graze upon the fresh grass, away from the arid lowlands. This transhumance can be on an enormous scale. An English traveller, writing in the 1830s, describes flocks 'plodding across the valley of Abruzzo, as far as the eye can see', while, on the plain of L'Aquila, they 'slowly passed by the carriage for a space of a mile or more'.[8]

The conflict between the demands of the lowland shepherd and the upland farmer, with his sparse resources, will be apparent from the Saepinum inscription that we mentioned earlier. Indeed, mountain and plain still remain in opposition, underlining the immense difficulties that Rome faced in attempting to bring unity and control to the Italian peninsula: it was no accident that during the Social War of 91–88 BC, when an Italian federation attempted to topple Rome from her perch, the rebel headquarters lay at Corfinio – ancient Corfinium, briefly renamed Italia – high in the Abruzzi sheep-country near the Gran Sasso.

It is appropriate to give space to the Apennines, for they have played a central role in Italy's long history. Even the dramatically engineered modern *autostrade* have tamed, but not conquered, these massive impedimenta to communications. But we must now turn our attention to the lowlands that stand in such sharp contrast with the country's lofty backbone. Pliny, who included a long account of Italy in his *Natural History*, took as his basis the eleven administrative regions that were created in the reign of the emperor Augustus.[9] Pliny compared Italy with the shape of an oak leaf, 'being far longer than it is broad'.[10] The analogy may not seem botanically exact, but it shrewdly picked out Italy's geographical advantage, being an immensely long finger of land, jutting out into the Mediterranean, where, given the right circumstances, it could take a central role. But what was needed was a richness of resources that could be manipulated in the country's favour: here the lowlands were to be of critical importance.

The area that was most transformed by the Roman state was the flatlands of the Po Plain, in northern Italy. Known until 42 BC as Cisalpine Gaul, the name harks back to the incursions of Gallic warriors from the Celtic world to the north-west of the Alps in the late fifth and fourth centuries BC.[11] Indeed, contemporary place-names, like that of the town of Senigallia, north-west of Ancona on the Adriatic, still bear witness to these invasions. Under Augustus the north was divided up into four regions. Regio VIII (Gallia Cispadana, modern Emilia) included a series of rich towns, mostly Roman foundations, along the edge of the Po Plain. This productive landscape, where, in Pliny's words, 'the Po deposits its spoil… [and] … bestows bounteous fertility',[12] was largely drained and brought under control by Roman engineers, enabling the cultivation of huge quantities of wheat, millet (a fodder crop now mainly replaced by maize) and also vines.[13] There was in addition good grazing for sheep in the nearby mountains (Modena and

Parma were both noted for their wool trade), so that the region as a whole prospered hugely in Roman times. Indeed, most of the Emilian Roman towns, such as Bologna, remain today as thriving and affluent centres.

Regio IX, Liguria, encompassed the north-west stretch of the Apennines, which remained fairly backward. But the flatlands between the northern flanks of the mountains and the Po did develop rapidly with, as the most successful urban foundation, Turin (ancient Augusta Taurinorum). Genoa, first settled still earlier, became a major port: wood for table-making (very costly items in antiquity) was taken there for export, 'as well as flocks, hides and honey ... [The people] ... receive a return cargo of olive-oil and Italian wine: The little wine that they have in their country is mixed with pitch, and harsh' – in other words, resinated wine like Greek retsina.[14]

Regio X was a huge area, stretching up through the Veneto and into the Austrian Alps. As today, this was a rich and fertile region, with as its principal river the Adige. Venice was not to emerge as a major urban centre until post-Roman times; but it was the successor to a series of important ports along the north and north-western coast of the Adriatic. Of the once rich and celebrated city of Spina, probably an Etruscan foundation which lies near modern Comacchio, little visible trace remains. But Ravenna, now completely land-locked, was an important harbour in Imperial times, while Aquileia, some thirty kilometres to the north-west of Trieste, was once one of the most populous cities of Roman Italy. Today there is a mere village, stranded in a plain created from upland silts washed down by the rivers; but in its time it was a great emporium, athrong with traders, just like contemporary Trieste. Many Roman cities of the north survived the upheavals of the Middle Ages, but not all.

Then there is the far north-west, known in antiquity as Regio XI, Gallia Transpadana, with its lakes, Alpine mountains and, for its southern fringe, some of the Po Valley. Today partly Piedmont, partly Lombardy (from the Germanic tribesmen who invaded Italy in AD 568), here grew major Roman frontier towns, strongly fortified, such as Aosta and Ivrea; and places like Como, home of Pliny, who was born there about AD 23, and of his even more famous nephew, Pliny the Younger. Many of the streets still follow the Roman grid in this attractive lakeside town, which was noted for its ironwork. 'I wonder how our darling Comum is looking?' wrote Pliny the Younger in a wistful letter to his friend, Caninius Rufus. 'And your lovely house outside the town, with its colonnade, where it is always springtime, and the shady plane trees, the stream with its sparkling greenish water flowing into the lake below, and the drive over the smooth firm turf.'[15]

Pliny was a senator and a rich landowner, with at least three villa estates on the shores of Lake Como, a house on the Esquiline Hill in Rome, a villa at Laurentium near Ostia, and a further estate at Tifernum, modern Città di Castello, in the Tiber Valley south of Sansepolcro. This was quite normal for a senator, or other high-placed person, whose life was exceedingly peripatetic.[16] We can imagine him setting off from Como, first to Milan and

Piacenza, then down the Via Aemilia to Bologna and over the Apennines to Florence, a route that would be little different today. He would by now have arrived in Regio VII, the great volcanic belt of western-central Italy, modern Tuscany and northern Lazio, ancient Etruria.

We shall have more to say of Etruria, the homeland of one of Rome's early opponents, the Etruscans, in our next chapter. It was and still is a very favoured land. Its volcanic origin is immediately apparent from the sharp-pointed hills and ridges, and the lakes, large and small, which fill the mouths of extinct volcanoes. Some, like the Baccano crater, just twenty kilometres to the north of Rome, were drained in Roman times; but many more, such as Bracciano, Lago di Vico and Lake Bolsena, remain as small inland seas, well stocked with fish. Moreover, the volcanic soil is exceptionally fertile, particularly for vines, olives and cereals: these are even today often grown together, side by side in the same field, known in Italian as 'promiscuous cultivation'.

The volcanic stone can be easily cut by hand, making it an invaluable building material, and lending cities like Rome that warm brown shade to its edifices, major and minor. There is also travertine in the Tiber Valley and, in central Etruria, rich mineral deposits of copper and iron. These ores attracted Greek traders from as early as the eighth century BC, and help to explain how the Etruscan cities rapidly expanded in both size and prosperity. The towns of Roman Etruria, on the other hand, were not on the whole notably successful, particularly in the north. Many now lie abandoned, especially those in the vicinity of the coast, where malaria — still very prevalent as recently as D. H. Lawrence's day — was undoubtedly one factor that contributed to their desertion.[17] But there are exceptions. Arezzo was to become a major Roman industrial centre, whose pottery (the so-called 'Arretine') is found as far afield as India and England, while Civitavecchia, provided with a great harbour by the emperor Trajan in the early second century AD, was to become as busy a port as it is today.

We shall be looking in some detail at the history of the countryside in Etruria, particularly in the vicinity of Cosa, a Roman town close to modern Orbetello, and in the territory to the north of Rome. Rome itself will also frequently claim our attention. Just why it should have achieved such pre-eminence is a matter that continues to inspire debate and research; but its geographical advantages were as obvious in antiquity as they are today. Built beside a river that, in its lower reaches, was thoroughly navigable, it also enjoyed an axial position within the peninsula; it would be hard to find a more logical site.[18] Moreover, it lay close to the natural eastern corridor into the interior, up the Aniene Valley, a route that had been used for millennia before Rome became a city. It is, perhaps, too easy to apply retrospective geographical logic to the emergence of the site as a 'central place', to employ modern jargon; but, in terms of topography, it is not difficult to understand why Rome became so important.[19]

To the south of Rome lay Regio I, Latium and Campania. Latium, the more northerly, was the homeland of the Latin tribes, which were forced into alliance with Rome at an early stage of their history. Many of the more prominent cities lay in the country of the Alban Hills, the volcanic belt that overlooks the wide, drab coastal plain bordering the Tyrrhenian Sea: these were positions with strong natural defences, usually enhanced with stout masonry walls. Two ancient routes headed south from Rome, both still in existence, albeit in modified form. The older was the Via Latina, which ran down the valley of the River Sacco, through Latin territory. It then entered the Liri Valley, eventually to arrive in the fertile Campania countryside to the north of Naples. The other was the Via Appia, which took a course across the marshy coastal flatlands not far from the Tyrrhenian Sea, down to the town of Terracina. It then cut across the Gaeta Peninsula (where there are still substantial traces of the old Via Appia beside the modern road), joining the Via Latina at Capua. This was ancient Casilinum, a town that was to become the heir to nearby Roman Capua, a city of great pre-eminence but now the site of what was until recently a mere village, S. Maria di Capua Vetere.

These journeys take us into Italy's *Mezzogiorno* or South, a region with a long history of poverty. In Roman times, however, matters were very different. Campania – the rich volcanic terrain that stretches from the Sorrento Peninsula in the south to the Garigliano River in the north – was in antiquity regarded as one of Italy's most favoured areas.[20] Pliny the Elder (who met his death in the eruption of Vesuvius in AD 79 which engulfed Pompeii and Herculaneum) was amongst many ancient writers to extol its virtues, particularly its 'vine-clad hills with their glorious wine and drinking festivals, famous all the world over'.[21] It became, indeed, a great holiday resort, much favoured by emperors and the very rich. Tiberius, for example, built a great house, the Villa Jovis, in a cliff-girt position on the island of Capri. He was eventually to retire there, where, according to Suetonius (a not very trustworthy source), 'they still show you the place where Tiberius used to watch his victims being thrown into the sea after prolonged and exquisite torture'.[22]

Traces of some of these great 'maritime villas' still survive on the ground today, while their ornate and affluent appearance is evident from pictures of them on the walls of houses in places like Pompeii. The wealth derived above all from Campania's highly fertile land, which yielded not only highly praised wines, but also excellent olive-oil and abundant cereals. Moreover, Pozzuoli – ancient Puteoli, to the west of Naples – was Italy's major port until eventually eclipsed by Ostia in the second century AD; this was where the grain fleet from Alexandria in Egypt arrived, together with a host of other goods. Campania, therefore, had every reason to prosper in antiquity.

The earliest towns in Campania, as along the coasts of other parts of south and south-western Italy, were mainly founded by settlers from Greece. The main thrust of this colonising movement took place in the eighth to sixth centuries BC, introducing a great wave of new ideas and fashions. Many of these towns developed into internationally important centres, both economically and intellectually, so that the Greek areas of south Italy came to be known as Magna Graecia. As Pliny remarked (a man not noted for his pro-Hellenic views): 'The Greeks themselves, a people most prone to gushing self-praise, have pronounced sentence on the land [of southern Italy] by conferring upon it ... the title of Great Greece.'[23]

South of Campania, however, the landscape changes dramatically. This was Augustan Regio III, ancient Lucania and Bruttium, roughly equivalent to modern Basilicata and Calabria. Here we are once more in mountainous terrain, the south-western extension of the Apennines. It is a country of high peaks and remote tangled valleys, so that even today many of the settlements seem isolated and cut off. There are echoes of this in Strabo's description of the region,[24] and it is no accident that for the most part he takes his reader on a voyage along the coast, for, where the mountains do not come down to touch the sea, there are just a few places where the upland is fringed with a narrow coastal plain. One such is Reggio di Calabria, the Greek town of Rhegion which, together with Messina, was founded to control passage through the straits between peninsular Italy and Sicily. Both towns were in existence by 700 BC and have remained as important centres down to this day.[25]

Other Greek cities of Italy's south-western peninsula have fared less well. Paestum and Velia remain as attractive ruins, Locri was destroyed by the Saracens, and Hipponion has given way to Vibo Valentia. But none met its end so dramatically as Sybaris, which was obliterated about 510 BC when the people of neighbouring Croton are supposed to have diverted the River Crati so that it covered the site.[26] Neither of Sybaris' successors, Thurii and Copia, survived into the Middle Ages, for reasons that topography makes clear. The successive cities lay towards the head of a triangular flood plain that stretches back twenty kilometres from the coast, in the western corner of Italy's 'instep', the Ionian Sea. However fertile the land, flood prevention was always a problem, and recent work has shown that the most ancient Greek settlement now lies buried a full three metres below sea-level – recovering these remains is an archaeologist's nightmare.[27]

Further up the instep there were other major Greek cities. To the north-west lie more of the Lucanian Mountains, drained by a series of great river valleys, including the Basento and the Bradano, which form great corridors into the interior. It was at the mouths of these valleys that the early Greek colonists chose to lay out their cities: places like now-abandoned Heraclea (near modern Policoro), Metaponto and, above all, Taranto. Strabo is continually at pains to stress Italy's poverty in harbours (as any Greek might, coming from a world with safe anchorages everywhere); but Taranto, together with Brindisi, are major exceptions. Both have fine and sheltered ports which, if prone to silt up (the great entrances to Taranto's land-locked 'Mare Piccolo', a lagoon eight kilometres across, are comparatively modern features), nevertheless provide excellent facilities for shipping. Taranto, founded by Sparta in 706 BC, was to become one of the most important cities of Italy before Rome conquered the peninsula, with a rich agricultural and industrial base and a far-flung trading network. When Brindisi was opened up by the Romans as a great mercantile centre, and (as today) as the port for ferries across to Corfu and Greece, Taranto's importance declined; but it continued to play a major role in Italy's history throughout medieval times and, as many British sailors know, into the modern age.

With Brindisi, however, we have moved into another Augustan Regio, II, that of Apulia and Italy's 'heel', the Salento Peninsula. Rather confusingly, this was known in antiquity as Calabria, now the name given to the south-west part of the peninsula. Apulia is a fascinating region. Writing of the Brindisi area, Strabo notes that the terrain 'appears rough', but, once ploughed, is found to be 'deep-soiled and, although rather lacking in water, is manifestly good for pasturage and for trees'.[28] Indeed, for Horace the region was *siticulosa* – 'parched Apulia' – a tag that is as apt as it is well known; for not only is the average rainfall very low, but there are geological difficulties too.[29] This is the consequence of a limestone crust, seamed by fissures which drain away the water with little benefit to the soil. As a result the landscape is better adapted to grazing than to arable cultivation, and the Apulian sheep flocks have always formed an essential element in the local economy, particularly in the same transhumance network of *tratturi* (drove-roads) that we described earlier. Even so, with the help of irrigation (the contemporary Apulian aqueduct, with 2,700 kilometres of channels, is the largest in the world) cereals and vines, as well as olives and almond trees, do well, and the appearance of much of today's countryside is fertile and prosperous.

Topographically, Apulia is a land of contrasts, as anyone who has travelled the *autostrada* from Naples to Taranto will know. After the long stretch through the rugged terrain of the Apennine Mountains, the contours of the landscape gradually become softer and more rounded, and cultivated fields increasingly frequent. Once down in the foothills, one has only to strike a short distance northwards to enter a huge, flat, treeless plain. It is known as the Tavoliere, 'the chessboard', a reference to the grid-like way in which the landscape is divided up. Superficially the Tavoliere resembles the Fenland of eastern England, but geologically the two regions are quite different. Whereas the Fens comprise a vast basin filled with peats and marine clays and silts, the Tavoliere is a great limestone plain. What they do share is the remarkable way in which the now buried traces of older buildings, settlements and field systems show up from the air, due to soil changes and differential growth in the crops. In the Tavoliere Plain a great many of the sites belong to the Neolithic period; but equally apparent are the farms, field boundaries, and even the pits and trenches for olive trees and rows of vines, of a highly organised Roman landscape.[30]

Some of the Tavoliere towns originated in Roman times. One such is Lucera; the town is perched upon a hill, 220 metres above the surrounding plain, and crowned by Frederick II's great castle, built in 1233. The capital, Foggia, is of much more modern aspect (although an old foundation), but in

The arch of the emperor Trajan at Ancona, built of Hymettos marble in AD 115. Trajan greatly improved the harbour, to which the steps descend.

the evening one still encounters long lines of carts, driven by the farmers, returning from the fields; they remind us that in the south it is a time-honoured tradition to work the land from the towns, one of the many features of daily life that divide the *Mezzogiorno* from the more northerly parts of the peninsula.[31]

Towering over the north-east part of the Tavoliere is a great limestone promontory, 1,000 metres or more in height, known as the Gargano. Still densely wooded, it forms that distinctive spur on the maps of Italy's eastern seaboard. It will play little part in our story, however, and is still difficult of access, as it was in Roman times. But we have diverged from the Naples to Bari *autostrada*, and must rejoin it at the south-eastern corner of the Tavoliere, near Canosa. Canosa is another ancient foundation, lying close to one of Apulia's major rivers, the Ofanto. It is built on a hill overlooking the valley, and prospered as a centre for wool production from as early as the third century BC. It also lay on the main road between Rome and Brindisi, and was something of a gateway to the long plateau that stretches down to the south-east, known as the Murge. This is fine, rolling countryside, bordered by long-established upland towns, often defensively situated, like Gravina, Altamura and Matera. Matera is particularly fascinating, for until quite recently upwards of 18,000 people lived in caves set into the sides of ravines. Similarly well known are the celebrated Apulian *trulli*, beehive houses made of rough, undressed stone, built without mortar. As one travels south-eastwards they become ever more frequent until, at places like Alberobello, they cluster together to form whole townships. We can hardly doubt that here is a building tradition that extends back far into prehistory.[32]

Apulia's coastline is low and flat and rather monotonous: a series of dull-seeming towns, many of them rapidly expanding in the modern age. Bari was only a small village in Roman times, but Brindisi, as we saw earlier, was an important place, and towns in the Salentine Peninsula, such as Lecce and Otranto, also became fairly affluent municipal centres. What is perhaps surprising is that the Greeks did not colonise this eastern seaboard, although their influence was nevertheless marked. Perhaps the local tribes made strong resistance for then, as now, Apulia retained its own peculiar individuality – a geographical identity which continues to be reflected by both the people and their settlements.

From Apulia we might travel north-westwards up the motorway that clings to the coast on its way to Pescara, Ancona and back to the Po Plain. Running into the mountains, in parallel lines, are the long valleys of Molise, natural corridors into the mountainous interior. We shall later see what recent archaeological investigation has to tell us about the effect of Roman colonisation of these still remote areas. But we may now rest from our geographical sketch of the peninsula, and start to people it with the amazingly diverse mosaic of tribes and city-states that emerged in the days before Roman domination. If in these few pages we have conveyed something of Italy's topographical diversity – and of the contemporary variation of culture and tradition – then that will be sufficient as a back-drop to the narrative and argument that will follow. It was not to be a simple story, for Italy is much too complex a country for that; but it is a very fascinating one.

FURTHER READING

The two principal ancient sources are Strabo's *Geography*, books 5 and 6, and Pliny the Elder's *Natural History*, book 3; both are available in the Loeb edition.

There are many fine works that introduce the geography, from both a modern and an ancient viewpoint. H. Nissen, *Italische Landeskunde* (two vols, 1883, 1902) remains essential, while very useful is M. Cary, *The geographic background of Greek and Roman history* (1949). The Admiralty Handbooks on Italy (1944, 1945) are a mine of statistical information, while D. S. Walker, *A geography of Italy* (1967) is a sound survey. G. W. W. Barker's *Landscape and society. Prehistoric central Italy* (1981) is a fascinating analysis of, amongst other things, transhumance; R. Thomsen, *The Italic regions from Augustus to the Lombard invasions* (1947) is essential for the history and location of the boundaries of the regions; and C. Delano-Smith, *Western Mediterranean Europe. A historical geography of Italy, Spain and southern France since the Neolithic* (1979) is an absorbing study. There are many outstanding regional surveys: M. W. Frederiksen's *Campania* (1984) is amongst the best.

The handiest set of maps are published by the Touring Club Italiano: *Atlante stradale d'Italia.* Vol. 1 *(Nord),* vol. 2 *(Centro),* vol. 3 *(Sud);* they are constantly being updated.

ROMANS, ETRUSCANS, GREEKS AND ITALIANS

The Latini at the outset were few in number and most of them would pay no attention to the Romans; but later on, struck with amazement at the prowess both of Romulus and of the kings who came after him, they all became subjects. And after the overthrow of the Aequi, the Volsci, the Hernici ... the Rutuli, the aborigines ... the Rhaeci, the Argyrusci and the Preferni, the whole country was called Latium.[1]

The peoples of the Italian peninsula who were eventually unified by Rome were immensely cosmopolitan. It has been estimated that at least forty different languages and dialects were being spoken in Italy in the fourth century BC, an astonishing diversity which clearly underlines the country's tendency to divide up into regional groups.[2] In a political sense many of these were fiercely inclined towards independence; at the same time, however, the diffusion of Hellenistic ideas, fashions and styles in the later centuries of the first millennium BC created a fascinating range of hybrid cultures. But it was only the unification brought about by Rome that initiated any sort of cultural uniformity and, with it, the use of a common language: Latin. Even so, many of the peoples retained something of their individual traditions well into Imperial times, so that in places like Naples Greek was still the *lingua franca* as late as the fifth and sixth centuries AD. Here, therefore, we shall set the scene by identifying the main ethnic and regional groups and by saying something of their history and culture.

The origins of Rome itself – and of the Romans – is a question that was as hotly debated in antiquity as it is today. The consensus amongst ancient writers was that the city was founded about the middle of the eighth century BC – in 753 according to Varro, who was writing very much later (about 47 BC).[3] Certainly the archaeological evidence confirms this as a period of considerable expansion; but there is still older material. This includes burials of the tenth to ninth centuries BC, as well as even earlier Bronze Age pottery, which suggests that the site was already by this time an important focus of settlement, exploiting its position on the River Tiber and close to the corridor into the mountainous interior, up the Aniene Valley.[4] By the beginning of the sixth century BC Rome was recognisably urban, with intermittent occupation over an area approaching 300 hectares; there were temples, sanctuaries and, in the area that was to become the site of the Forum, a great public square. The structures coincide chronologically with the reign of the Etruscan king Tarquinius Priscus, who, according to tradition, ruled from 616 to 579 BC; in antiquity he was credited as a great builder of public works. It is significant that there are inscriptions of this period in both archaic Latin and in Etruscan and a good deal of other evidence, material and literary, for close contacts with some Etruscan cities at this time.[5] Tarquin II, for example, commissioned a cult statue for a great temple to Jupiter from one Vulca, a sculptor from the nearby Etruscan city of Veii, and Etruscan influence in architecture, engineering and the arts appears to have been strong. On the other hand, Rome was no vassal of the Etruscans, but maintained a strong political independence. Although ethnically diverse – for instance, the acquisition of a strong Sabine element (echoed in the celebrated legend of the 'Rape of the Sabine women') – the population of Rome was basically Latin; that is, one of a group of settlements that extended across the plains to the east and south of Rome and into the Alban Hills – the region known as Latium. These Latini, who spoke an Indo-European tongue, have a firm archaeological context. It is known as the 'Latin culture' and archaeologists distinguish four main chronological phases.[6] In part these phases are seen as a progression and development from Bronze Age times, but it is also clear that there were substantial influences from outside which stimulated change, both in material terms and in ideas.

The first phase, known as the 'Final Bronze Age', dates roughly speaking to the eleventh and tenth centuries BC. The settlements were generally of modest size and, in numerical terms, were comparatively sparse; we cannot therefore envisage a particularly large population. Excavation of the cemeteries has shown that the dead were cremated and the ashes placed in urns, which often reproduced the form of an oval, timber-framed house; this marks the beginning of a long tradition in central Italy whereby, in architectural terms, the world of the living was perpetuated in the tombs of the dead. Normally, however, few goods were placed in the graves – although occasionally weapons are found – and archaeologists reconstruct this period as a time of few social divisions, whilst recognising that it can be very difficult to define a 'class structure' from the material remains.[7]

Around 900 BC, at the beginning of the early Iron Age, there were significant changes. Some tombs where the dead were not cremated but inhumed appear in the cemeteries, which suggests to some that a form of social differentiation had begun to emerge. At the same time the settlements were expanding in size, pointing to a growing population, and trading contacts were being set up with southern Etruria, across the Tiber, as well as with areas of Campania, well to the south. Phase II, therefore, marks the beginning of a period of momentous growth.

Around 770 BC, the start of phase III, there were still further changes. It is beyond doubt that the foundation of Greek colonies, especially Pithecusa on the island of Ischia in the Bay of Naples, was the major contributory factor. Greek traders came northwards in search of metals and other goods and as a result Greek objects, especially pottery vessels, start to appear in the graves of Latium and southern Etruria. Many of these pots were brightly painted and highly attractive, and local craftsmen soon began to make their own imitations of them. Before long some graves in the cemeteries become conspicuously richer than others; this is now generally interpreted as a sign of the way in which some individuals were achieving social pre-eminence, creating a new form of class structure. Then, from about 730 BC (the start of phase IVA), a well-defined aristocracy commanding immense wealth becomes apparent. It is manifested by a series of fabulously rich tombs, filled with fine imported goods, many of them brought in from the oriental world of the east Mediterranean: hence the period is known as the early Orientalising. Correspondingly rich tombs are also known from Etruria and Campania at this time, pointing to the development of an élite class all along the coastal strip of western-central Italy. Moreover, the artefacts further suggest that within this region there also came into being a group of highly talented specialist craftsmen who imitated and then evolved the styles of the imported objects: these artisans form, therefore, a further social class of importance. Similarly, there were important changes in agriculture, par-ticularly the widespread introduction of the cultivation of the vine. This, too, must be a Greek-inspired innovation, with all its immense implications for changes in social habits and customs: wine-drinking and production will be a constant theme in this book.[8]

Phase IVB, the so-called late Orientalising period, began about 640 BC. This marks the time when proper urban centres were being laid out – places like Gabii, Satricum (modern Conca), Lavinium and Rome itself. Domestic buildings were now being constructed with stone footings, and all the major centres had public buildings. Meanwhile, in the cemeteries tombs with multiple chambers came into fashion; they were undoubtedly designed for families, and show how the inheritance of wealth – and, no doubt, social position – had become well established. Moreover, olive cultivation was also initiated, another agricultural staple of the Mediterranean world which, like wine, will constantly recur in these pages.

This fourth archaeological period can thus be seen as a decisive time. Towns were by now widespread amongst the Latini and defences have been recognised at a number of them; they reflect the fact that, with an expanding population, competition for the best territory was by now inevitable. Before long a pecking-order was in formation, a league-table that in Latium Rome was soon to lead.

The massive east gate, built in limestone polygonal masonry, of the important early Latin town of Norba (modern Norma). The walls probably date to the first century BC.

A not dissimilar pattern can be traced in the area to the north of Rome, Etruria. Here there was at least one tribe with close linguistic and cultural ties with the Latini, namely the Faliscans; but the bulk of the population from Rome's northern boundary as far as Florence and the River Arno would have called themselves Etruscans. Some of the Etruscan towns and cities may have been first occupied, like Rome, in the latter phases of the Bronze Age; however, the great majority were created by peoples known archaeologically as the Villanovans. These Villanovan sites were settled mainly from the ninth century BC, and the main centres like Veii and Tarquinia are conspicuous both for their size and for the strength of their natural defences – river valleys or hilltops. Within the area of settlement there were very often a number of small dispersed nuclei, best regarded as villages, which were eventually to coalesce into a single centre. The cemeteries generally lay outside the line of the natural defences and display a clear pattern of evolution. During the ninth century (phase I) the corpse was cremated and the ashes placed in a distinctive type of funerary urn, covered with a lid, and accompanied by a few objects of bronze. In phase II (from *c.* 800 BC) inhumations began gradually to supersede the cremations, and the grave-goods became richer and more diverse. Soon afterwards the first objects of east Mediterranean origin appear in the tombs, indicating that, as in Latium, much wider markets with the Greek colonies to the south had been established. By phase III (*c.* 720 BC) these trading contacts had been enormously expanded, and conspicuous divisions between the very wealthy and the less wealthy burials had become manifest.[9]

This picture, which can be traced at many of the sites that were to become major Etruscan cities, is therefore a close match for the sequence in Latium – even though many of the local artefact types are rather different. During the

31

seventh century Etruria further mirrors Latium in that many of the large Villanovan settlements began to take on distinct urban characteristics: some instances of town defences, major public buildings, much more elaborate private houses and, linking town and country (and, eventually, one town with another), the beginnings of a proper road network, adapted to wheeled transport. At the same time chamber tombs appear in the cemeteries. These were furnished with fabulously rich grave-goods, suggesting that an immensely affluent aristocracy had come to the fore as rulers of these incipient city-states.

We can now legitimately call these people Etruscans, since, from the beginning of the seventh century, the first inscriptions appear. The alphabet derives from the Euboean Greek used by the colonists in the south; but, in contrast, the language is not Indo-European in its roots, a feature that has always seemed to give good reason to follow Herodotus and to regard the Etruscans as originating in some shadowy homeland in the east Mediterranean. In fact, the archaeological evidence is decisive in affirming that Etruscan roots lie firmly in Etruria and that, whatever the source of their language, we cannot postulate any large-scale migration from Asia Minor or anywhere else at this time.[10]

In the course of the sixth century BC Etruscan history (insofar as it can be reconstructed) is one of expansion both to the north, beyond the Apennines, and into Campania. At the same time the aristocratic rulers of the previous century seem to have merged with a new class of merchants and craftsmen, witnessed by cemeteries with very little differentiation of tomb type or of contents. Some smaller towns seem to have come to a violent end in this period, suggesting to some scholars that their aristocratic rulers – perhaps to be compared with the feudal lords of medieval castles – may have met their end at the hands of more powerful neighbours.[11] But, whatever the truth of that hypothesis, there can be no doubt that a city-state system, based mainly on Greek models, was in the process of emerging.

The Greeks themselves had by this time been established in parts of southern Italy and Sicily for nearly two hundred years. The earliest colony had been founded by Euboeans at Pithecusa, on the island of Ischia in the Bay of Naples, early in the eighth century BC. That it was primarily a trading settlement is clear from the cemetery of Valle San Montano, which has yielded pottery from Crete, Rhodes and elsewhere; seals from Cilicia; faience and scarabs from Egypt; and a clay flask from Syria. One late eighth-century cup in the late Geometric style depicts the scene of a shipwreck, with an up-ended ship and drowned sailors, one of whom is being decapitated by a shark. There are also pottery vessels from Etruria and, significantly, areas where the working of iron-ore, apparently deriving from Elba, was taking place. The clear implication is that these Greeks were exploiting the rich metal deposits of Etruria, thus explaining the presence of Greek objects in central Italy at this time.[12]

The Euboeans soon expanded their colonial base. A settlement was

1 Gate of the third century BC at the town of Falerii Novi, founded soon after 241 BC to replace the old Faliscan centre of Falerii Veteres.

2 The sanctuary of
Hercules Curinus,
overlooking the Abruzzese
town of Sulmona (ancient
Sulmo), the birthplace of
Ovid. The sanctuary is
terraced into the hillside in
the manner of some of the
great temple complexes of
Latium.

3 Excavations in progress
at Tuscania, in central
Etruria. Visible are Roman
houses, flanking a street,
with medieval structures on
top. Occupation on this site
came to an end about
AD 1400, by which time the
town's nucleus had shifted
to its present position
(background).

founded on the mainland opposite Ischia at Cumae, and before long they had established a hold in eastern Sicily, with colonies at Naxos, Leontini, Catania, Zancle (modern Messina) and Mylai. A further colony at Rhegion (modern Reggio di Calabria) gave them firm control of the straits of Messina. Meanwhile, other Greek cities were also sending out colonies, so that the northern, eastern and southern coasts of Sicily and the south-western shores of peninsular Italy were gradually settled. Although they only founded one colony themselves – Syracuse – the Corinthians were to play a particularly important role in the trade of ceramics in the seventh and early sixth centuries, before Athenian potters slowly won over their markets. But Spartans, Achaeans and Megarians were there too as colonialists, while individual colonies also created new settlements. Thus it was that the region eventually to be known as Magna Graecia – Great Greece – was in fact to be comprised of a series of small city-states, independent both of each other and, indeed, of the mother cities whence they originated.[13]

We shall come to say something of the form of these settlements, and of their territories, in chapter 4. Here, it will suffice to make it clear that the great majority of the sites were chosen for the excellence of their harbours and for their rich farming land; and, too, that it is in Magna Graecia that the first attempts were made to lay out towns in a formal manner. This is a matter of some importance, since it was to influence the Etruscans in the planning of some of their 'new towns', like Marzabotto near Bologna (founded *c.* 500 BC), and was ultimately to have a highly significant effect on the form of many Roman towns. Part of the reason for so effective a diffusion of Greek ideas lay in their readiness to promote their goods through trading posts and other means. Mixed communities of natives and Greeks, as at Torre Galli near Hipponion (modern Vibo Valentia), may have been quite common in parts of southern Italy, while in Etruria there seem to have been Greek quarters at Caere, Gravisca and probably elsewhere. Some 'Greek' products were undoubtedly made in Etruria, recalling the story of Demaratus, who emigrated from Corinth about 650 BC and settled at Tarquinia, bringing with him a painter and three clay-modellers. Similarly, at the town of Spina, on the Adriatic coast close to Ravenna, the Greek presence was so considerable that it is not clear whether it should be regarded as a Greek or as an Etruscan foundation. What is important, however, is that Greek ideas, religious beliefs and taste were so deeply to permeate parts of Iron Age Italy that there are times when it is hard to know whether to attribute a work of art to native or to Greek craftsmen. Some of the so-called 'Etruscan' painted tombs at Tarquinia are a case in point; here there is good reason to suppose that both Greek and Etruscan craftsmen were at work almost side by side. These tombs underline the fact that, as a catalyst to change and development in pre-Roman Italy, the Greeks were to play a crucial role.[14]

It is now time to turn our attention to the much less well-documented, but no less absorbing tribes who made up the 'Italic' population of Iron Age

Italy. Archaeology has hardly begun to do justice to these peoples in the sense that systematic, large-scale exploration of their settlements is only just beginning, and for many areas we lack the detailed cultural framework of the sort that we can set out for regions like Latium and Etruria. Moreover, there has been a tendency (also reflected in many ancient writers) to relegate most of the Italic peoples to some minor league, since their towns, sanctuaries and cemeteries seem rarely, if ever, to approach the sophistication of their more advanced Roman, Etruscan and Greek neighbours.[15] The powerful Samnites, for example, were *montani atque agrestes*, 'rustic mountain people', for Livy, or 'deprived mountain-dwellers' for one modern authority, a view that it is important to test by the arguably more objective means of archaeology.[16]

In a linguistic sense many 'Italic' peoples shared a close affinity with Rome and the Latini. Many of the dialects of much of central and large parts of southern Italy (Etruscan apart) derived from a common Indo-European root. Generally known as 'Italic', this developed on the one hand into Latin and Faliscan, and on the other into Oscan and Umbrian. Oscan-speakers were known to the Romans as Sabelli, and their inscriptions, written in an alphabet closely related to that used by the Etruscans, are distributed widely in the mountainous Apennine terrain of Samnium, and in Campania, Apulia, Lucania and Bruttium (present-day Calabria). The oldest inscriptions occur on coins dating to about 450–350 BC, while graffiti scratched on the walls of buildings at Pompeii between AD 63 and 79 show that the language was still current some four hundred years later. Numerous peoples spoke Oscan in one form or another and were to achieve some sort of political status in the course of the Iron Age, but the best known were undoubtedly the Samnites.[17]

Rome was to fight three bitter wars against the Samnites, who, according to Strabo, could field an army of eighty thousand infantry and eight thousand cavalry.[18] They won a reputation as hard and implacable warriors, toughened by the exigencies of life in their homeland, the central-southern Apennines. Politically they comprised a confederation of four tribes, the Caraceni, Caudini, Hirpini and Pentri; each was administered by a high-ranking magistrate, known as a *meddix*. In times of war a supreme general was appointed. It has been estimated that in the mid-fourth century their mountainous territory encompassed over 15,000 square kilometres, making Samnium the largest political grouping in Italy at that time. In addition, from the mid-fifth to mid-fourth centuries the Samnites exercised a measure of control over large parts of Campania and Lucania, taking over such lowland towns as Capua in 432 BC, Cumae in 420 BC, as well as Pompeii, and possibly north Apulian settlements like Lucera. When in the fourth century they pushed into the Liri Valley, close to the borders of the area under the domination of Rome, a territorial and political conflict became inevitable: the First Samnite War (343–341 BC) was the consequence.[19]

As we noted above, both ancient and modern authorities have been quick to dismiss Samnite culture as rustic and backward. They are supposed mainly to have lived in 'hamlets' and have been recently described as 'a nation of peasants and herdsmen'.[20] Current work is tending, however, to refine and modify this picture. Although the upland nature of the Samnites' territory favoured a stock economy, and sheep rearing in particular is well attested, it would seem that cereals, legumes, vines and olives were also widely produced in the valleys. Smallholdings may well have been common, and we can probably envisage a quite large rural population.[21] At the same time there were many larger settlements, some of them occurring only a few kilometres apart. Excavations at Saepinum have shown how that site began as a cluster of buildings around a crossroads, the main road being a *tratturo*, a track which led between summer pastures in the high Apennines and lowland winter grazing. Substantial expansion soon followed. As at many Samnite towns, this began in the fourth century BC and was especially conspicuous in the third century. Massive defences are a particular characteristic of these Samnite centres, and are usually assigned to the period of the Samnite wars with Rome, that is between 343 and 290 BC. These strongly fortified centres (*vici*) underline the way in which the Samnite political structure developed into comparatively small territorial units, *pagi* ; but our historical sources are eloquent of the way in which the Samnites were able to confederate in times of war, and it is clear that an important factor in this was the unity brought about by a series of tribal religious sanctuaries. The best known is at Pietrabbondante, a site located high on a mountainside,

The theatre at the major Samnite religious sanctuary at Pietrabbondante, in the Abruzzi Mountains. The theatre, which is of Hellenistic type, dates to the second century BC.

twenty kilometres north-east of Isernia. Although the theatre and two temples visible on the site are Hellenistic in date, the sanctuary originated in the Samnite period and seems to have been a religious focus for all of the Pentri Samnites. Nearby, on Monte Saraceno, was a large fortified settlement. Like most Samnite settlements, little is known of the internal arrangements, but there is no reason to expect any very formal layout. Concepts of urbanisation, as developed in contemporary Greek cities of southern Italy and elsewhere, hardly touched these mountain fastnesses. Similarly, while from about 400 BC Greek (and Etruscan) ideas about art and religion slowly permeated the region, the mix was geographically uneven and indigenous traditions remained strong. Only Roman municipalisation was to bring about any very lasting change.[22]

Further south matters were rather different. The Apulian coastlands in particular had been open to trans-Adriatic traffic from far back into prehistoric times. Especially abundant are objects that originated in Mycenaean Greece, and it has been conjectured that a site like Scoglio del Tonno at Taranto, which has yielded very large quantities of Mycenaean pottery, may have been established as a Greek trading post. Certainly, it was a Greek presence that seems to have stimulated the development of the Apulian tribes. Massive stone-built defences surrounding settlements in comparatively vulnerable lowland positions are characteristic of the region from the later phases of the Bronze Age, and there are other hints of the evolution of a more sophisticated style of living. At the same time the growth of these defended centres argues for the development of clearly defined territories – so much so that in most parts of Apulia the later Greek colonisers were unable (or unwilling) to achieve any firm foothold.[23] Instead a vigorous local culture with, amongst other things, distinctive forms of painted pottery rapidly emerged. In the much more mountainous terrain to the west and south of Apulia, on the other hand, the preference in the last phases of the Bronze Age and early part of the Iron Age was for hilltop settlements. With the foundation of the Greek colonies during the eighth century BC, many of these were either abandoned or taken over by the Greeks. For example, soon after Sybaris was founded by the Achaeans, about 720 BC, the nearby hilltop settlement was converted into a sanctuary to the goddess Athena, a pattern that can be traced at other sites in the Sybaris region and elsewhere. Those native settlements which did survive began increasingly to purchase Greek objects and, no doubt, to absorb Greek ideas. By about 500 BC it is often hard to distinguish locally made goods from Greek products, a telling comment on the way in which indigenous traditions were rapidly submerged by the culture of the colonists.[24]

The extension of Greek control over many of the native sites of south-western Italy was matched by a gradual diffusion of Greek ideas through large parts of Apulia. At the large native site of Monte Sannace, near Gioia del Colle, for example, Corinthian and Attic vases of the seventh and sixth centuries BC are found in the tombs, together with native-style pottery. By

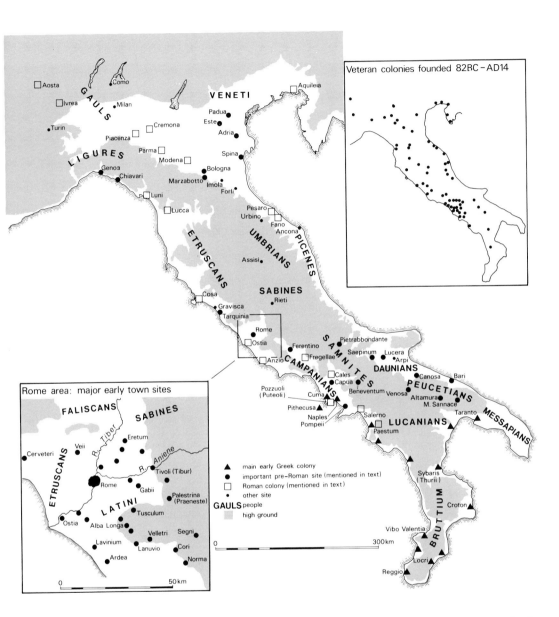

Veteran colonies founded 82BC – AD14

Rome area: major early town sites

FALISCANS
SABINES
Cerveteri
Veii
Eretum
R. Tiber
R. Aniene
Tivoli (Tibur)
ETRUSCANS
Rome
Gabii
Ostia
Palestrina (Praeneste)
LATINI
Tusculum
Alba Longa
Velletri
Segni
Lavinium
Lanuvio
Cori
Ardea
Norma

▲ main early Greek colony
● important pre–Roman site (mentioned in text)
□ Roman colony (mentioned in text)
· other site
GAULS people
high ground

0 — 50km

0 — 300km

Aosta
Como
VENETI
Aquileia
Ivrea
Milan
Padua
Este
GAULS
Turin
Cremona
Adria
Piacenza
Parma
Spina
LIGURES
Modena
Genoa
Bologna
Chiavari
Marzabotto
Imola
Luni
Forli
Lucca
Pesaro
Urbino
ETRUSCANS
UMBRIANS
Fano
PICENES
Ancona
Assisi
SABINES
Cosa
Rieti
Gravisca
Tarquinia
Rome
Ostia
Ferentino
Pietrabbondante
SAMNITES
Saepinum
Lucera
Anzio
Fregellae
Arpi
CAMPANIANS
Cales
DAUNIANS
Canosa
Bari
Capua
PEUCETIANS
Pozzuoli (Puteoli)
Cuma
Beneventum
Venosa
Altamura
Pithecusa
M. Sannace
Taranto
MESSAPIANS
Naples
Salerno
LUCANIANS
Pompeii
Paestum
Sybaris (Thurii)
BRUTTIUM
Croton
Vibo Valentia
Locri
Reggio

The pre-Roman peoples of Italy, together with the principal sites mentioned in chapters 2–4. The inset (top right) shows veteran colonies founded between 82 BC and AD 14.

the later fifth century the site was walled, and Greek notions of urban planning had begun to make themselves felt in the layout of the settlement. In part this was the result of direct contact with the Greek colonies; but there were also close connections with both Greece itself and Illyria, just a short distance away across the Straits of Otranto. The Illyrian element was especially conspicuous in the Salentine Peninsula, where the Messapians were to emerge as the dominant tribe. They spoke an Indo-European language, but one that is thought to be distinct from the Oscan and Greek of their neighbours; it may well be a dialect of Illyrian.[25]

To the north of the Messapians were first the Peucetians and then the Daunians.[26] Both were speakers of Oscan, and were collectively known as Apuli. Many of their centres are known, like Arpi, Canosa, Lucera, Siponto and Venosa (all Daunian) and Altamura, Bari and Monte Sannace (Peucetian). Massive defences are to be found at most of the Apulian towns, and some have been firmly dated to the fifth century BC. These fortifications were erected with good reason. Quite apart from the threat posed by the Greek colonists of Magna Graecia, the Oscan-speaking group of the central Apennines, of whom the Samnites were to become the most powerful and best known, undertook a rapid territorial expansion in the fifth century BC: Campania fell about 450–420 BC, the mountainous country of Lucania about 420–390, while Bruttium – modern Calabria – emerged as a Sabellic (= Oscan) tribal unit by the mid-fourth century. Apulia was no less at risk. Towns like Lucera and Venosa came under the Samnite yoke and others were at times hard pressed. Equally, there were conflicts with the Greek colonies. Thus, about 490 BC Taranto inflicted a great defeat upon the Peucetians – commemorated with a dedication at the sanctuary at Delphi in Greece – while less than twenty years later the native forces in turn won a great victory over them. Nevertheless, by then Hellenisation was well advanced and the swings and roundabouts of the political and military history of the period made little impact upon cultural life.

Much the same is true of Campania and Lucania. Once the Etruscans had been ousted from Campania in the late fifth century BC, most of the towns came under Samnite rule. Even so, there is little sign of any break in the archaeological record, and Hellenistic styles continued to prevail. Even the coins retained their legends in Greek. However, a new nation was in the making. During the period of the Etruscan and Greek hegemony there was always a very sizeable sub-stratum of local peoples; in the markets of towns like Capua, for example, there is no doubt that one would have heard an extraordinary babble of different tongues. With the demise of Greek and Etruscan power and the Samnite move down to the plains, these different ethnic groups gradually merged. Eventually Oscan rose to be the main language, and the people became known as Campanians, with Capua (modern S. Maria di Capua Vetere) their chief city. Only Rome's intervention in their affairs, brought about by a further threat from the Sabellic population of the Samnite mountains about 343 BC, prevented the development of what was potentially a very powerful political confederation.

The Hellenisation that is characteristic of so much of southern Italy becomes much less marked as one travels northwards. The Etruscans are, of course, a conspicuous exception, but their neighbours across the Tiber to the south-east – the Sabines – are not. Their rustic character was widely noted in antiquity, as was a tradition of close links with Rome. Both comments find some confirmation in the archaeological record, although the early history of Sabine towns like Rieti remains little known, and it may turn out that they were rather more than the 'hamlets' referred to by Strabo.[27] Similarly, the sites of central Italian tribal groups like the Vestini, Frentani, Marrucini, Paeligni and Marsi, and of the Umbrians, have so far yielded limited evidence for external contacts. Of these peoples probably the Umbrians were the most advanced. They spoke a language which differed in important respects from Oscan, as can be inferred from a lengthy religious tract written in letters borrowed from Etruscan, known as the Iguvine Tables.[28] Some of the sub-groups into which this extensive people was divided issued coins, and the indications are that certain of the Roman towns, such as Asisium (Assisi) or Urvinum (Urbino), originated as Umbrian centres. It may be, then, that urbanisation was more advanced than is sometimes supposed. Nevertheless, it was their conservative tendency towards regionalism – influenced, no doubt, by the hilly nature of their terrain – that is perhaps the most marked feature of Umbrian culture. In this, their eastern neighbours, the Picenes, provide a close parallel. They were a tribal group whose territory bordered the Adriatic Sea and included a considerable number of large settlements. Inscriptions in what may be a form of Oscan are known, and the cemeteries are characterised by a comparatively rich array of finds and by some distinctive forms of local arts – not least a remarkable series of engraved stelae, with scenes of battles on both land and sea. Greek influence becomes apparent from about 500 BC with the appearance of imported vases in some of the tombs; but it is the relative imperviousness of Picene culture to these foreign traditions that is so striking. Despite the proximity of Greek trading posts at sites like Spina, there seems to have been a strong resistance towards copying the work of the Greek craftsmen.[29]

To the north of the Umbrians and Picenes was another complex mosaic of peoples of diverse origins. In the flatlands and Alpine slopes of north-east Italy were the Veneti. Archaeologically they are best known through their cemeteries, which manifest a gradual development from the ninth century BC. The preferred rite of burial was by cremation, and the grave-goods show an increasing degree of technological competence, as well as becoming more numerous during successive archaeological periods. Conspicuously beautiful are sheet-bronze *situlae* – tall, shouldered, bucket-like vessels – decorated with warriors, animals and scenes of everyday life; they were in production by the late seventh century BC. There is some evidence for family burial plots, and eventually many graves came to be marked with stelae inscribed in a local script (but with a form of letters derived from Etruscan); but it is interesting to note that, generally speaking, the tombs reveal little indication of social stratification. Equally, Greek objects are by no means common, although whether through choice or for economic reasons is not clear.[30]

The chief town of the Veneti was at Ateste (modern Este), so that their archaeology is referred to as the Este or Atestine culture. Later Padua (Roman Patavium) rose to importance, but little is known of the overall layout of either site (although it is thought that neither possessed defences). Similarly, the Iron Age culture of Lombardy is again best known from a series of cemeteries which cluster around lakes Maggiore and Como.

Divided into three main periods (I: *c.* 900–600 BC; II: *c.* 600–500 BC; III: *c.* 500–15 BC), this 'Golasecca' culture does show regional variations in tomb type and contents. But there is consistent evidence for sporadic contact with the Etruscans and Greeks – and for more sustained links with peoples north of the Alps – and, moreover, for the emergence of so-called 'warrior-chieftains', some of whom were buried with elaborate chariots or carts.[31]

These 'Golaseccan' burials should be regarded as archaeologically distinct from the sites of the Ligures, a tribally very complex people who inhabited large parts of north-western Italy (and, according to tradition, some of what is now south-eastern France). Ligurian communities developed differently in response to variations in the topography. In the more mountainous regions of the Apennines there appear to have been a large number of fortified hilltop centres, probably of no great cultural sophistication. These were the sites where the wiry and skilful guerrilla fighters, much noted by Roman writers, lived their comparatively independent lives. Those who occupied the narrow band of coastal land, on the other hand, had much wider contacts. The finds from the eighth-century cemetery at Chiavari, for example, show close links with Etruria, while at Genoa tombs of the period between about 475 and 325 BC contain both Greek and Etruscan objects, as well as other finds which hint at connections further afield. Here, therefore, maritime trade was a considerable factor in the growth of this highly commercial – and successful – emporium.[32]

So far, we have been considering some of the indigenous peoples of northern Italy. Now we must turn to those who came into the region as colonisers or invaders. Tradition has it that towards the end of the sixth century BC the Etruscans created a federation of twelve towns in the Po Plain; Mantua, Modena, Parma, Piacenza, Rimini and Ravenna have all been suggested as possibilities. Only two are certain, however: Bologna (Etruscan Felsina) and Marzabotto (Etruscan Misa). Under Etruscan control, Bologna was to develop into a prosperous commercial and manufacturing centre; its cemeteries have yielded a rich array of Greek and Etruscan objects. Marzabotto also had an important industrial role, with evidence for smithing, smelting and pottery production; unlike Bologna, it was laid out in the early fifth century BC as a carefully planned 'new town', organised on the lines of some Greek settlements in the south. Elsewhere in the north Etruscan influence is less conspicuous, with the exception of two Adriatic harbour towns, Spina and Adria. Interestingly, ancient writers could not agree whether these sites were founded by Greeks, Etruscans or Italic peoples, and it is certain that both were thronged with people of very diverse nationalities. But the plan of Spina – a regular grid, not of streets, but of canals, covering some 230 hectares – is essentially Greek, and the cemeteries are crammed with Greek objects, something which implies that it was traders from Greece and southern Italy who controlled much of the marketing.[33]

If it was Etruscans and Greeks who provided the dominant 'external' influences in many parts of northern Italy in the fifth century BC, then it was the Gauls who took over that role in the fourth. The archaeological evidence suggests that Gallic Celts from north of the Alps were already beginning to move south during the fifth century; but, despite inconsistencies in our historical sources, it seems clear that the main thrust of Celtic expansion belongs to the period after 400 BC. These were not peaceful times. The Celts were a warrior people to whom prowess in battle was important: the weaponry in their graves is ample archaeological confirmation of this, and the literary evidence extensive and explicit. Indeed, within a dozen years or so of 400 BC Melpum (apparently a rich unidentified town, probably Etruscan) and Felsina had fallen and Rome itself was sacked. Nevertheless, the situation began slowly to stabilise. Different tribal groups (whose migration into Italy was spread over a fair amount of time) began to create territories in the north, and a series of new settlements was founded; Milan, Bergamo, Brescia, Cremona and Verona are likely to be amongst them. Bologna maintained its importance, although Marzabotto, which was occupied by a tribe called the Boii, fell rapidly into decline.[34]

Archaeologically, it is a fascinating task to attempt to trace the Gauls in Italy and to measure the cultural amalgam that resulted. The late phases of the Este, Golasecca and Ligurian cemeteries all include Celtic-type objects – brooches, weapons and the like – and some burials are very clearly those of Gallic warriors. These are not especially numerous, however, and it seems clear that many tombs of this period are those of indigenous people whose taste was influenced by Celtic styles. What is perhaps more striking is the comparatively even spread of fairly small cemeteries with Celtic material across large parts of northern Italy; this implies the creation of many small agricultural communities of a sort familiar in northern Europe. Certainly, there must have been substantial change in some areas: for example, the territory of the tribe called the Insubres – the coastal strip between, roughly speaking, Rimini and Ancona – was eventually to be termed the Ager Gallicus, while the Taurini are recalled by the name of the modern city of Turin (Italian Torino, Roman Augusta Taurinorum), and the Po Plain came to be known as Cisalpine Gaul, that is, 'Gaul this side of the Alps'.

The migrations of Gauls were to be the last major incursion into Italy of pre-Roman times. Their rapid expansion in search of new homelands mirrors the fact that the first millennium BC in the Mediterranean was a time when many populations were growing rapidly and territories were often being radically reshaped. At the same time fundamental changes were taking place in the nature of many societies, not least that of Rome itself. But in so topographically diverse a country such as Italy the pace of change was uneven, and the diversity of peoples, cultures and political and economic systems a far more telling factor than the uniformities. Indeed, even as Rome began to expand its territorial base, there were occurring developments of far-reaching political importance in most parts of the peninsula – something that underlines Rome's achievement in ultimately unifying this cosmopolitan country.

Further reading

Much of the archaeological evidence for early Rome is collected in E. Gjerstad, *Early Rome* (6 vols, 1953–73); but see Pallottino in D. and F. Ridgway (eds), *Italy before the Romans* (1979) and H. H. Scullard, *History of the Roman world* (4th edn, 1981) for major modifications to the interpretation. There is a useful summary of the evidence from Latium in T. J. Cornell, *Journal of Hellenic Studies* 100 (1980), 71ff; see also the important study of A. M. Bietti Sestieri, *Ricerca su una communità del Lazio protostorico* (1979).

There are many excellent works on the Etruscans, amongst them M. Pallottino, *The Etruscans* (1975); M. Cristofani, *The Etruscans: a new investigation* (1979); M. Grant, *The Etruscans* (1980); and R. M. Ogilvie, *Early Rome and the Etruscans* (1976). The *Progetto Etruschi* exhibition catalogues of 1985 are also particularly useful; there are eight in all, including M. Cristofani, *Civiltà degli Etruschi* (Milan).

The best introduction in English to the Greek colonists is J. Boardman, *The Greeks overseas* (1980). There is much of importance in D. and F. Ridgway (eds), *Italy before the Romans* (1979); see also M. W. Frederiksen, *Campania* (1984) and D. Ridgway, *Alba della Magna Grecia* (1984), with full bibliographies.

The literature on the Italic peoples is expanding rapidly. *Popoli e civiltà dell'Italia antica* (7 vols, 1974–8) are standard text-books; see also M. Pallottino, *Genti e culture dell'Italia preromana* (1981). E. Pulgram, *The tongues of Italy* (1958) is very useful, as is E. T. Salmon, *The making of Roman Italy* (1982). There are many important regional studies, amongst them E. T. Salmon, *Samnium and the Samnites* (1967), together with G. Barker in *Antiquity* 51 (1977), 20ff. and forthcoming (on his Molise survey); and the exhibition catalogue, *Sannio, Pentri e Frentani dal VI al I sec. a.c.* (1980). Splendidly illustrated are M. Mazzei (ed.), *La Daunia antica* (1984) and R. Bianchi Bandinelli and A. Giuliano, *Etruschi e Italici prima del dominio di Roma* (1979). For northern Italy, see L. H. Barfield, *Northern Italy before Rome* (1971); and for the Gauls, the exhibition catalogue, *I Galli e l'Italia* (1978).

—3—

THE RISE
OF ROME

So great is the glory won by the Roman people in their wars that . . .
they declare that Mars himself was their first parent and father of the man
who founded their city.[1]

Rome's rise as a world power is a story that has been told so many times that
it is not necessary to reiterate it here in any detail. What is important for our
purposes is to set out a broad chronological framework and to explore some
of the implications. In particular, it is illuminating to see how the innovatory
attitudes and policies adopted by Roman statesmen in the early centuries of
expansion were to create a model for the control of an empire: that the ideas
developed in the period of the Roman Republic were to become the basis of
the Imperial strategy of government.

The Roman Republic was created in 509 BC, following the expulsion of the
Etruscan King, Tarquin 'the Proud'. To replace the regal system a political
structure was devised which, for once, seems to have owed nothing to Greek
(nor, indeed, Etruscan) ideas. Briefly stated, the executive role was placed in
the hands of two magistrates, later known as consuls, who were elected for a
period of one year. They were drawn from a group of aristocrats, the
patricians, who formed what was in effect the governing body of Rome, the
Senate. Close controls were imposed on the consuls to prevent them from
abusing their power, and they were in due course given assistants, such as
censors, who carried out censuses and assigned citizens to their appropriate
tribes. The oligarchic or 'patrician' nature of their system soon came under
attack, in particular from the urban masses, known as the plebs. Their
oppression – especially a lack of land and heavy debts – was such that in 494
BC they withdrew from the city, established an assembly, and elected their
own officers. Called tribunes, they were granted considerable powers to fine

and imprison malefactors and, in return, were expected to intercede with the patricians on behalf of the plebs.

Not unnaturally, this provoked what was to become a bitter class struggle, lasting some two hundred years. But by the late Republic both patrician and plebeian families were to be numbered amongst the rich, although the patricians, broadly speaking, held their own. This was largely due to an important facet of life in ancient Rome, namely the patron–client relationship. This was a mechanism whereby the affluent took under their wing certain dependents on whose support they could count. In return, the clients received certain favours, not least financial inducements, which enabled them to raise themselves out of the mire of abject poverty. They could therefore afford to buy new weapons and enrol in the citizen army, and thus rise in social status well above their fellows – an incentive of great importance in the world of this ambitious young Republic.

Social conflicts apart, war was the dominant theme of the early history of the Republic. Even under the sixth-century kings Rome had achieved political and military domination over many of the other cities of Latium, and it is interesting to see how religious festivals were employed to maintain some sort of unity amongst the Latini – interesting since religion was to be exploited politically throughout Roman history.[2] With the foundation of the Republic in 509 BC, a treaty was made with Carthage, already a strong overseas power with an interest in protecting the Latin cities of central Italy. Soon after there ensued a lengthy military struggle between the Romans and the Latins. In 499 BC Rome won – narrowly – and a treaty was signed, creating a Latin league. A joint army was soon in action. Italic mountain tribes, especially the Sabines and the powerful Aequi and Volsci, initiated what was in effect a clash over territories, particularly the fertile lowlands to the east and south of Rome. Our sources make it clear that many of the battles were close fought and that Rome was often hard pressed; but, in the end, the allied armies won the upper hand and the threat was averted.

These victories were crucial, since Rome had an enemy of great power and influence only ten miles away: the Etruscan city of Veii. There had been intermittent clashes with the Veientines throughout the fifth century; now, with the threat from the Apennine tribes temporarily stifled, the time had come to deal with the problem of this much too near Etruscan neighbour. The war became legendary in Roman history, supposedly lasting from 405 until 396 BC and culminating in a great siege; but, as archaeology confirms, in the early fourth century Veii fell, and from then on lapsed into the status of a minor half-forgotten place. Propertius' description, in an elegant sonnet, of the sheep grazing within its walls is perhaps truer of Veii today than of its Roman past; but there is no doubt that the war effectively erased Veii from the political map.[3]

No sooner had Veii capitulated, however, than a new menace was at hand. As we have seen, the Gauls had been gradually infiltrating the north of Italy from before 400 BC, and in 390 one group mounted an attack on Rome itself.

This story, too, achieved legendary status, although the archaeological evidence does not support the assertions by ancient writers of widespread damage at the hand of the Gallic warriors. What is important, however, is that the Romans were able to hold out – unlike many cities in the north – and recover rapidly. Within a few years they were enclosing Rome within a massive stone wall (a long section of which is to be seen as one emerges from Rome's main railway station), and had begun to establish colonies at some of the major cities of Latium, such as Satricum (385) and Tusculum (381). Rome's wall, ten kilometres in length, symbolised its power. It was now a very big city, and its inhabitants must have been conscious that it was within their grasp to achieve great things.

Unfortunately, our sources for the next period of Roman history are exasperatingly thin. Nevertheless, the main outlines of the story are clear. In 354 BC hostilities broke out for the first time between the Romans and the Samnites. The outcome was, in the long term, hardly decisive, but it raised the curtain upon a military conflict that was to be of crucial importance for Rome's territorial ambitions. Happily for Rome, this first skirmish with the Samnites was soon over, for a more immediate threat was at hand: a potentially very dangerous coalition of tribes, including the Campanians and Volsci, and led by a group of the Latins. This war broke out in 340 BC and lasted for more than two years. It was undoubtedly a hard struggle, but Rome's eventual victory had implications that extended far beyond achievement on the field of battle. The Latin War resulted in a very considerable extension of Roman-controlled territory and it was therefore necessary to decide how this – and its inhabitants – should be administered. Eventually a novel and ingenious series of solutions was worked out, the form of which varied with the history, ethnic make-up and nature of each subject community. Some of the Latin cities were quite simply incorporated into the Roman state and the inhabitants made Roman citizens. Deprived of their independence, a good many of these settlements rapidly dwindled into insignificance. Other Latin cities retained their independence, but were required both to forfeit some of their lands and to supply Rome with military support as and when necessary. They had, however, the important guarantee of *commercium*, namely the right to enter into a legally protected contract with a Roman, and *conubium*, the right to marry someone from another state without giving up rights of inheritance or paternity. Elsewhere, especially in the territory of the Campanians and the Volsci, a rather different formula was imposed. Here major towns were defined as *municipia* that were *sine suffragio*, that is without the right either to vote in the Roman assemblies or to hold public office in Rome. This was an elegant solution in that it effectively released Rome from any administrative burden, and yet worked very much to Rome's advantage in military and financial terms.[4]

Rome also created new settlements, known as *coloniae*. These were designed both to make land available for the Roman poor and to safeguard the interests of the Republic. Some colonies had been founded during the

fifth century BC, but the main thrust came after the Latin War. Some were military foundations — three hundred families of citizens were, for example, sent to Ostia and to Antium (modern Anzio) to provide garrisons along the coast — but the great majority of the colonies were those of 'Latin' type, namely settlements whose inhabitants possessed the 'half-rights' of Rome's Latin allies. These were not thought of as high-ranking towns — *municipia*, being existing centres of importance, were considered to be of much greater status — but in the long term they were to play an immensely significant role in the unification of Italy and, eventually, in the Empire as a whole.[5]

The imaginative and flexible policy that Rome adopted towards its subject territories was a decisive factor in its success. Communities could develop independently within the Roman state, and yet maintained important ties with Rome. It was a formula that was soon to be tested. In 327 BC hostilities again broke out with the Samnites, following the foundation of a colony at Fregellae. Fregellae, near modern Ceprano, lay in the strategically vital corridor between the territories at Latium and Samnium, the Liris Valley. Together with another early colony at Cales (modern Calvi), founded in 334 BC, it clearly posed a very tangible threat to Samnite freedom of movement and, consequently, the Samnites attacked and took Fregellae. This initiated a very long struggle that carried on intermittently for nearly forty years. The war divided into two main phases, the first lasting from 327 to 304 BC and the second from 298 to 290. For a long time things did not go smoothly for the Romans. After a few years of inconsequential skirmishing, a Roman army of between 12,000 and 16,000 men was sent to invade the

The strongly defended site of Ferentino (ancient Ferentinum), on the Via Casilina. Taken by Rome in 361 BC, it became a prosperous town.

territory of the Samnites. The enemy was well informed, however, and managed to block the Romans in a defile, the Caudine Forks, and force their surrender. Following this disaster, the Samnites seem to have imposed terms, and there was a brief pause in the hostilities. In 316, however, the Samnites invaded Latium, and were only finally halted when they had reached Ardea, less than thirty-five kilometres to the south of Rome. Thereafter the tide turned and the Romans scored a series of successes, including the recapture of Fregellae. When the important Samnite centre of Bovianum (modern Boiano) fell in 305, the so-called Second Samnite War came to an end.

By then, however, Rome's war-front had widened considerably. Many of the tribes of the Abruzzi had been subdued and from 302 BC there was regular campaigning both in Etruria and in Umbria. Attack was evidently seen as the best form of defence and, significantly, was accompanied by the founding of a number of Latin colonies in the newly conquered territory. There was also a programme of road-building – most notably the Via Appia, which was to link Rome and Capua. But the Samnites were not yet beaten and hostilities reopened in 298 BC. Matters came to a head when a coalition of Samnites, Etruscans, Umbrians and Gauls was formed. In 295 the rival armies met in battle at Sentinum (modern Sentino) in Umbria, where, partly due to a Roman ruse, the result was a decisive defeat of the allies. It was a victory of far-reaching importance. Samnite resistance soon crumbled, and by 290 the Sabines and the Praetuttii had also capitulated. Rome now controlled a vast tract of central Italy, from the Tyrrhenian to the Adriatic seas, and wasted no time in consolidating its hold over these precious territorial gains. The imposition of allied status upon the Samnites and most other tribes of central Italy – which meant, in effect, a total loss of independence – combined with the spread of settlements with either full or half-citizenship, was to prove a powerful instrument of Romanisation. Loyalty towards Rome was not guaranteed by these moves; but it was clearly expedient to throw in one's lot with this powerful Republic. The use of Latin started to spread amongst the Italic people; the local aristocracy (who were often bolstered by Rome in the face of popular discontent) came increasingly to represent Roman interests; and a structure of government for a very diverse range of peoples began slowly to emerge.[6]

Indeed, following the Samnite Wars the emphasis started to shift towards conflict with some of the Greek cities of southern Italy – Magna Graecia. Rome had become politically involved with the Greeks as early as 326 BC, when the city of Neapolis (modern Naples) threw out its Samnite garrison and placed itself under the protection of the Roman Republic. This alliance set a valuable precedent in that, in the 280s, other Greek cities, including Thurii, Locri, Rhegion and Croton, also invited Roman support against the native tribes.[7] At this time the leading Greek city was Taras (Roman Tarentum, modern Taranto), a place made rich by virtue of its fine harbour and its extensive industries, particularly in ceramics and metalwork. The Tarentines became increasingly disquieted by the attitude of some of their countrymen towards Rome's role in their affairs, and decided to ask Pyrrhus, King of Epirus in north-west Greece, to intercede on their behalf. It was a disastrous decision. Landing in 280 BC, Pyrrhus fought the Romans at Heraclea (modern Policoro, not far from Taranto) and at Ausculum (modern Ascoli Satriano in Apulia). Although victory was formally his on each occasion, in neither case was it decisive and, more importantly, none of Rome's allies defected to him. Consequently, his resources became increasingly depleted, so that when a third and final encounter took place between Pyrrhus' army and the Romans, he was conclusively defeated. This battle, which was fought at Malventum (subsequently renamed Beneventum, modern Benevento), saw the end of Greek resistance. Pyrrhus returned to Greece and in 272 Tarentum was besieged — and succumbed. From then on all of southern Italy was under Roman control, a victory marked by a spate of colonial foundations, backed up by road-building and land-development schemes. It was a crucial step towards the unification of Italy, the spirit of which is well summed up by the epitaph of the consul of 298 BC, L. Cornelius Scipio Barbatus, who was 'a brave and a wise man, whose good looks matched his gallantry, who served you as consul, censor and aedile, captured Taurasia and Cisauna in Samnium, overran all Lucania and brought back hostages'.[8] It was achievement of this sort that acquired land and booty for Rome — and her allies — and provided a firm economic and military base for the conflicts that lay ahead. Indeed, by about 260 BC Rome exercised direct control over more than twenty per cent of peninsular Italy and, in the capital itself, conspicuous display of its new wealth was made by the construction of aqueducts, temples and other lavish public works.[9]

The victory over Pyrrhus brought Rome very much to the centre of the world stage. People, particularly in the Greek world, were now taking notice of this abrasive and militaristic new power, while Hellenistic ideas (as well as a taste for classical Greek and Hellenistic art) became increasingly fashionable in Rome itself. Before long there was conflict overseas: the First Punic War (264–241 BC). This began innocuously enough. Rome was asked to intercede on behalf of a group of Italian mercenaries, who had earlier taken control of the Greek city that underlies modern Messina on the north-east tip of Sicily and who now found themselves under attack by King Hieron of Syracuse. The Italians were at first undecided whether to call upon Rome or upon Carthage for support; but, when they finally opted for Rome, the Carthaginians (who had a long-standing interest in Sicily) realised that they must side with King Hieron and repel this Roman threat. The outcome was a protracted struggle which, for the Greek historian Polybius, was 'the greatest war in history'.[10] It saw not only an unprecedented scale of destruction — and Rome's first deployment of naval forces — but also the realisation that the Carthaginians could be expelled from Sicily once and for all. That this was eventually to happen was in part due to the extraordinary level of resources available to Rome, not least the funds to build and rebuild an enormous fleet; it is a reminder that so often the outcome of a major

4 Court and pool at Hadrian's villa near Tivoli, c. AD 118–34.

5 General view across the Roman theatre at Ostia, looking towards the Piazzale delle Corporazione; this was the heart of the town's mercantile activity.

6 The Capitoline temple at Brescia (Roman Brixia), erected under Vespasian in AD 73. It overlies an earlier temple to the Capitoline triad, Jupiter, Juno and Minerva.

The Via Flaminia, where it passes through the centre of the Umbrian town of Carseoli (ancient Carsulae). To the right is the Capitolium, the temple to Jupiter, Juno and Minerva.

conflict depends much more upon reserves of wealth rather than upon individual military success. Wealth was something that Rome had in abundance, and the addition of the rich country of Sicily – the first province – to its territorial holdings further strengthened the Republic's position.

Sardinia and Corsica were also soon added to Rome's possessions, after which the war arena once more reverted to Italy. Here the distribution of land to Roman citizens in the Rimini–Ancona area, the so-called Ager Gallicus, again provoked conflict with the Gauls. In 225 BC a huge Gallic force marched south across the Apennines and met the Roman army at Telamon (modern Talamone), not far from Grosseto in central Etruria. We know that Rome viewed this development with considerable alarm, and made plans to mobilise half a million men, should it prove necessary – no small comment on the strength of their resources.[11] In fact, the emergency was decisively resolved in the battle at Telamon with the rout of the Gauls, and was followed by a bold advance into Gallic territory. This brought further successes, and within a short space of time substantial parts of Cisalpine Gaul, from Piedmont to the north-east Adriatic, were in Roman hands. Colonisation was rapidly put in hand, with Latin foundations at Cremona and Piacenza (Roman Placentia), and in 220 BC construction was begun on a great road linking Rome and Rimini (Roman Ariminum). Still

known as the Via Flaminia, after the censor Gaius Flaminius, who built it, this superbly engineered road was to stretch for a distance of 336 kilometres; it illustrates very effectively how good communications were by now regarded as an essential component in the exercise of tight military control.[12]

Even as this was happening, however, other moves were afoot. After the First Punic War the Carthaginians had decided to re-establish themselves by securing land in Spain. Operations began as early as 237 BC but only became a threat to Roman interests when in 219 Hannibal attacked a town that was under their protection, Saguntum (modern Sagunto), near Valencia. Retaliatory moves, either in Spain or in North Africa, were no doubt considered, but these were pre-empted by Hannibal's famous march over the Alps into Italy, with a force of 20,000 infantry, 6,000 cavalry and even a number of elephants. Vital to Hannibal's plans was the attitude of Rome's Italian allies: were a proportion to defect to him, then his chances of ultimate victory would be considerably enhanced. As it happened, the Gauls immediately threw in their lot with him, and he was able to gain several resounding victories in 218 and 217; but in general Rome's allies remained loyal. Only after Hannibal's triumphant defeat of the Romans at Cannae (modern Canne, between Canosa and Barletta in Apulia) in 216 did any of the Italians join him: most notably the powerful city of Capua, in Campania, but also various towns in Apulia, as well as a good many of the Samnites, Lucanians and Bruttii.

This should have spelt disaster for Rome; as Livy commented: 'no other nation in the world could have suffered so tremendous a series of disasters and not been overwhelmed'.[13] But the fact of the matter was that many of Rome's allies did remain steadfastly loyal, providing both troops and, when necessary, places of refuge. This was not because of their belief in any heady concept of Italian nationalism; rather, it reflected a pragmatic conviction that, in the long run, Rome was more powerful than Hannibal and would ultimately win. And so it proved to be. There ensued a long drawn-out struggle, fought on many fronts in Italy and abroad, and gradually Rome gained the upper hand. In 203 Hannibal, although undefeated, decided to withdraw from Italy and return to Africa. This was precipitated by the fact that a Roman army under Scipio (later 'Africanus') had arrived there the previous year after a series of successful campaigns in Spain. Hannibal's Waterloo came at Zama, in central Tunisia; it was a close-fought battle but in the end Scipio's troops were victorious and, at long last, terms could be imposed upon Carthage.

We shall explore some of the consequences for Italy of the Hannibalic War in more detail elsewhere. Here it will suffice to note the severity with which the disloyal were treated: Capua, for instance, was reduced to the lowly status of a *pagus*, its territory confiscated and its leading citizens either executed or disciplined in other ways. It was a disgrace that the Capuans never forgot. Equally, we must bear in mind the devastating consequences of sixteen years of warfare upon Italian soil, and the implications for change in society of this protracted disruption. Not the least of these was the multiplication of the landless and impoverished, whose discontent was to be a major feature of the subsequent century. Not that the victory of Zama was to bring long-lasting peace; rather it was to usher in a period when Rome's rapacity became notorious, and its treatment of the conquered unconcern-edly brutal. Indeed, there was still unfinished business in the north of Italy, where campaigning had been disrupted by Hannibal's invasion. In 203 BC a Roman force was dispatched to the Po Valley and over the next twenty years or so much of the region was brought under control. This was accompanied by the foundation of further colonies, amongst them Parma, Mutina (modern Modena) and Bononia (Bologna), which were linked by a road that ran close to the northern flanks of the Apennine Mountains, the Via Aemilia. Significantly, some of these colonies were not of the Latin type but settlements of citizens; they reflect the fact that Romans were by now unwilling to give up their rights of citizenship in return for land in the territory of a Latin colony, and it was becoming increasingly hard to populate the new foundations. Only three thousand colonists could be persuaded to settle at Bononia, for example, created a Latin *colonia* in 189 BC on the site of the very important Etruscan city of Felsina. Hence there was a need for a new sort of citizen colony, where there would be both grants of land and the retention of all the rights of citizenship. Thus it was that no Latin colony was founded after 178 BC, when Luca (modern Lucca) was built, and the citizen type became the model for the future.[14]

Meanwhile, other colonies were being created around the southern shores of Italy, primarily to guard against the possibility of an invasion by Antiochus III, King of the Seleucids of Asia Minor. This underlines the way in which Rome's perspectives had become wholly Mediterranean, with overseas involvement on many fronts. There was vigorous campaigning in Spain, Sardinia, Corsica and, later, in southern Gaul (some of it in response to rebellions), as well as aggressive attempts to establish control in Greece and other parts of the east Mediterranean. With Italy secure, the Romans could indulge what was unquestionably a taste for imperialism – this an undeniable fact despite their historians' claims that they fought only 'just wars'. Given an efficient army and almost unlimited resources, success could only breed success. The total devastation of Carthage, the awful sequel to the short-lived Third Punic War (150–146 BC), was a highly evocative statement of attitudes in this militaristic and by then very powerful Republic: 'Remember, Roman, that it is for you to rule the nations. This should be your task: to impose the ways of peace, to spare the vanquished and to tame the proud by war', as Virgil was later to write in his *Aeneid*.[15]

But the story of the middle period of the Republic is far from being a narrative that recounts only the growth of an empire. Of equal importance are the social problems that this engendered. Since only Roman citizens holding a certain amount of property could serve in the army, many of the adult male population were away fighting for long periods of time. This brought about neglect of the land and, very often, severe problems of debt. What happened then is described for us by historians like Appian: 'the rich ... getting possession of adjoining strips, together with the allotments of their poor neighbours, partly by purchase and persuasion, partly by forcible means, came to farm vast tracts, using slaves as farm-workers'.[16]

We shall examine the archaeological evidence for these large slave-run villa estates in chapter 5. Their existence can be demonstrated with certainty in some parts of the peninsula, although it is still very difficult to ascertain just how common they were. Nevertheless, it does seem clear that the population of many towns swelled considerably in the second century BC and that this was due in large part to a migration of dispossessed peasants from the country into the urban centres. A plethora of building programmes ensued, reflecting the injection of new wealth that the wars of conquest brought about and an abundance of cheap labour. Indeed, there are those that think that the development of a new technique of building, involving the use of concrete, came about partly because of the ready availability of unskilled workmen, who could easily adapt to this comparatively simple method of construction.[17]

Even so, the agrarian problem remained. In particular there was a steady rise in the size of the slave population. This was very largely due to the fact that military successes ensured a ready supply of slaves, coupled with the firmly held belief in the profitability of slave-run estates. As a result, there was an enormous investment in slaves, the scale of which may be judged from the estimate of one modern authority that in 43–42 BC there were about 3 million slaves out of a total population of no more than 7.5 million.[18] Inevitably, so high a proportion of slaves led to trouble, not least in 136 BC, when a very serious rebellion in Sicily was just one symptom of widespread discontent amongst the slaves. This provoked grave concern in some quarters, as did another feature of the period: the fact that the dispossessed peasantry, being without property, were no longer eligible to serve in the army. Most scholars believe that there was a sharp decline in the number of these *assidui* (the term given to those who could enrol), and that this, in combination with the growth of the slave-run estates, was a powerful catalyst for a reforming movement.

Its champion was Tiberius Gracchus, tribune in 133 BC.[19] His proposal was that a long-standing restriction limiting holdings of public land (*ager publicus*) to a maximum of 500 *iugera* (125 hectares), should be revived. Since many landowners had acquired much in excess of this, the intended legislation provoked rapid and profound opposition from the rich, but the poor were overjoyed by the idea and flooded into Rome to vote. We need not dwell upon the events which were to lead to the assassination of Gracchus and three hundred of his supporters. What mattered was that a land commission was set up and soon began its work – something that can be demonstrated through archaeological evidence.[20] Moreover, Gracchus also set another important precedent in that he attempted to ensure that the revenue from the Kingdom of Attalus III of Pergamum, who had bequeathed his realm to the Romans, should be distributed to those receiving new land allotments. It was a munificent subsidy that was to be imitated later by other popular leaders, not least by his brother, Gaius Gracchus. Gaius held the tribunate in both 123 and 122 BC, in the course of which he initiated an extraordinary range of new legislation. His targets were both social and political. On the one hand were measures designed to protect the plebs from the abuses of mismanagement and corruption by the senate and the magistrates; these were coupled with laws that ensured a state-subsidised supply of grain at fixed prices for distribution to the citizens of Rome, as well as a programme of public works and improved terms of service in the army. At the same time further agrarian reform was enacted in association with the foundation of new colonies, both in Italy and at Carthage, as well as an attempt to extend the citizenship. Not all of these measures were to meet with success, and Gaius Gracchus and his followers were to suffer a grisly death at the hands of their opponents. Nevertheless, much was achieved, not least a powerful and necessary assertion of the rights of the plebeian poor.

Other changes soon followed. In 108 BC C. Marius, a nobody from Arpino in the mountainous region south-east of Rome, was elected to the consulship. His principal brief was to fight the army of Jugurtha, leader of the Numidians of North Africa, and long campaigning abroad created so disciplined a force as to make it virtually professional.[21] Thus it was that the property qualification was swept away and soldiering, for the first time, became a fully fledged occupation. This in turn led to demands for proper rewards, particularly a grant of land upon retirement, perhaps in conjunction with a colonial foundation. This, however, was too much for the patricians to stomach and, despite strong popular support – especially from the tribune of 103 BC, Saturninus – no such allotments were made.

Meanwhile, other events were afoot, for Rome's allies were becoming increasingly discontented with their lot. The burden of taxation and military service, the absence of political control and the dispossession of lands at the hands of the Gracchan commissioners gradually brought about disaffection. Had they gained some form of citizenship, as Gaius Gracchus and others had proposed, then things might have gone differently. But this was not to be, and in 91 BC the Samnites, Lucanians, Marsi and others proclaimed an independent state, Italia, with its capital at Corfinio in the mountains of the Abruzzi. Support was not universal, but the Social War (from *socii*, allies) was hard fought. In 90 BC Roman citizenship was bestowed upon all loyal groups and to those who laid down their arms throughout the entire peninsula; by 89 the contest was effectively over.

Already the first century BC had a stamp of violence and deep conflict upon it; but worse was to follow. In 88 BC L. Cornelius Sulla was consul. A patrician noble with little regard for niceties, he was asked to lead an army to the east Mediterranean to put down Mithridates, King of Pontus and champion of the many who were suffering at the hands of the Romans. The events of the period between 88 and Sulla's death in 78, with the Civil War of 83–82 between Sulla and the supporters of Marius, need not be traced here in any detail. The defusing of the eastern problem, the defeat of the 'Marians', Sulla's infamous purges and ruthless dictatorship and the reinforcement of the authority of the oligarchy (which, in the words of one modern commentator, 'governed with a guilty conscience') set a pattern for the final decades of the Republic. Despite settling (according to our ancient sources) 120,000 army veterans in a large number of *coloniae*, Sulla did nothing to weed out the deeper causes of social discontent. Violent solutions were to bring a violent response.[22]

One of the figures to emerge as a formidable general during Sulla's period of power was Gnaeus Pompeius, called Magnus (Pompey the Great) after 81. A charismatic man, he commanded widespread support: in the words of his biographer, Plutarch, 'some seriously gave him the name of Alexander, and he did not refuse it'.[23] Pompey's rise to power was the outcome of an outstanding series of military successes, combined with a shrewd approach to politics. His campaigns in Spain and against Mithridates in the east, his role in quelling the slave revolt led by Spartacus and in suppressing piracy, as well as his determination to secure land for the veterans of his army, were all factors that helped to make him both immensely powerful and popular. Eventually, in 60 BC, he, Crassus and Julius Caesar formed what came to be known as the First Triumvirate.

Although only an informal arrangement between three rich and powerful aristocrats, it clearly demonstrated how the future fortunes of the late Republic now lay in the hands of a very few ambitious men. In 60 Caesar was elected consul, and departed soon afterwards on his wars of conquest in Gaul. Meanwhile, further attempts were made to alleviate the problems of debt and land shortage which, in 63, had brought about the conspiracy engineered by L. Sergius Catilina: he, in Sallust's words, 'openly took up the cause of the dispossessed', albeit with little success. Nevertheless, this episode underlined the acuteness of the problem, and led to further measures, including the creation of a free dole handout of corn in Rome.[24]

In 53 Crassus was killed while fighting in the east and in 49 the Senate voted that Caesar should relinquish his command. Caesar's response was to invade Italy at the head of his triumphant and loyal army, and the inevitable conflict with Pompey soon followed. The showdown came at Pharsalus in Greece the following year, where Pompey was comprehensively defeated and then murdered soon afterwards. Caesar was declared dictator, and pursued the armies of Pompey's supporters all over the Mediterranean; but he also found time to settle veterans and poor citizens in Italy and abroad and to introduce other wide-ranging legislation. His assassination in 44 BC deprived Italy of a great statesman who, in many senses, anticipated the monarchy that was to follow: indeed, it was precisely that fear of Caesar taking on the full trappings of *rex* (king), together with his undisguised contempt for the Republic, that led to his murder. But, whatever the chaos of the times, the Republic was not yet ready to place the supreme power in the hands of one man.

Caesar's appointed heir and adopted son was his great-nephew, C. Octavius, a nineteen-year-old from Velitrae (modern Velletri), a town some thirty kilometres to the south-east of Rome. His decision to claim his inheritance, changing his name in the process to C. Julius Caesar Octavianus (hence 'Octavian'), immediately sparked off conflict. As Caesar's heir, his position was strong; but he was soon at war with the surviving consul, Mark Antony. There was fighting in the north of Italy, but towards the end of 43 the differences were patched up and a Triumvirate of Octavian, Antony and another of Caesar's supporters, Lepidus, was set up. The war arena now widened, with campaigns against Caesar's murderers, Brutus and Cassius. At the same time there ensued a terrible pogrom against their opponents, in which thousands are said to have been slaughtered. Meanwhile, Antony — like Caesar before him — was becoming increasingly infatuated with the Queen of Egypt, Cleopatra. The union was viewed with great suspicion, an opposition that Octavian systematically exploited; when the inevitable finale came, at the battle of Actium in 31 BC, Octavian was to emerge the victor and the stage was free for him.

Octavian's triumph was finally to bring to an end all the turmoil and chaos of the previous decades. It was also to usher in an era of extraordinary prosperity. First, however, a formula had to be worked out so that he could

The great mausoleum of L. Munatius Plancus at Gaeta, Campania. Plancus, who was from a senatorial family, was much involved with late Republican politics and had served with Caesar. *c.* 20 BC.

A bronze mask, worn by a cavalry trooper. It was found on the face of a corpse at Nola, the town in Campania where Augustus died. Second century AD. *(British Museum)*

rule within the framework of the constitution. Thus, he was nominated as *princeps*, ('first person'), and in 27 BC the title of Augustus was bestowed upon him. Moreover, time was on his side, for his rule was to last for forty-five years; as a result, he was able to devote much skill and care towards ensuring that the monarchical system would survive well after his death – as indeed it did, not just for years, but for centuries.

We shall examine the archaeological evidence for the Augustan period in subsequent chapters. Suffice it to say here that the legacy of the period is conspicuously rich. In his autobiography, the *Res Gestae divi Augusti*, 'the achievements of the divine Augustus', he tells how he embellished Rome and other cities, settled more than 300,000 soldiers, to whom 'I assigned lands or gave money as rewards for their military service', and founded twenty-eight colonies in Italy alone.[25] Taking the army out of the political arena was an important step. Soldiers now enlisted for a fixed twenty-year period and received a parcel of land or a lump sum upon discharge; military service became in effect a full-time profession. At the same time senators came increasingly to take on the role of senior administrators, while the *equites*, knights, began to fulfill other 'civil-service' type jobs, such as that of procurator (finance officer). Significantly, they derived from all over Italy, underlining the increased social mobility and unification of the age. Religion, too, was pressed into service as a way of focusing loyalty to the state, symbolised by the consecration in 13 BC of the *Ara Pacis Augustae*, the altar of the Augustan Peace, by the Campus Martius in Rome. It can still be seen in reconstructed form, standing on the bank of the River Tiber, close to Augustus' mausoleum. When, years later, a temple dedicated to the emperor Claudius was built at Camulodunum (Colchester), the leading city in the newly conquered province of Britain, it was intended to have precisely the same symbolic significance. Taken in conjunction with Augustus' determination to stamp out moral laxity – even his own daughter was banished for her unbecoming behaviour – it lends a somewhat Victorian flavour to the age.

For one modern commentator the Augustan era 'carried with it the end of the will and the capacity to innovate further' – a verdict that it is important to test by archaeology.[26] Historically the first principate was a watershed, and studies conventionally start or stop at this point. Archaeology, with its happy way of so often ignoring the period divisions of history, demands that the story be taken further. A glance at those innumerable sites where walls and floors of the Imperial period all too clearly overlie those of Republican date assures us of that. Augustus died at Nola, near Naples, in AD 14 at the age of seventy-seven, and a month later he was deified by order of the Senate. His successor, Tiberius, had much to build upon: an extended network of towns, an efficient system of roads, an increasingly developed structure of commerce and, by now, a largely pacified empire. In addition, a full treasury, a relatively small but excellent army, skilfully disposed around the provinces, and a stable society all lent optimism for the future. Inevitably, much would rest upon the character and abilities of future emperors, as the historian Suetonius was vividly to bring out in his *Twelve Caesars* – a work made entertaining by its scurrilous observations – but the auguries must have seemed good.

By now, however, perspectives had totally changed, as the emphasis of events switched away from Italy and towards the provinces. We shall be alluding to some aspects of provincial history elsewhere, but here we shall concentrate upon Italy itself. In fact, in comparison with the Republican period, the first centuries of imperial rule were relatively uneventful, apart from the Civil War of AD 69 which was to bring Vespasian to the throne. They could easily be written up as a chronicle of benefactions and building

programmes by the emperors: the great monuments of Rome, to take an obvious instance, are very largely creations of the Augustan period onwards. But this would be to ignore trends of considerable interest. Augustus had divided Italy into eleven administrative regions (including Cisalpine Gaul, incorporated in 42 BC), but they were to develop in a very uneven way. The Po Valley, for example, prospered immensely, while much of the south apparently went into a steady decline: '[In AD 60] the settlements at Tarentum [Taranto] and Antium [Anzio] were augmented by ex-soldiers; but this did not arrest their depopulation, for most of the settlers emigrated to the provinces in which they had served, leaving no children', remarked Tacitus.[27]

The use of veterans to put new blood into needy areas was a policy adopted by more than one emperor in the first century AD, including Nero and Vespasian. But, as Tacitus implies, it does not seem to have been a success, if only because the number of Italian legionaries was falling away steeply in favour of provincials, and in any case many soldiers formed an attachment with the country in which they served. Nevertheless, these measures emphasise the way in which Italy was beginning to lose its pre-eminence. As we shall see, the provinces were slowly capturing some of the markets for manufactured goods and for produce, and there is evidence for significant changes in some rural areas from about AD 100, if not before. Nerva, who ruled for just sixteen months between AD 96 and 98, did attempt to do something about this, spending 60 million sesterces on land allotments

The tomb of the Plautii (AD 10–14) near Tivoli, and a Roman bridge, the Ponte Lucano. Aulus Plautius commanded the invasion army of Britain, in AD 43.

The forum at Velleia, a small town in hilly country not far from Piacenza. It was paved in sandstone at the expense of Lucius Lucílius. A bronze tablet recording Trajan's attempts to promote agriculture was found in the basilica, to the left of the forum.

for poor citizens and reorganising dole handouts in Rome. More significant was the contribution of his successor, the first non-Italian emperor, Trajan (AD 98–117). He was born in Spain and was from a 'new' family – a clear sign of the way in which social patterns were changing. An innovative thinker, Trajan had money to spend – 5 million pounds of gold and 10 million of silver, won in what is now Romania in the second Dacian War (AD 105–6), it is said – and initiated many building programmes in Italy and abroad. One important scheme that he seems to have been responsible for was the *alimenta*, which provided for the public payment of subsistence in Italy. It worked by making state loans to landowners, the interest being used to finance the allowances. These were specifically for poor children, with the intended aim, according to Pliny, of raising the Italian birth-rate. At Velleia, in north Italy, for example, inscriptions show that an annual sum of 55,800 sesterces was distributed to 263 boys, 35 girls and 2 illegitimate offspring – a very considerable handout. Indeed, it is a measure of the success of the scheme that it is attested at more than fifty Italian towns, and that a special branch of the civil service was created to administer it.[28]

Whether the *alimenta* was also intended to help the smallholder in particular and Italian agriculture in general is a matter that is much debated; but it did encourage some of the rich to make their own private provision for the poor. The Younger Pliny tells us in one of his letters how he endowed an alimentary foundation with a value of 500,000 sesterces at his home town of Como, a move that was no doubt welcomed, if not initiated, by the emperor.

Similarly, we learn from the same source of legislation which obliged senators to invest one third of their capital in Italian land.[29]

Trajan died on 8 August 117 and his nominated successor was Hadrian. It was a highly significant appointment because Hadrian, like Trajan, was of Spanish birth. Although he immediately remitted the tax traditionally levied upon the accession of an emperor, wrote off no less than 900 million sesterces of debts, laid on shows and gave out grants to people such as poor senators, he was determined to show Italy no favouritism. Hadrian's view, shaped by his foreign background and by his love for Greece and all things Greek, was that Italy was essentially one province among many. Although he embellished Rome – Hadrianic monuments include the Pantheon, the temple of Venus and Rome, and his mausoleum, now Castel S. Angelo – and built an extraordinary villa near Tivoli, in the foothills of the Apennine Mountains, twenty-five kilometres to the east of Rome, his main concerns were with the Empire as a whole. To this end, he travelled to most parts,

The arch of Trajan at Benevento, dedicated in AD 114. The relief commemorates the emperor's achievements in Italy and in the provinces, and the arch marks the beginning of the Via Traiana, which led to Brindisi.

leaving a spate of building programmes in his wake. He also ordained that soldiers should be recruited from the province in which the unit was serving, a further pointer to the enhanced role that the provinces were now playing.

We shall attempt to assess Italy's agricultural and manufacturing output at this time in later chapters and, for some regions at least, will be able to demonstrate the onset of a decline. Other producers, particularly Gaul, Spain and North Africa, were now vigorously exploiting some of the more lucrative Italian markets, something which helps to explain why there was so much building and replanning in Rome's harbour town, Ostia, in the Hadrianic period. In economic terms, however, Italy was beginning to stagnate, a situation that was in no sense arrested by the Antonine rulers who followed, Antoninus Pius (138–61), Marcus Aurelius (161–80) and Commodus (180–93).

Whereas Hadrian had been the restless traveller, Antoninus Pius was the quiet stay-at-home. It is thought that once he became emperor he never left Italy, and it is recorded how he enjoyed life at his villa at his home town of Lanuvium. His contemporary, the writer Aristides, depicted his reign as a time of harmony, peace and prosperity. Fighting there was, brought about in the main by uprisings in a number of provinces: but in Italy life was more tranquil. Relations with the senate were good, tight control was maintained in Italy by means of an increased bureaucracy and, despite a good deal of public building – particularly on roads and harbours – public expenditure was kept down. It may not have been an exciting or innovatory period, but at least the helm was held steady.

Marcus Aurelius, by nature and training a Stoic philosopher, found himself by contrast involved in almost continuous campaigning. Increasingly, tribes like the Germans and Parthians were testing the strength of the frontiers and finding it wanting. In 166, for example, German forces swept across the Danube and into northern Italy. For a time havoc reigned, and it was two years before they were repulsed. At the same time there was a severe plague with, it is said, two thousand deaths a day in Rome itself.

These wars dragged on and did little for the citizens of Italy, except to empty the coffers. Still worse, Marcus' appointed successor, his son Commodus, was simply not fit to be *princeps*. It is probably fortunate that he elected to buy peace along the frontiers – only in Britain was there any real trouble – for he rapidly fell out with the senate. Persecution and conspiracy soon followed, exacerbated by Commodus' increasing insanity. Rome he renamed Colonia Commodiana and himself he regarded as the reincarnation of Hercules. His assassination by strangulation on 1 January 193 can have come as no surprise, nor the Civil War that was soon to ensue.

The war itself need not detain us. What matters is that it brought to the throne a new dynasty of African-born emperors, the Severi, who in many senses paved the way for the Italy of the late Empire. The first emperor, Septimius Severus, an ambitious, perceptive but essentially humane man, came from a well-to-do family from Lepcis Magna, in what is now Libya. His eventful reign from AD 193 to 211 has provoked all manner of evaluation, ancient and modern, flattering and critical. Pragmatic he certainly was: Cassius Dio tells us that on his death-bed in far-off York he is said to have advised his sons to 'give money to the soldiers and despise everyone else'. In other words, a loyal, contented army meant peace, a lesson that he had learnt in a long career of campaigning, particularly on the Empire's frontiers.[30]

With Septimius Severus, however, it is time to pause from this long historical narrative and begin to flesh out this bare historical skeleton with some archaeological matter. The story that we have been unfolding is a complex but fascinating one, a stage peopled with all manner of colourful, brilliant characters. That the Romans were able to achieve mastery, firstly, over their immediate environs and, then, over the rest of Italy and beyond is a tribute both to their genius as a group and to the many strong and talented leaders that emerged. Now we must see what contribution archaeology is making to our understanding of this absorbing and important period of world history.

FURTHER READING

Amongst many excellent works on the Republic, M. H. Crawford, *The Roman Republic* (1978) is highly readable, while standard works (the *Cambridge Ancient History* apart) include H. H. Scullard, *History of the Roman world* (4th edn, 1981) and his *From the Gracchi to Nero* (5th edn, 1982). See also M. Beard and M. H. Crawford, *Rome in the late Republic* (1984); J. Heurgon, *The rise of Rome to 264 BC* (1973); E. S. Gruen, *The last generation of the Roman Republic* (1974); D. Stockton, *The Gracchi* (1979); and Cl. Nicolet, *Les structures de l'Italie romaine* (1977). The *Atlas of the Roman world* (1982) of T. Cornell and J. Matthews is especially useful.

For population studies see P. A. Brunt, *Italian manpower* (1971); for constitutional matters, A. N. Sherwin-White, *The Roman citizenship* (1973); for social history, P. A. Brunt, *Social conflicts in the Roman Republic* (1971); and for Hellenisation, P. Zanker (ed.), *Hellenismus in Mittelitalien* (1976). On imperialism there is W. V. Harris, *War and imperialism in Republican Rome* (1979), discussed by J. A. North in *JRS* 71 (1981), 1–9; K. Hopkins, *Conquerors and slaves* (1978); and Cl. Nicolet (ed.), *Rome et la conquête du monde méditerranéen*, II (1978).

For Imperial Italy, F. Millar, *The emperor in the Roman world* (1977) and *The Roman empire and its neighbours* (1981) are both useful; see also A. Garzetti, *From Tiberius to the Antonines* (1974) and C. Wells, *The Roman empire* (1984). Of many biographies, see A. H. M. Jones, *Augustus* (1970); B. M. Levick, *Tiberius the politician* (1976); M. Griffin, *Nero, the end of a dynasty* (1984); and A. R. Birley, *Septimius Severus, the African emperor* (1971).

—4—

CITIES
AND
URBANISATION

More than four hundred Roman towns are known from Italy, as well as an uncounted number of villages and road stations.[1] Many lie buried beneath modern cities and towns, like Milan, Bologna and Florence, vividly illustrating the skill with which the original sites were chosen. Others are now deserted, their presence marked by rubble, tile and pottery and, more often than not, by standing remains from the defences or some other major structure. Pride of place, however, must go to the great monuments of Rome itself, the lava-fossilised towns of Pompeii and Herculaneum and the immense sprawl of buildings and streets that is the harbour city of Ostia.

It is perhaps natural that these most spectacular sites, about which so much is now known, should dominate discussion of Roman towns in Italy. Taken together, they provide a picture of urban life that is incomparable, not just in Italy, but in the whole Empire. However, our purpose is different, namely to look at Italy as a whole. This is an aim that immediately poses problems. Not the least is that with such a vastness of archaeological evidence to examine the picture is inevitably patchy and highly incomplete; in short, there are centuries of work to do — should the sites survive the onslaught of modern civilisation. Moreover, it is only very recently that more sophisticated methods of excavation have began to make a real impact, particularly in the study of historic town centres.[2] As a result there are very few sites where we can say much about the historical development as disclosed by meticulous study of the layers and the objects they contain. Nevertheless, a start has been made and a story *is* slowly unfolding.

It should be said at once that, in a geographical sense, urbanisation in Italy progressed in a very uneven way. In some favoured areas towns flourished everywhere, while in others they were few and far between, and were comparatively modest affairs. This pattern of course changed with time, but

it is worth beginning by looking at towns as they were before Rome established control.

It was claimed in antiquity that the fifth-century Greek architect Hippodamus was the father of town-planning. Our main source for this view is no less an authority than Aristotle, who tells us that 'the arrangement of private dwellings is thought to be more agreeable and more convenient if they are laid out in straight streets, after the modern fashion, that is, the one introduced by Hippodamus'.[3] Certainly Hippodamus planned Athens' harbour town, Piraeus, and probably designed the successor to the ill-fated Sybaris – Thurii, an Athenian colony founded in 443 BC on the instep of Italy's southern coast. However, there is now good reason to think that he

The forum and adjacent buildings of the Roman hilltop town (a colony) at Roselle. It was a major Etruscan city, and some buildings of that period have been uncovered; they are preserved beneath the modern shed.

may have been putting into effect ideas that had been developing for some time, particularly in southern Italy and Sicily. For example, at Poseidonia – later to become the Roman colony of Paestum – there was by about 500 BC a reserved central space with a piazza (agora) and temples, while three broad avenues and at least thirty-two cross-streets divided the city into rectangular blocks – the so-called orthogonal planning. A not dissimilar arrangement of streets can be detected still earlier – by about 600 BC – at Sicilian sites such as Selinunte and Megara Hyblaea, and it is clear that this sort of layout rapidly became popular in many Greek cities, especially in the late seventh and sixth centuries BC.[4]

The Greek colonies in Italy were, of course, largely restricted to coastal positions in the south and south-western parts of the peninsula. However, in many regions, particularly in the Apennine Mountains and in large parts of the Po Plain, town-building did not properly begin until after the Roman conquest and, even then, was sometimes on a rather muted scale. The incentive to create what a Greek would have called a 'city', or *polis*, simply did not exist. In other areas, especially in Etruria, Latium and Apulia, there is a rather different pattern. By about the year 1000 BC many quite extensive local centres had begun to emerge. Often these were situated in positions with strong natural defences and, at a few, stone walls enclosed the settlement. Not all were to prosper, but a high proportion remained in occupation during the centuries that followed and also became increasingly affluent. This much is clear from the cemeteries, many of which have been extensively excavated. Much less attention has been devoted to the settlements themselves, but where they have been explored, the pattern is normally that of a scatter of buildings, dispersed in a haphazard manner across the site. Despite the absence of formal planning, stone buildings became prevalent during the seventh century, and public works such as temples were being constructed in some towns by the beginning of the sixth century. If rather different in appearance from many of their Greek contemporaries, these sites can in many respects be regarded as urban.[5]

The impetus for further change appears to have been brought about mainly in Campania, a cosmopolitan region where Greek and Etruscan communities co-existed side by side. The Etruscans learnt much from their Hellenic neighbours, including the concept of orthogonal planning. Settlements like Capua (today S. Maria di Capua Vetere) probably received the first systemisation of their street-plan whilst under Etruscan control, and in Etruria itself the sixth century sees regular planning of the cemeteries in some cities.[6] But it is in the new Etruscan colonies in the north-east of Italy that the most spectacular advances were made. At Marzabotto, for example – a settlement founded about 500 BC on the side of a valley – architects were brought in at an early stage to lay out a regular pattern of streets in the Greek manner. Similarly, at Spina, built towards the end of the sixth century BC close to the Adriatic coast, the Etruscans combined their skills in hydraulic engineering with the new ideas of town-planning to create a grid of canals in an area of coastal fen. There was a 'grand canal' linking the settlement with the sea and, carrying the obvious analogy with medieval Venice still further, the houses were constructed on wooden piles, driven deep into the silts.[7] Spina was a port town, athrong with traders of many nationalities. The cemeteries are full of rich burials, accompanied by costly imported goods, particularly Greek painted pottery. It was an affluent and, above all, a cosmopolitan place – so much so that in antiquity opinion was divided as to whether it was a Greek or an Etruscan foundation. But, whatever the truth of that, the influence of Greek ideas is abundantly manifest, and it was to prove one of the key factors in shaping the future of town-planning.

Rome itself had grown up in an unplanned and haphazard way, and was never to achieve a very ordered layout. It was first settled well before 1000 BC, and seems to have developed into a series of separate hilltop villages, with those on the Palatine, Esquiline and Quirinal (flanking the valley where later the Forum was to be sited) as the most important. Under the Etruscans (who, according to tradition, ruled Rome from 616 to 509 BC) these different villages coalesced into a single centre. The Forum valley was drained, Servius Tullius reputedly erected a defensive circuit, and specific areas, such as the Aventine Hill, were designated for religious or public use: the culmination was a great temple on the Capitol to Jupiter, Juno and Minerva. It was dedicated in 509 BC, the first year of the Republic. With the new Republic, the city developed rapidly. The valleys – the natural routes of communication – soon began to fill in with housing, and by the third century BC tenement dwellings were becoming increasingly common, as pressure on space grew. Much of Rome must have been ever more slum-like, a harbinger of the inner-city problems that lay ahead. Markets grew up beside the Tiber, serving the busy throng of river traffic bringing produce into the town, while the Forum and its environs became established as the civic centre. About 378 BC a stone wall was built to enclose Rome's four administrative quarters or *regiones*, while munificence, public and private, endowed the city with temples, and the Palatine emerged as an area of smart housing. By the late fourth century BC the first aqueduct, the Aqua Appia, had become necessary; it was soon to be followed by a second, built in 272 BC. Rome was well on its way to becoming a splendid city.[8]

Just why this site should have been so favoured is a matter that has been much debated. There is no easy answer, for all manner of factors, both geographical and human, no doubt played their part; however, it would be hard to deny the River Tiber an important role, for it was Rome's principal link both with the sea and with the interior of central Italy. Equally, it is not surprising that amongst the earliest foundations was a fortified *castrum* at the mouth of the Tiber at Ostia, founded in the fourth century BC, probably by three hundred citizen colonists, it was designed to safeguard this important outlet to the sea against hostile marauders.[9] One of the gates and the line of the walls are still visible at the heart of the later Roman city. They were laid out in the form of a rectangle covering 2.2 hectares, a plan that was later to become standard for military bases. The early date is immediately obvious from the use of blocks of unmortared volcanic *tufo*, which stand out from the prevalent brick-and-concrete construction of the buildings of the Imperial period. Little is known of the internal arrangements of the *castrum*, save for its main streets (the east–west *decumanus* and north–south *cardo*), but the way in which it shaped the growth of what was destined to become one of the major harbour towns of the ancient world is immediately obvious from the plan.

We shall return later to Ostia to review its subsequent development. With the young Republic of Rome poised to begin its expansion, it is now time to say something about the different types of town. Here we immediately move into a complex world, which differs sharply from ours today. For us the distinctions between cities, towns, villages and hamlets are matters of degree, and also measures of varying levels of architectural embellishment, as well as of the range and quality of services for the community: whether resident in a city or a village, one's status as a citizen is the same. In antiquity matters were very different, as St Paul's celebrated remark 'I am a Roman citizen' reminds us. This meant special rights, privileges – and, not least, social and legal obligations.[10] These we need not pursue in detail, for the important thing is to emphasise the fact that people were strongly ranked in the ancient world. Moreover, these distinctions were rigorously applied to what became a well-defined hierarchy of towns. This is not an easy matter to summarise, however, if only because the Romans, as more and more territory fell to them, had to devise formulae that fitted a highly diverse range of situations.

Originally Roman citizens belonged to one of four urban or seventeen rural 'tribes', denoting the area in which they were formally enrolled. With new territory in the vicinity of Rome, these tribes were extended by four in 387 BC and a further two in 358. As the Latins came under the Roman yoke – a people with a large concentration of major settlements, many with their own defences – their towns had to be provided with an appropriate form of incorporation into the Roman state.[11] The problem was that Rome had neither the manpower nor the resources to put in administrators, and had, therefore, to devise other means. The answer was a type of town that they called a *municipium* (from the noun *munus*, 'a duty' or 'service', and the verb *capere*, 'to take'). This meant that the inhabitants became full Roman citizens, being liable both for taxation and military service, while the town remained locally autonomous, with its own traditions and laws. However, not all towns were deemed sufficiently elevated or friendly to merit this full status, and their citizens were consequently designated *sine suffragio*, without voting rights. The old Etruscan city at Cerveteri (Roman Caere) is an example, where the people held rights in Roman law (particularly as far as trading and marriage were concerned), but were not allowed either to vote or to hold office in Rome. Later, of course, if things went well, the town could be promoted to full status, so that the inhabitants became *cives Romani optimo iure*, Roman citizens with full rights. However, it was not until 268 BC that the first non-Latin communities – in this case certain Sabine towns – were to benefit in this way.

Other towns and their dependent states were treated differently. Here a treaty, *foedus*, was agreed upon, so that they became allies, *socii* and *foederati*. Normally speaking, this followed a Roman conquest – the magnificent hilltop site of Praeneste (modern Palestrina) is an example – and entailed both the giving up of some land and, when called upon, the provision of soldiers. Otherwise, such towns were nominally independent, and escaped the onerous burden of taxation, although Rome in effect exercised close control.

Archaeology has a long way to go in defining these political changes in material terms. The fact of the matter, however, is that they applied to a comparatively restricted number of towns, and the main importance is that, for the time being at least, they ensured the survival of many pre-existing Latian urban communities in the new order of things. Many other centres were not so lucky. To the north of Rome, for example, the Roman conquest was to result in the abandonment of many of the old large settlements.[12] This was partly the result of direct political action, but also because from an early stage the Romans began to create a network of colonies, bringing about a completely novel social and economic framework.

The word colony, *colonia*, derives from the Latin verb *colere*, 'to cultivate', so that the inhabitants of a colony, *coloni*, were designated 'tillers of the soil'. Colonies, ultimately to be the highest ranking of all Roman towns, were the major instrument in changing the urban face both of Italy and of large parts of the Empire. Appian, a writer of the second century AD, put it as follows: 'As the Romans subjugated the people of Italy successively, it was their habit to confiscate a portion of land and establish towns upon it, and to enrol colonists of their own in the towns already on it. They intended these for strongholds ... either to hold the earlier inhabitants in subjection or to repel enemy inroads.'[13]

The first colonies were founded in the fifth and fourth centuries BC. The great majority were created jointly with the Latins, at any rate until the Latin League was laid to rest in 338 BC. They were in effect new Latin cities, each with a military force of its own, and most lay fairly close to Rome. Nepi, ancient Nepet, is a good example. A settlement in existence from at least as early as the eighth century BC, it occupied (as it still does today) an impregnable ravine-girt position, in the heart of Faliscan territory. Although Nepi is barely forty kilometres to the north of Rome, the Faliscans were not finally subjugated until 241 BC, and there must have been some uneasy times in this frontier region. In fact, Livy describes Nepi, and its neighbouring colony, Sutri, as 'places sited to face Etruria and, as it were, both its barriers and gateways'.[14]

After 338 BC, as more and more territory accrued to Rome, the pace of colonisation increased immeasurably. Exact numbers are disputed, but one source, Asconius, tells us that when Placentia (modern Piacenza) was founded in May 218 BC it was the fifty-third colony.[15] Moreover, many of these were intended as large towns. Cales (modern Calvi), which was created in 334 BC as the first colony in Campania, was provided with 2,500 settlers. The site, which fell to the Romans by siege, had already been occupied for several centuries by the Aurunci. It was strongly defended by river valleys, and lay on the route that was eventually consolidated into the Via Latina. With a Samnite stronghold, Teanum Sidicinum (modern Teano), only a few miles away, it must have been deemed essential that the *coloni* should take over a position that was immediately defensible, especially as Cales lay some 150 kilometres to the south of Rome. Piacenza, too, was a vulnerable foundation, particularly as it was situated beside an important crossing of the River Po in flat and open terrain. Here the number of settlers was much larger, namely 6,000 (although it should be remembered that a good many were dispersed through the town's *territorium*). Nevertheless, the settlement was of necessity large and strongly defended, taking the form of a *castrum*, measuring 480 metres square. It was a particular target of attacks by Ligurian tribesmen, Gauls and Carthaginians, and the *coloni* led a precarious existence, suffering, in 200 BC, heavy plundering of the town at the hands of a Gallic force.

Piacenza was a 'new town', laid out – so far as we know – on virgin ground, whereas many of the older Latin colonies involved little more than the physical dispossession of the inhabitants' site and land. Other sites, like the Latin colonies of Alba Fucens (overlooking the Fucine Lake in the Abruzzi Mountains to the east of Rome) or Cosa are chronologically closer to the transition. Alba Fucens was founded in 303 BC, and Cosa just thirty years later, and the two sites share many points of comparison, not least the fact that both have seen a good deal of archaeological investigation. Both are perched on hilltops and were enclosed within defences; both share undulating territory inside the walls (rather like the troughs and hills of medieval Urbino); and in each the architects imposed a grid of streets upon the difficult terrain. Alba Fucens was much the larger – it measures some 1,150 × 675 metres – and was set up with 6,000 colonists, while Cosa covers an area of only 500 × 400 metres and probably had many fewer colonists (the exact number is not recorded). But both were frontier towns, where defensible qualities were combined with careful planning of the layout.[16]

Frank Brown, the excavator of Cosa, has given us an evocative picture of a long column of men, women, children and baggage carts, stretched out over some twenty-five kilometres, wending its way northwards along narrow, twisting Etruscan roads: the great Roman highways had yet to be built.[17] It was no accident that their destination lay on the coast 120 kilometres away; the Etruscsans were noted pirates, and Rome's western seaboard needed guarding. But the position was not a secure one, for nearby Orbetello was an Etruscan stronghold and Cosa lay in the territory of one of Rome's old enemies, the Etruscan city of Vulci. Not surprisingly, therefore, the colonists

were soon building strong walls, which extended for some two kilometres and were constructed – in the Latin manner – with massive polygonal blocks of limestone, pierced by three gates. In addition, the more vulnerable south and west sides, which face the sea, were furnished with great rectangular towers, eighteen in all. Within the town the two hills became the sites of temples, while the forum was laid out in the saddle between.

Excavation of the forum has disclosed a complicated history, extending down into the fifth century AD. As originally planned, it was a long, rectangular square, measuring some 90 × 35 metres which, as time went on, became increasingly built up with shops and offices. More importantly, there was a circular *comitium*, in effect a small amphitheatre with eight rows of seats, where the town council met in debate, and a *curia*, a rectangular town hall. Both were constructed in the early days of the colony; later a temple and a basilica were added, as were other public buildings. Even today it is not hard to imagine the hubbub of life in Cosa's civic centre, the ancient counterpart of thousands of town squares in modern Italy.

Later on the forum often became the principal religious focus of the town.

The centre of the Roman colony of Alba Fucens, situated close to the Fucine Lake, in the central Apennines. Founded with 6,000 colonists in 303 BC, the town was an important early military base.

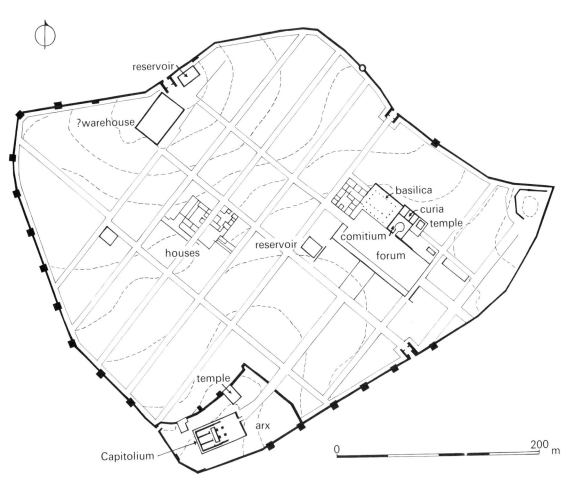

reservoir

?warehouse

basilica

curia

temple

comitium

reservoir

forum

houses

temple

arx

Capitolium

0   200 m

Plan of the Latin colony of
Cosa, founded in 273 BC.
Contour intervals: 4 m.

At Cosa the main temple lay on the southern hill. It is a steep climb to the *arx*, where a separately walled enclosure was built around first a temple to Jupiter; this was then replaced by a *capitolium* – a tripartite sanctuary for the triad of Jupiter, Juno and Minerva, matching, appropriately enough, the principal temple of Rome itself. Water tanks on this barren hilltop point to the additional role of the *arx* as a temporary refuge, and the excavators also found what they believe to have been the sacrificial deposits that accompanied the inauguration of the colony. Etruscan-style terracottas embellished the Capitoline temple, endowing it with an elegance that in some senses foreshadows the gracious cathedrals of Italian towns of the Middle Ages. Cosa was not, in the end, sufficiently successful to boast a theatre and an amphitheatre; but in its early heyday, it did its best to show a prosperous front.

Initially the houses were austere and somewhat regimented in design: uniform plots and uniform design, reflecting perhaps equality in status of the first colonists. Fortune, however, played its part, as some adapted to their new role more successfully than others. Today one can visit the house of a well-to-do later Republican burgher, with its garden and courts, a more provincial residence, perhaps, than that of his contemporary in Pompeii, but, nevertheless, the family had seized its opportunities and done well. Later we shall see why (chapter 7); but the archaeological evidence evokes very clearly both the difficulties and the achievements of those colonists who with either hope or resentment set out from Rome in 273 BC. The way in which Cosa's territory – which covered some 550 square kilometres – was organised and farmed will be considered in the chapter on the countryside. Like Cosa itself, it has seen much recent research, with results of outstanding importance.[18]

Cosa had a sister Latin colony, also found in 273 BC, at Paestum, ninety-six kilometres south of Naples. This settlement had originally been established by Greeks from Sybaris, down in the flat and fertile plain around the mouth of the River Sele. They had named it Poseidonia in honour of the god of the sea, and magnificent Greek temples, some still standing today, pay tribute to the city's distinguished past. Paestum's maritime advantages (as at Cosa) were clearly recognised by the Romans, who imposed the condition that it should provide both ships and sailors, if the need arise: to have taken control of this already strongly walled and prosperous centre can only have brought considerable satisfaction.[19]

Something of the Roman buildings at Paestum is known. There are some simple houses, with deep wells and layouts that hark back to the modest architectural tradition of the Samnites. These houses are just one of many reminders of the city's pre-Roman antecedents: the grid of streets, for example, is essentially that of the Greek architects, while there is good reason to suppose that the Roman forum lies directly over the agora of Poseidonia. This was a rectangular piazza, somewhat larger than that of Cosa – it measures 150 × 57 metres – and was lined with small *tabernae* (shops) and public buildings. These include a structure with an apse that rests on a Greek temple, beside which was a hall, with a semicircular arrangement of seats inside; in all likelihood this was where the town council met. Opposite, on the other side of the square, was the Capitolium, the temple to Jupiter, Juno and Minerva. Construction on this began when the colony was founded, although the plan was subsequently much modified. Next door to that was a rectangular building containing a circular setting of seats, rather like Cosa's *comitium*. Opinion is divided as to its role: was it a meeting place or could it have been used for ceremonies and sporting contests? In Imperial times an amphitheatre was put up close to it, unusually as these foci of rowdy behaviour were normally tucked away in the corner of town or even beyond the walls. This does suggest that performances and contests were also held in the *comitium*, and were accorded special prominence – interestingly, since the oldest amphitheatres so far known are found in Campania and may well have been developed there.

Another addition to the forum area was a complex of baths, erected by one M. Tullius Venneianus, and later reconstructed by his son after they had been damaged in a fire. The inscription which gives us these details also tells us that Venneianus paid for the building out of his own pocket, reminding us that private benefaction was a highly important factor in the development of the towns of antiquity. It brought renown to the donor but was almost a social obligation and a way of advancement for the wealthy citizen. Modern parallels are not hard to seek, but the role of the rich in promoting the towns of the ancient world is important to remember, especially when viewed from our modern perspective of a world where the role of the state is so totally pervasive in shaping urban development.[20]

Paestum, therefore, was a town where, as the archaeology so clearly demonstrates, Roman innovation was blended with what already existed; it was a formula which was to be applied again and again in later centuries. Moreover, it was just one in a series of Latin colonies that over a period of a century or more created a widespread network of towns through central Italy and, to a lesser extent, down to the south and up into the northern plains. All had some strategic purpose, and many could and did provoke hostile reactions. One need only mention Fregellae, founded in 328 BC some hundred kilometres south-east of Rome, and the catalyst that sparked off the Second Samnite War, which began two years later.[21]

However, the half-rights of the citizens of Latin colonies and the dissatisfaction that their status brought about, combined with the often difficult and dangerous lives of the colonists, gradually ushered in significant change. Colonies peopled by full Roman citizens were initially rare: according to Livy, just ten were created between 338 and 241 BC. Like Ostia, these normally lay on central Italy's western coast, earning them the title of 'maritime colonies'. In the aftermath of the Second Punic War, with Hannibal finally defeated by Scipio Africanus in 202 BC, another eight citizen colonies were founded. These were mainly spaced out around the south-western coast, at places such as Puteoli (modern Pozzuoli) and Salernum (modern Salerno). Although individually small, their combined effect was to create a powerful chain down this long and vulnerable shore-line. At the same time reinforcements were sent to Latin settlements in the north, such as Cosa, Piacenza and Cremona, to help stem the tide of incursions by Gallic tribesmen.[22]

Recruiting for these Latin colonies had by now become extremely difficult, even with the carrot of a large piece of land, and almost the last to be founded was Aquileia in 181 BC. This provoked a good deal of debate in the Senate, so Livy tells us, as to whether it should be Latin or citizen.[23] Being close to the modern Yugoslav border, Aquileia was very much out on a limb, over 630 kilometres from Rome. Its military importance, at the head of the Adriatic and at the eastern corner of the Po Plain, was obvious: could it be entrusted to Latin colonists? In the event it was: each was offered 50 iugera (12.5 hectares of land), and it was to grow into a very major city with some 70,000 inhabitants or more. Its harbour brought wealth through trade and the exaction of customs duties, but its exposed position also meant vulnerability: it is no accident that today the site is occupied by a modest settlement of just 3,342 inhabitants, reflecting a long history of enemy invasions.

Something is known of the brick-walled *castrum*, built by the original 3,000 colonists, and there is much more, still visible today, that attests the city's prosperous history in Imperial and late antique times. Aquileia was, in fact, to become one of the major emporia of the ancient world.[24] Nevertheless, it was the creation of new citizen colonies that now came to the fore in the urbanisation of the peninsula – inspired in some cases by particular individuals who perceived that there was political advantage to be gained by such enterprises. Some of the names of these new towns are still famous ones, like Parma, Modena (Roman Mutina) and Pesaro (Roman Pisaurum). Others are less well known, such as Saturnia and Gravisca in the southern half of Etruria, and Luni.

Luni (Roman Luna) lies in the shadows of the Carrara Mountains, not far from La Spezia in north-western Italy.[25] Its interest is neither scenic – it is situated on a rather dreary tract of coastal plain – nor does it lie in the quality

The amphitheatre at Luni. Beyond are the Carrara mountains, which provided the marble that was a major source of the city's wealth.

of the surviving remains, for there is little that is spectacular; rather, it is the careful investigation of the site in recent years that confers such importance upon it. Later we shall examine its archaeology in Imperial times, and see how it prospered from shipping Carrara white marble, as well as huge cheeses and excellent wine, through a fine harbour which was greatly celebrated in antiquity. It was founded in 177 BC, and was to be the springboard for the conquest of the Ligurian tribes in 155 BC. The town, as Strabo notes, was not particularly large – it is laid out, one corner apart, as a *castrum*-shaped rectangle 420 × 580 metres – and it was settled by 2,000 colonists, each of whom was offered 6.5 *iugera* of land (1.6 hectares).[26] The discrepancy between this allotment and that offered to the Latin colonists of Aquileia (50 *iugera*) underlines how highly valued the possession of the full rights of a Roman citizen was now thought to be.[27] Moreover, as roads that linked Rome with the colonies began to be built, so the new settlements became ever less isolated: the Italian peninsula was increasingly turning into the unified whole that Roman Italy became.

For a number of decades after 177 BC, however, the creation of new

Plan of the Roman colony at Luni, founded in 177 BC.

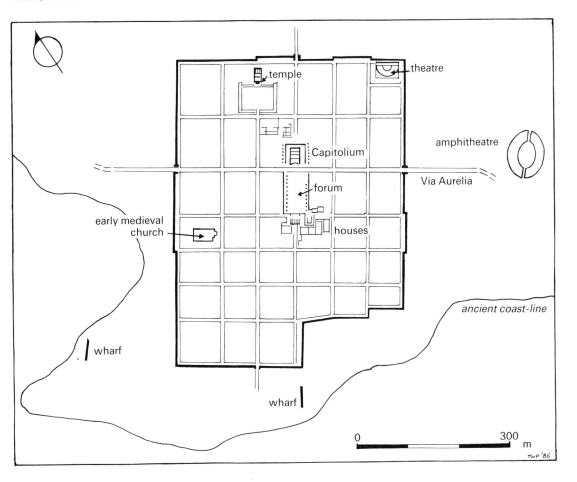

colonies dwindled away to nothing. Italy itself was comparatively peaceful, and there was a need to consolidate the new towns and to develop the lands around them – a matter that we shall consider in chapter 5. But there were also other problems, which came increasingly into focus as the century wore on: one was the steady rise in the numbers of ex-soldiers who required resettling, and the other was an ever more vocal demand by citizens of the Latin colonies for full Roman rights. When the Latin colony at Fregellae, a city heavily populated by Samnites and Paeligni, rose in rebellion against the unjustness of their position in 125 BC, the Roman response was drastic: Fregellae was flattened and replaced with a completely new settlement on another site.[28] Many Latin colonies, on the other hand, were emerging as strong foci of Romanisation and, with the passing of the generations, found that their loyalties were now more Roman than Latin. The eventual outcome, as we saw earlier, was that many were given the franchise in 90 BC and created *municipia*. Henceforth, towns with municipal status were to rank as autonomous, but second in rank to full *coloniae*, a distinction that was perpetuated down into late antiquity.

Towards the end of the second century BC several foundations were made with vital strategic considerations in mind. They lay mainly either in the far south or in the distant north. One was at Tarentum (Taranto), a Greek city already then six hundred years old, with a fine harbour. Another was Eporedia (modern Ivrea), which lies en route for the Aosta Valley and the Mont Cenis and St Bernard passes over the Alps – crossings that had been in use far back into prehistory. Here was a site well chosen to monitor through-traffic and to keep an eye on the dissident local tribe, the Salassi. Moreover, it was a region rich in gold and iron ore, in itself no mean incentive for colonisation in an increasingly greedy age.[29]

It is striking when looking at the new foundations to see how the planners of these second-century BC towns so often eschewed the safer but inconvenient hilltop position favoured by their predecessors. Unlike, say, Cosa, there is no natural defensive advantage to be had at Ivrea or Taranto, a measure of the confidence that lay behind the choices of site. However, during the earlier part of the first century BC other factors came into consideration. This was largely brought about by the general Marius, who was the first to admit landless proletarians into the army. This greatly altered both its size and its social status, and in turn created a problem of major dimensions: namely, what should be done with these impoverished soldiers once they had been demobbed.[30]

The solution, adopted both by the other great generals of the first century BC and by many of the early emperors – most notably Augustus – was the creation of a series of 'veteran' colonies of Roman citizens who had been retired from the Roman army. Their distribution is in stark contrast with that of the maritime colonies. Now what was needed was a site surrounded by good land, to be purchased or confiscated as necessary. Marius himself is credited with only one foundation, on Corsica; but from 82 BC Sulla was utterly ruthless in depriving his enemies of their territory, a policy later followed in particular by the Triumvirs, who were responsible for at least twenty foundations in Italy. Caesar, on the other hand, sought to place many of his veterans abroad – some 80,000 according to Suetonius – although he, too, was active in Italy itself. However, probably the most active creator of these new towns was the first emperor, Augustus. More than 120,000 men were demobbed after the Battle of Actium in 31 BC, and Augustus in his autobiography, the *Res Gestae* (literally, 'things done'), proudly proclaims how he 'founded 28 colonies in Italy alone'.[31]

Between about 80 BC and AD 14 veteran colonies spread over much of the Italian peninsula. The ever-fertile landscape of Campania was particularly favoured (the Bay of Naples fast became a Riviera of classical times, lined with luxury villas); and so too was the Po Valley.[32] Here extensive land reclamation created rich farmland out of fen and marsh, and the enterprising colonist could do especially well. Etruria and the far south were exploited less, but, overall, the urban face of Italy was changed remarkably. That said, it should be stressed that many of the veterans were placed not in new towns, but in or near to settlements that already existed. Pompeii is a case in point. By the time that colonists were sent there, about 80 BC, it had been a Samnite town for several centuries. The quartering of colonists at Pompeii, together with the provision of land for them to farm, was a harsh penalty for the town's residents, a deliberate reprisal for opposing Sulla in the Social War. Hardly surprisingly, there emerged a two-tiered society, although according to Cicero some of their differences had been settled within twenty years.[33] Nevertheless, the arrogance and generally insufferable behaviour of many of the veterans all over the Empire was to become notorious and a cause for very real grievances – a prime cause, for example, of the revolt of Queen Boudica and the Iceni tribe in Britain, much later on in AD 60.[34]

Even so, the veteran settlements did an enormous amount to promote the Romanisation of Italy. Formal inscriptions and graffiti scratched upon both walls and objects from Pompeii show very clearly how Latin rapidly became the *lingua franca* there, and much the same process was taking place all over the country. *Coloniae* were no longer the unpopular option that they had been in times past, but were fashionable places in which to reside, bringing high social status and possibilities for advancement. Archaeology, too, is beginning to highlight these changes. Although many regions of the peninsula were to develop their own distinctive 'Roman-Italic' culture, mass-produced Roman goods nevertheless made their appearance everywhere. Black-slipped pottery table-ware (the so-called 'black-glaze'), for example, turns up on almost every site occupied in the mid–late Republican period. Along with amphorae for transporting wine and oil, and various forms of kitchen pottery, it is one hallmark of 'Romanisation' regularly encountered by almost all field archaeologists wherever they work in Italy.[35]

Our understanding of the layout and history of these later Republican and early Imperial military colonies remains, however, at a very preliminary stage. The architect and engineer Vitruvius, who was writing early in Augustus' reign, had clear ideas about what was desirable. The situation of the site was seen as being of paramount importance: 'cold winds are disagreeable, hot winds enervating and moist winds unhealthy', he comments acerbically, while fenland locations are castigated because 'the morning breezes bring with them the poisonous breath of the creatures of the marsh'.[36] Here may be lessons learnt from the string of new settlements in the Po Valley and in other flatlands, like the Pomptine Marshes to the south of Rome. Moreover, Vitruvius sets out particular rules that govern the arrangement of the streets and the placing of the public buildings – the forum and senate house, the temples, theatre, circus, market and baths. It is not hard to discern the voice of long and solid experience behind these remarks.

Vitruvius, in fact, tells us something of his own work, particularly the construction of the great basilica that he personally superintended at Fano, on the Adriatic coast. The building's position is no longer known, but Vitruvius' somewhat immodest comment, namely that 'basilicas of the greatest dignity and beauty may be constructed in the style of the one which I erected', is amply supported by his description of this lofty and elegant structure. Placed next to the forum and close to the temple of Augustus (an unimpeded view of which is carefully arranged by omitting two columns),

Aerial photograph of Fano (ancient Fanum Fortunae), an Umbrian town on the Adriatic coast. Both the rectangular town blocks and the Via Flaminia (which runs from left to right) are preserved in the modern layout.

The arch of Augustus at the Alpine town of Aosta (Roman Augusta Praetoria). It lies 320 metres from the Roman colony's east gate, and is made of limestone; the dedicatory inscription and original top of the monument are now missing.

this was in effect a two-storey building; but 'the carrying of the columns directly up to the beams which support the main roof seems to add an air of sumptousness and dignity to the work', writes its architect, adding that he designed it so that those appearing before the magistrates' tribunal, in the centre of one side of the basilica, should not get in the way of all the businessmen elsewhere.[37]

The way in which 'public' architecture burgeoned in the Roman towns of Italy, old and new, is one of the striking features of the second and first centuries BC. Naturally, it took a long time for a single place to acquire all the buildings that an architect like Vitruvius would have desired. Calculations based on inscriptions from the Imperial cities in North Africa suggest that, in practice, it took about 120–140 years – should the place be successful and prosperous.[38] Under the Empire many new towns did not 'make it'; but Republican Italy, enriched by the wars of conquest, had a full treasury and numerous individuals with money in their pockets. There was ample scope for private endowment.

Moreover, it was a time of architectural experiment and change. To be sure, in a frontier town like Aosta (Roman Augusta Praetoria), which was founded in an Alpine valley in 25 BC, it was the older *castrum* plan that was selected. It had a basic grid of sixteen main building blocks, enclosed within a strong wall, which was 10 metres high, and provided with twenty towers. Overall it measured 572 × 724 metres. But Aosta lay in dangerous territory and was a veterans' settlement in the old tradition, founded by three

Part of the Roman town wall, together with one of the towers, at Fondi (ancient Fundi), in Campania. The Roman masonry, in *opus incertum* (the predecessor of the more regular reticulate work, *opus reticulatum*), can be clearly made out along the lower part of the wall.

thousand Praetorian Guards. Even the amphitheatre was placed within the walls.[39] Elsewhere in Italy, however, both the *coloniae* and other towns display all manner of invention. Fundamental was the discovery of concrete, a rubble mix which derived its strength from the admixture of volcanic dust, today known as pozzolana. Its use is first attested late in the third century BC; by the middle of the second century BC it was widespread, particularly in the volcanic region of Italy's west coast. Concrete enabled architects to realise novel ideas in design, most noticably in the construction of spectacular lofty vaults. One has only to wander around a site like Pompeii to appreciate the importance – and the durability – of this fundamental advance in architectural engineering.[40]

The technique of later Republican concrete work is instantly recognisable, for the walls were normally faced with small squarish stones. Initially, these were somewhat haphazardly arranged, giving rise to the term *opus incertum*; but by the mid-first century BC a much more regular design, where the facing stones were set in a diamond pattern – reticulate work (*opus reticulatum*) – came into use. This was to remain common until the middle of the first century AD, and was still being used in some second-century complexes such as Hadrian's villa, built between about AD 118 and 134. By this time, however, brick-facing had largely taken over, underlining how notorious rules of thumb can be in architecture. Even so, it is useful to bear in mind that, in visiting a site in, say, central Italy, buildings with large blocks of brown *tufo* masonry will often date to the early or mid-Republican period; those with reticulate work to between about 50 BC and AD 50–100; and brick-faced concrete structures to the first century AD onwards. These are very crude distinctions, but they make a handy start in sorting out the often bewildering sequence of building that confronts one at so many ruined towns of Roman Italy.[41]

The development of the concrete-and-reticulate technique of construction can also be viewed in other interesting ways. Whereas building in masonry is a skilled business, the use of concrete is technically much less demanding, given an adequate labour force and a good foreman. Italy in the second and first centuries BC had an expanding population and a changing urban face: the demand for new building was very considerable, and it must have become increasingly clear that concrete offered a relatively inexpensive and rapid solution to the problem. At the same time good use could be made of the glut of unskilled labour that was so abundant amongst the urban poor.[42]

We will not go far wrong, therefore, if we envisage the period of the late Republic and early Empire as a time of intensive building activity over large parts of the country. It was a spurt which really began in the second century BC and continued almost unabated into the second century AD. It applied, of course, not only to the new colonies, but also to the towns with municipal rank and, to a lesser extent, to settlements of lower status. There were an enormous number of *municipia* but also myriad smaller places with some urban characteristics. A good many were pre-existing settlements which were assigned judicial duties, so as to assist the local authorities in the *municipia*. These were called *praefecturae* or assize towns, although they were largely abolished during the first century BC in a reshuffle that placed all administrative responsibility for a district in the hands of the municipal towns. Similarly, there were *conciliabula*, or large villages, which until the time of the Social War (up to 90 BC) served as political centres in the country where, for example, official notices might be displayed.[43]

As with any developing system of local government, however, the system is not easy to unravel in detail: the existence of so many archaic survivals in the urban structure of present-day England – for example, the 'city' of Ely, in reality a very small town – is a reminder of the difficulties in interpreting such terminology. Much less ambiguous is the archaeological evidence, which almost everywhere attests the formation of new roadside centres and villages. Many of these may well have resulted simply from people drifting away from old redundant centres to places from which it was easier to exploit the new through-traffic. It is a phenomenon that is particularly clear in southern Etruria, and has its modern-day counterpart in the same area, as more and more of the old medieval centres are left vacant and replaced by new settlements.[44]

A large number of these new roadside stations were very small, and remained so; others were officially inspired, in particular a class of settlement called a *forum*. Although the same word as the central square of a town, here the term was used to denote a place that was founded as an administrative

The main gate at Fano (ancient Fanum Fortunae). As the inscription records, it was a gift of the emperor Augustus in AD 9–10. The second storey, which had seven windows, is now largely missing.

and market centre for a region. Many lay on major highways, and sometimes took their name from the road (or its founder), such as Forum Cassii (modern Vetralla) on the Via Cassia. There was a notable string along the Via Aemilia, which ran along the north-east edge of the Apennine Mountains, serving the settlements in the Po Valley. Amongst them were Forum Cornelii (modern Imola), which was possibly founded by Sulla (whose full name was Lucius Cornelius Sulla Felix); Forum Livi (Forlì); and Forum Popoli (Forlimpópoli). 'Forum-type' towns were still being founded in the provinces as late as Hadrian's reign, the 120s and 130s AD, and many were promoted to municipal status, underlining the success that often attended these new foundations.[45]

Whatever the political discord of the late Republic, therefore, the period was in some senses an entrepreneur's dream. Every town of any consequence needed paved streets and drains; an aqueduct to supply running water; public and private baths; an amphitheatre and a theatre; the forum and temples, town council chamber, commemorative arches, porticoes and the great basilica; if possible, town walls, both for security and to demonstrate civic pride in the community's achievement; and statues set up by the principal citizens. All of this took a good deal of time – and money. For some communities there was help. Augustus, for example, was a considerable benefactor, particularly in the veteran colonies. The walls and gates at Fano (where Vitruvius worked) were put up at his expense, as were many aqueducts, including those at Venafro (Molise), Sutri in Etruria and, most spectacularly, the enormous Serino Aqueduct in Campania.[46] Although this was probably started before Augustus became emperor (and was no doubt intended to win him allegiance in this area), its construction must have taken a very great deal of time, for it ran for no less than ninety-six kilometres, and served a whole series of towns, including Pompeii, Naples and Pozzuoli.[47]

The list of known imperial benefactions, both by Augustus and by his immediate successors, would indeed be long. Town walls were particularly popular, for obvious military reasons, but the emperor's generosity could and did extend far wider. Nowhere benefited more than Rome, of course, with the great fora (five in all: of Julius Caesar, planned *c.* 54 BC; of Augustus, *c.* 10–2 BC; of Vespasian, AD 69–79; of Nerva, dedicated in AD 97; and of Trajan, dedicated in AD 112–13); huge baths like those of Caracalla (AD 212–16); the Colosseum, begun under Vespasian and dedicated under Titus in June AD 81; the massive system of aqueducts; and the city walls, especially those of Aurelian, begun in AD 271, which are so magnificently preserved today.[48] But many smaller towns also did well, especially as priorities changed in the wake first of Italian unification and then of the building of a vast empire.

State subventions of this sort would, of course, today be considered commonplace; in antiquity, however, matters were very different. There were civic funds available, which, as inscriptions show, were sometimes used for major public works. However, many enterprises were paid for by private individuals. Thus, at Pompeii, while the small theatre and part of the forum baths were financed by the town, it was individuals who paid for the building of the large theatre, the amphitheatre and much of the great Stabian baths. Similarly, at the charming small town of Veleia, which is situated in

The amphitheatre at Pompeii, built by two magistrates for the veterans of the colony (the Colonia Cornelia Veneria), founded in 80 BC. It is the oldest known example of an amphitheatre. Vesuvius lies in the background.

hilly terrain thirty kilometres to the south of Piacenza, the paving of the forum, the basilica at one end and the portico were all built with monies donated by affluent citizens.[49]

Sometimes it was pride in one's home town that prompted such generosity. The younger Pliny, for example, who died about AD 112, left money in his will to build and maintain a library, to decorate and maintain baths and to feed poor children in his town of Como, in the north Italian lake district.[50] Normally, however, motives were far from altruistic, since a display of conspicuous munificence usually brought about social and political advantage. Towns chose their own chief magistrates and a council, or *ordo*, which was supposed to number one hundred elected decurions, men of wealth and high standing in the community. Competition for these places could be fierce, and it helped greatly if one had embellished the town in some way (not forgetting, of course, to advertise the fact with appropriately worded inscriptions). Indeed, chief magistrates were obliged to pay for games, although putting up a public building was usually considered a suitable, and more permanent, alternative.

It was not only councillors (or those who aspired to such offices) who provided benefactions. Freedmen (former slaves) were barred from serving on the *ordo*; but there were other offices that they could hold, such as that of *augustalis*. This was an honorary priesthood, one of a board of six, the *seviri augustales*, which supervised and promoted the cult of the emperor. Amongst them was P. Eros Merula, a doctor, surgeon and eye specialist of Assisi, who records how he paid 50,000 sesterces for his freedom, and spent another 67,000 sesterces on paving streets in the town and erecting statues in the temple of Hercules. Another *augustalis* from Veii earned the privilege of the right to sit with the decurions at public banquets, an exemption from civic taxes, and a special seat at shows; while a Pompeian freedman, Numerius, earned a place on the *ordo* itself for his son (who was only six) by rebuilding the temple of Isis after the terrible earthquake of AD 62.[51]

The social climber, therefore, could do well – providing he dug deep enough into his pocket. Fortunately, there was a huge quantity of money around, the direct result of Italy's privileged position at the head of an expanding empire. Moreover, the overall level of the population seems to have been rising steadily during Republican times, to reach a peak in the Augustan period.[52] In other words, there was both cheap labour and ever-expanding markets, to set alongside the possibilities of social mobility. This is a matter that is clearly reflected in the architecture, both public and private. It is no accident that we see the construction of, for example, great amphitheatres like those of Capua, Pozzuoli, Verona and, of course, Rome itself. By the end of the first century AD every town of any consequence had its own amphitheatre, some of them admittedly small and simple, but witness to the ubiquity of public entertainment, paid for more often than not by private generosity.[53] Theatres, too, became popular; these originated for the most part with ideas generated by the Greek cities of southern Italy and

The vast amphitheatre at Verona. Known as the Arena, and now capable of holding 22,000 spectators, it is one of a series of great masonry amphitheatres, which were probably built following the construction of the Colosseum in Rome, inaugurated in AD 80.

provided the perfect setting for that mix of religious ceremony and entertainment so favoured in antiquity.[54] However, it is domestic housing that is perhaps the best barometer with which to measure some of the changes of late Republican and early to mid-Imperial times.

Naturally, it is easy to oversimplify the picture grossly: private houses, as a wander around the Pompeii of AD 79 reminds us, are above all prone to reflect individual taste and fortunes. The prevalent style there was a building which had a central hall or *atrium* lit by an opening in the roof, beyond which was a peristyle, an open courtyard or garden surrounded by porticoes. However, most of the town blocks at Pompeii incorporate a building history that stretches back over several centuries before the city's demise in AD 79. One that has been recently studied is that containing the House of the Menander, named after the painted portrait of the celebrated Athenian playwright, found in a recess in the principal house. The block measures some 52 × 65 metres, about 3,500 square metres in all. The oldest structures date to around 300 BC, when the House of the Menander already existed as ranges of rooms around an imposing court. The block was extensively built up during the third century BC, reflecting the increase in the population of the town, while in the second century BC the House of the Menander acquired a colonnaded garden or peristyle. This was an introduction from the world of the Greek east, an innovation adopted by many Pompeians at this time. At the same time, wall plastering simulating ashlar masonry (the so-called First Pompeian Style) appears, and there was some rearrangement of the properties, creating a new house in one corner. About 50 BC a splendid house (called the House of the Lovers, after a graffito scored in the plaster

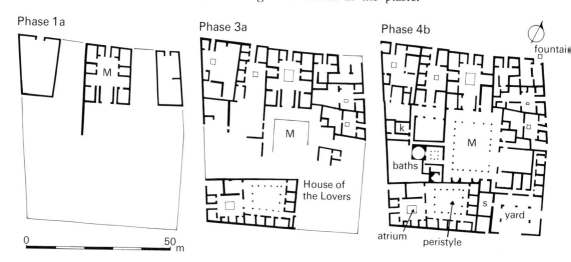

remarking that 'lovers like bees lead a honeyed iife') was built in the south-west corner, and soon afterwards the House of the Menander was enlarged. The extensions included the construction of a private bath-suite, and the wall decorations are in the Second Pompeian Style, including some splendid scenes from Greek mythology: clearly, the owner was now extremely well-to-do. Within the course of a generation, however, there were important changes. Upper storeys were added to a number of the houses, including that of the Lovers, shops were opened in some of the front rooms, and running water, supplied by the new Augustan aqueduct, fed a fountain at the north-east corner and was immediately exploited by one of the shop-owners. This symbolises both the increased level of the population and the spirit of commercial enterprise of the age. Nevertheless, around AD 50 the rich owner of the House of the Menander was adding new reception rooms, including a great dining-room (triclinium), as well as stables and servants' rooms. A cart, farm tools and wine jars from the stable area show that he must have also owned a country estate, no doubt to his great profit. The dreadful earthquake of AD 62 seems to have damaged comparatively little of his property, but by AD 79 the character of this town block was changing: next door were now a carpenter, a weaver and a fullery for preparing cloth; an

Successive phases in the build-up of the *insula* containing the House of the Menander at Pompeii, as revealed by detailed study of the masonry and decorations. In phase 1a (early fourth to early third centuries BC) the House of the Menander (M) was already the principal building. By phase 3a (c. 50–40 BC), it (M) had been considerably enlarged and at this time the House of the Lovers was constructed. In phase 4b (c. AD 50), the House of the Menander included baths, kitchens (K), stables (S) and new reception areas to the east, and the whole block was very densely built up.

upstairs flat had apparently become a brothel; and close by lived a retired gladiator, who may well have patronised the two on-street bars in the block. We do not know if the House of the Menander was occupied by the same family over these four centuries, but, if so, they must surely have turned up their aristocratic noses at such developments.[55]

Old-style town-houses, *domus*, designed with *atria* and peristyles, survived a very long time: they were still to be found, for example, on the great map of Rome, carved on marble in the early third century AD.[56] But the building of upper storeys onto Pompeii's elegant houses, the equivalent of today's loft conversions, marks an important change in attitudes towards town-planning. Everyone – social climbers particularly – wanted a house in the town centre: the problem was to find space. Eventually the really smart families also acquired villas in the suburbs or nearby countryside, while in towns such as Pompeii parts of the older houses, like that of the Menander, were increasingly divided up into apartments and shops and workshops.[57]

These developments at Pompeii were, of course, fossilised by the lava from the eruption of Vesuvius in AD 79, and one must go to Ostia to trace the subsequent history of urban housing. Large parts of the harbour town were replanned in the first decades of the second century, in the reigns of Trajan and Hadrian, providing an excellent insight into contemporary design. Two features are immediately striking. One is the ubiquity of brickwork, replacing diamond-shaped *opus reticulatum*. This is a reflection of a massive expansion in brickyards, particularly in the Tiber Valley; most helpfully, many bricks were stamped to identify the manufacturer (*figulus*), and some list the consuls of the year, giving us a date.[58] There is some evidence to suggest that the brick surfaces remained unstuccoed, lending that warm red hue that is so enduring a memory of a visit to Ostia. Secondly, much of Ostia, the warehouses apart, is dominated by huge, tall apartment blocks (*insulae*). These had been known in Rome from as least as early as the third century BC – Livy has a story about an ox finding his way up to the third floor of a house near the cattle market – and were very much the product of horrific overcrowding in the city. Indeed, Vitruvius has a good deal to say about the advantages of such blocks, and gives advice on how to build them. Stability was one problem – regulations limiting their height to 60 Roman feet (some 20 metres) had to be introduced – and another was fire. 'Town property brings good returns but it is terribly risky', observes Aulus Gellius, adding; 'If there was any way of stopping houses perpetually burning down in Rome, I would sell my farms and buy town property every time.' At least forty fires are recorded in the ancient sources, and none was more serious than that of AD 64, gloated over by Nero, who watched the conflagration from the tower of Maecenas. But they were an incentive to build new apartment blocks, if only because bricks and concrete were in general more fireproof.[59]

The long-term impact of these new forms of apartment blocks in Rome may be measured by the fact that fourth-century catalogues record 46,000 of them, as opposed to only 1,790 single-family residences, *domus*.[60] They

A typical brick-faced *insula* or apartment block in the Via di Diana at Ostia, with shops on the ground floor and apartments above.

became in effect a standard form of inner-city middle-class housing, certainly in parts of central Italy. Normally there were shops on the ground floor, and staircases leading up to the apartments. The rather plain façades were often embellished with balconies, and on each floor was a lavatory and chutes for disposing of rubbish. Behind was a court, which provided light, and a place for a water cistern, which supplied a communal tap. In the cheaper houses these courts were diminutive; but some apartment blocks were more prosperous. The so-called Garden Houses at Ostia are an example; here two identical blocks were set within a, no doubt, elaborately laid-out garden, each block containing flats with spacious and lofty rooms.[61]

Such architectural developments were inspired above all by utilitarian considerations. As today, crowded cities had to expand upwards, matched by rising rents. Surviving advertisements have a surprisingly modern ring; to take an example from Pompeii: 'To let from the fifteenth of next July, shops with their stalls, high-class second-storey apartments, and a house. Prospective lessees may apply to Primus, slave of Gnaeus Alleius Nigidius.'[62] Such advertisements must have been common, at any rate in the larger towns, where real estate was at a premium. Nor is it surprising that shops should exist cheek by jowl with flats on the upper floors: it is a phenomenon common to many Mediterranean cities of today, whether in the older quarters of Rome or in the Casbah of Algiers. Those narrow streets of contemporary Rome, lined with small shops, where, more often than not, the goods – brass dishes, furniture, fabrics or bread – are made on the premises by a family who live over the shop, all had their counterpart in the cities of antiquity. These *tabernae*, magnificently represented at Pompeii and Ostia, can be identified all over Roman Italy. The forum was often a major focus for them, as at Lucus Feroniae, to the north-east of Rome, where much of the west side was lined with bars, each with counters set with large jars to hold the wine. Along the side-streets are other shops, providing no doubt all the goods to be expected in a small country market town.

In the major towns some shops began to be grouped together from about 100 BC, doubtless facilitating the distribution of supplies. It would be wrong to exaggerate the significance of this; but it is true to say that as the fora of the more prestigious towns became embellished by public works, so there was increasing pressure to transfer some aspects of commercial life elsewhere. The meat market, where on-site butchery was commonplace, was one obvious target. In Rome the old meat market which underlay the Temple of Peace, next to the Forum of Augustus, was moved by Nero to the Caelian Hill; we can perhaps see why when looking at the plan of Pompeii, where the Capitolium, there as elsewhere the town's principal religious focus, was flanked by the vegetable market on one side and the huge meat market on the other: colourful certainly, but lacking perhaps in civic pomp, something which may well have offended some of the staider burghers.[63]

The complex which, in some senses, did most in Rome to reconcile the needs of shoppers and shop-owners with the demands of a civic centre, was the forum and market of Trajan, built in the early second century AD. A huge complex covering 120 × 200 metres, with an enormous piazza, a vast basilica, libraries, Trajan's celebrated column, and a temple, it seems somehow bizarre to have attached what in modern parlance was an enormous shopping centre – a great covered hall and some 150 individual shops. The grandeur of the project is extraordinary, and yet it is not difficult to visualise it as a logical development, on an Imperial scale, of what was happening in towns up and down the peninsula.[64]

That said, it should not be forgotten that there were many towns and villages where the scale of building work was modest, the streets more randomly planned and the community's perspectives little more than local. Indeed, in some areas, such as northern Etruria, there remained a comparative dearth of new towns, and instead old Etruscan centres such as Volterra, Chiusi, Vetulonia and Fiesole were maintained. In many areas, however, new foundations were made. Patient work, for example, by the French School at Rome at Bolsena, a delightful lake-side site in central Etruria, has brought to light large parts of a major Roman 'new town'. More importantly, a good deal can now be said about the way in which the town evolved. Founded in all probability to replace the nearby Etruscan city of Velzna (modern Orvieto), which had been destroyed by the Romans in 264 BC, Bolsena grew only slowly. The known forum belongs to the first century AD (although there must have been an older one); the theatre is early Imperial in date. Real prosperity did not fully come about until a major road that ran through Bolsena, the Via Traiana Nova, was constructed about AD 108. Thenceforth the town's burghers grew ever more affluent, as is attested by numerous splendid houses (still to be seen today), dating to the second and third centuries. In Etruria in particular Roman policy was flexible and geared as far as possible to local needs: Vulci, both a major Etruscan and a highly successful Roman city, and Bolsena, a Roman new town, clearly make the point.[65]

Nevertheless, the overall legacy of centuries of town development was a prodigious number of new sites and an enormous quantity of public and private buildings. Maintenance rapidly became a major problem. Few benefactors made provision for the upkeep of the works that they had paid for, and as Italy gradually lost its pre-eminence, funds became increasingly in short supply. After Hadrian, who died in AD 138, no emperor saw fit to create new towns either in Italy or elsewhere in the Empire, and Hadrian's successor, Antoninus Pius, introduced legislation seeking to restrain new building and encourage repair-work instead. Aqueducts and drains were in particular need of constant attention, especially in a country with heavy autumn rains and not infrequent earthquakes. Fire was also a hazard; but sheer wear and tear always took its toll. There is an abundance of inscriptions recording repairs to buildings, many simply observing that they had 'collapsed through old age' (*vetustate conlapsum*). This work could be very expensive (as those who have inherited the care of Victorian edifices, such as the British Museum, can all too readily attest), and it is not unrealistic to visualise the average Roman town as a rather grubby, smelly place, where a good many buildings were in need of some urgent maintenance. Another common formula on inscriptions is *longa incuria neglectum*: 'long left to rot', as we might say.

Inscriptions, in fact, show that there was heavy reliance upon private generosity in effecting repairs. The civic authorities carried out a good deal of day-to-day maintenance, but comparatively few major projects. However, after the end of the second century inscriptions commemorating individual munificence become infrequent, and they disappear completely by about AD 300. These are matters that will claim our attention later on, when we examine the later Roman period; however, it is worth noting here that the later second century marks the beginning of an overall decline of wealth in Italy, combined with many fewer opportunities for individual advancement except through the patronage of the emperor and his associates. Indeed, during the third century municipal officials known as *curatores* became increasingly common. These were not elected figures, but men appointed by the emperor to control the municipal purse and were thus answerable not to the people of the town, but to central authority. This must have sapped the spirit of local enterprise, so that purchasing status by conspicuous public-spirited behaviour became an increasingly profitless game: the rich were better advised to put their money into costly residences of their own, whether in the town or in the countryside. At the same time opportunities for 'conspicuous consumption' were fewer: most towns of any consequence already had their major public buildings by the end of the second century.[66]

A measure of Italy's declining wealth and investment is provided by meticulous study of the finds from the upper layers at towns like Ostia and Luni. Too little work has been done to permit anything more than very cautious conclusions; but there is a consistency in the results achieved up to now. Excavations in one of the bath complexes at Ostia, the Terme del Nuotatore (the Baths of the Swimmer), has shown for example that there was a steady decline in Italian products throughout the second century. Whether judged in terms of Italian pottery, lamps, oil- or wine-jars, or by marble quarried in Italy, the volume of finds gradually decreases. At first it is Spanish and, to some extent, Gaulish products that dominate the imports; but by the reign of the first African emperor, Septimius Severus, in the early third century AD products from Tunisia (where Carthage was now the second city of the Empire after Rome) become numerically overwhelming.[67]

A general decline in Italy's economic fortunes did not mean that there were no longer immensely rich individuals who lived there: far from it. The Greek historian Olympiodorus, writing in the first quarter of the fifth century AD, tells us that the estates of many senators at Rome brought in some 4,000 pounds of gold every year, as well as the equivalent of about a third of that sum in produce – wine, oil, cereals and the like. These estates were often widely distributed: one affluent lady, Melania, owned land in

Campania, Apulia, Sicily, various parts of North Africa, Spain and even far-off Britain. Her annual income was 1,600 pounds of gold: a millionairess for sure in our terms, but in antiquity a person only in the middle rank of the upper classes.[68]

The affluence of these late Roman aristocrats was obviously beneficial to those towns where they chose still to maintain a town-house and to bestow their patronage, and we shall say something in chapter 9 of the splendours of

The site of the amphitheatre at Lucca, where both the outline and the four main entrances are fossilised by later building.

places like Milan in the late fourth century, and Ravenna in the fifth and sixth centuries. However, the changing nature of patronage, combined with the rise of Christianity and the creation of ecclesiastical architecture, was to make the late Roman town a rather different sort of place. The role of the State, whether exercised through the emperor or through the governors of the new provinces established in Italy in the late third century, became of paramount importance; private initiative was of negligible consequence. In the process some towns dwindled away to insignificance, while others maintained their vigour or, indeed, emerged as important new centres, as we shall see in chapter 9.

The story of the urbanisation of Italy is a remarkable one. The sheer density of substantial towns, and the wealth and range of their buildings, are sufficient comment upon the drive and determination of those responsible for developing them, and of the abundance of wealth available to pay for the work. Equally, it is striking to see just how many of today's towns can trace their origins to classical times. It has been estimated that some two-thirds of Roman towns survived in occupation into the Middle Ages, a reflection of the care with which many of the sites were chosen. So we must now turn our attention to the countryside and examine the way in which it was developed into a profitable source of income for the towns.

FURTHER READING

Apart from basic reference works like *Enciclopedia dell'Arte antica* and the *Princeton Encyclopaedia of classical sites* (1976), see generally G. Schmiedt, *Atlante aerofotografico delle sedi umane in Italia* (1970); A. Rieche, *Das antike Italien aus der Luft* (1978); and J. S. P. Bradford, *Ancient landscapes* (1957). For early towns see A. Boëthius, *Etruscan and early Roman architecture* (1978); P. G. Guzzo, *Le città scomparse della Magna Grecia* (1982); and *Studi sulla città antica* (I, Bologna 1970; II, Rome 1983). For town-planning, see F. Castagnoli, *Orthogonal planning in antiquity* (1972) and J. B. Ward-Perkins, *Cities of ancient Greece and Italy* (1974). Types of town are discussed by A. N. Sherwin-White, *The Roman citizenship* (1973); see also E. Ruoff-Väänänen, *Studies on the Italian fora* (1978). For colonies see E. T. Salmon, *Roman colonisation under the Republic* (1969) and *The making of Roman Italy* (1982); L. J. F. Keppie, *Colonisation and veteran settlement in Italy* (1983) and in *PBSR* 52 (1984), 77ff; and R. Bussi, *Misurare la terra: centuriazione e coloni nel mondo romano* (1983). See also R. Chevallier, *La romanisation de la Celtique du Pô* (1980, 1983), and P. Tozzi, *Storia Padana antica* (1972). On architecture, see J. B. Ward-Perkins, *Roman Imperial architecture* (1981); M. E. Blake, *Roman construction in Italy* (1947, 1959, 1973); F. Coarelli in *PBSR* 45 (1977), 1–23. For costs and patronage, see T. Frank, *Economic survey of ancient Rome* (1933, 1940); R. P. Duncan-Jones, *The economy of the Roman empire* (1982); and B. Ward-Perkins, *From classical antiquity to the Middle Ages* (1984). Detailed site reports are listed in the bibliography: amongst the outstanding are Alba Fucens (Mertens 1981), Bolsena (Gros 1981), Cosa (Brown 1980), Luni (Siena 1985), Ordona (Mertens 1979), Ostia (Meiggs 1973), Pompeii (De Vos 1982, Jashemski 1979) and Velleia (Calvani 1984). See also J. Hermansen, *Ostia: aspects of Roman city life* (1981).

−5−

VILLAS, FARMS AND THE COUNTRYSIDE

There are many well-known villas from Roman Italy: Hadrian's fabulous villa at Tivoli; the great house, the so-called Grotte di Catullo, at Sirmione, which lies at the tip of a long peninsula jutting into Lake Garda; the Villa Jovis, a private retreat on the island of Capri for the emperor Tiberius, or the fabulously preserved villa at Oplontis, fairly recently discovered beneath the dull modern town of Torre Annunziata, near Pompeii.[1] These are all representative of a remarkable series of luxurious villas, built either by imperial families or by very rich aristocrats. Campania, and especially the Bay of Naples, was particularly favoured: Strabo, writing at the time of Augustus, describes the bay as 'entirely adorned partly by cities ... and partly by the residences and their gardens which, since they continue in such an unbroken succession, present the appearance of a single city'; for Cicero, writing a generation or so earlier, it was the 'Bay of luxury'.[2]

The sites of a good many of these seaside *villae maritimae* are known, like the great fifty-room mansion at Stabiae, the Villa San Marco, which is currently under renewed investigation.[3] Moreover, we are fortunate enough to have paintings of them as well, such as the colonnaded façade and central *exedra* (a large semicircular recess) of a seaside villa, depicted on the wall of a house at Pompeii, that of Marcus Lucretius Fronto. These were, in effect, the stately homes of Roman Italy, symbols of the power and status of the very rich senatorial families.[4]

Not surprisingly, the splendours of the luxury villas have tended to capture the imagination, and at times play a disproportionate role in discussions of the Italian countryside. The villas buried by volcanic deposits in the vicinity of Pompeii and Stabiae have also been given special prominence, partly because of the remarkable preservation of the buildings and their contents, but also because of the extraordinary insight that they

The great villa, preserved by the eruption of Vesuvius in AD 79, at Oplontis. Behind are the houses of modern Torre Annunziata; the garden (foreground) has been reconstructed as a result of recent excavations.

Wall-painting from a rich villa at Boscoreale, near Naples. It shows a coastal scene, with a maritime villa, boats and a man fishing with his rod and line. *(British Museum)*

provided into the social and economic life of the period. A classic study, published in 1931, sought to define the economic and social significance of these villas, developing a classificatory scheme devised by the great ancient historian, Rostovtzeff. A contrast was drawn between the luxurious *villae maritimae* and those in the vicinity of Pompeii, which was 'no garden city or suburb, but the scene of an intense industrial activity'.[5] These Pompeian villas (which are known by numbers) seemed to fall into three main groups.

One comprised conspicuously rich suburban or country houses (the *pars urbana*), but with attached farm buildings (the *pars rustica*): they seemed to provide archaeological confirmation of inferences drawn from Cato's agricultural manual, *De Agri Cultura*, for capitalist owners who invested in estates. They lived mainly in town, leaving a bailiff in day-to-day charge, and visited only occasionally; they were, in effect, old-style gentlemen farmers. Such properties contrasted with others where the owner was permanently resident in a 'real farm-house, modest, spacious and clean', running his own estate. These included buildings which served as country inns, like villa no. 28 at Boscoreale; here the owner served wine produced on his own land, and his guests sat on a bench along a wall facing the road, and sometimes recorded their presence with a scribbled remark such as *Cerdo hic bibit* ('Cerdo drank here').[6]

Finally, there were farms which were owned by absentee landlords and run by a bailiff who was in charge of a gang of slaves. Slave-run estates figure prominently in the literature, both ancient and modern. It was the famous journey of Tiberius Gracchus, up the Via Aurelia in the 130s BC, that revealed how in Etruria the free peasantry had been displaced by large estates, run by slaves; this journey was to lead to the attempts by the Gracchi to introduce land reform. Sites near Pompeii, like villa no. 34 at Gragnano, which had many small, bare rooms around a court, as well as a set of punishment stocks, seemed to provide archaeological proof of this notorious aspect of ancient farming (although there remains the distinct possibility of a still undiscovered, adjacent *pars urbana*).[7]

Probably the best-known villa, reproduced in many school-boy Latin books, was villa no. 13 at Boscoreale, also known as 'alla Pisanella'. The principal buildings cover an area of some 23.5 × 45.5 metres, making it a fairly substantial complex. It probably had a second storey, but nothing survived of that. At ground level there was a central court, surrounded on three sides by a portico. Beyond it, to the north, were a dining room, kitchen, baths and bedrooms, situated so as to take full advantage of the winter sunshine. There was also a bakery and a stable block, a not unusual juxtaposition in these villas. To one side of the court were the foundations for two wine presses, together with receptacles for the juice, and to the other was a further large court, about 13 × 15 metres, with containers for fermenting the wine. Further small cubicles for sleeping separated the wine presses from a room with a crusher for olives and an oil press, and there was also an adjacent barn and a threshing floor.

Calculations show that the wine vats could hold altogether 93,800 litres of wine; in addition to this was the oil, and the grain. This would mean an estate covering about 100 Roman *iugera*, the equivalent of 25 hectares. Certainly, the owner was well off. Apart from the painted walls and mosaics of the main rooms, a hoard of more than one thousand gold coins, as well as many pieces of silver table-ware, was found in the villa – no mean testimony to the affluence of a farmer who, no doubt, found it more convenient and desirable to reside much of the time in a comfortable house in Pompeii.[8]

In the last few years the investigation of these Pompeian villas – 103 of which are now known – has been further extended. Both at the Villa Regina at Boscoreale and at Terzigno, the substantial remains of other *villae rusticae* have been revealed. These again have rooms with great vats for the wine and other produce, while at other sites remarkable traces of the vineyards themselves have been identified. Indeed, it is especially striking to witness the way in which the archaeological findings seem to fit in with the ideas expounded in the farming manuals of Roman writers. We have already mentioned Cato, whose book was composed about 160 BC. Cato was a shrewd, practical man, much concerned with the production of wine and oil, as well as with fruit-growing and grazing. He was above all intent upon giving advice to those who planned to invest in farming, and offered dogmatic and occasionally somewhat unsound counsel. Varro's *Rerum rusticarum libri* were published in 37 BC, when he was eighty. They were written for his wife Fundania, who had recently bought an estate and who 'wished to make it profitable by good cultivation': it seems reasonable to suppose that she was a good deal younger than him! He was probably born at Rieti, to the north-east of Rome, and owned stud farms there for the breeding of horses and mules. He makes some important and useful distinctions between different sorts of farms. The villa, he notes, divides into the residential part (the *pars urbana*), the working areas (the *pars rustica*), and the storage part (the *pars fructuaria*). Further down the scale are the *casa*, the cottage of the smallholder, and the *tugurium*, the peasant's hut. The Pompeian sites may not have included those of the smallholder, but there was no difficulty, it seemed, in identifying the different sorts of villa as explained by Varro. The same sort of distinctions were recorded by Columella in his *De Re Rustica*, written about AD 60–65. Moreover, here was a writer who devoted a quarter or more of this book to the problems of viticulture. Columella was a Spaniard who owned estates in Latium and near Cerveteri in southern Etruria, and was deeply concerned about the declining state of Italian agriculture, as he saw it: too many absentee landlords, too much imported food, and too much pasture were his complaints. Thus his book was aimed at either the owners of large farms or those who possessed several estates, staffed and run by slaves; even the duties of the bailiff's wife receive a chapter.[9]

These manuals, together with the works of others, like Pliny the Elder's *Natural History*, published in AD 77, are obviously of extreme importance in assessing the nature and effectiveness of agriculture in Roman Italy. However, it is all too easy to assume that the remarks refer to all parts of the peninsula, and that the sort of villa found near Pompeii was typical of the country as a whole. In fact, the agrarian writers were describing what they knew about, namely a comparatively restricted part of western-central Italy. Even here there was a great deal of diversity in the approaches that were adopted towards agriculture in antiquity, just as there is today. We have to expect a picture that is complex to reconstruct, and one that contains all manner of variety. Similarly, it is not always easy to know just how much reliance to place on the often very general remarks made by ancient writers about the state of the land: it would be difficult enough today, even for a country like England, with a host of readily available information.

It is necessary to stress these problems, since work in Italy over the last twenty years has given rise to all sorts of furious debate about the nature and history of agriculture in Roman times. A lot of it is exciting stuff, not least because modern Marxist theories about the rise and fall of capitalist enterprise are quite explicitly applied to the evidence gleaned from the ancient writers, inscriptions, archaeology and other sources. Briefly and simply stated, one view of the agrarian history of the time envisages the gradual creation during the period between about 200 and 50 BC of large estates, which took the place of land worked by smallholders. These peasant farmers were dispossessed principally because they were heavily involved in the wars of conquest. In their absence the rich stepped in and snapped up their land. The large estates were worked in the main by slaves directed by a bailiff, and were owned by absentee landlords of the sort that Columella complained about with such bitterness. Appian, writing in the second century AD, sums it all up in these words: 'The rich came to cultivate vast tracts instead of single estates, using slaves as labourers and herdsmen, in place of free men who might be called from there on military service.'[10]

A further factor that encouraged the formation of these huge estates (later to be called *latifundia*) is thought to be Hannibal's invasion of Italy, and his prolonged occupation of the south between 215 and 203 BC. Historians are in dispute about the precise interpretation; one school stresses the devastation brought about by this long period of war and another points to the massive confiscations of land that were imposed upon people in Apulia and Lucania (that is, south-eastern Italy), who were imprudent enough to back the Carthaginians. But both schools unite in their interpretation of the sequel: that the literary sources imply the creation of huge ranches, devoted in the main to the raising of sheep. Again, these are thought to have been run mainly by slaves, a point that is buttressed both by the evidence of inscriptions (only one bailiff is known who did not have servile status), and by calculations of the size of the slave population in Italy in the late Republic. Naturally, such calculations are speculative, but the consensus amongst scholars seems to be that, out of a total population of between 6 and 7.5 million, no fewer than 2 to 3 million were slaves.[11]

Figures like this, however accurate, do of course shock, for slavery is an emotive word, especially if coupled with images of slave chains and *ergastuli* – 'correction houses for slaves', as one dictionary rather darkly puts it. In fact, slaves in antiquity could often achieve positions of power and responsibility – such as being a bailiff – and in the socially mobile world of the late Republic and early Empire many attained their freedom; indeed, in subsequent generations they might become highly respected pillars of the community. Nevertheless, the notion of slave-run, 'capitalist' farming enterprises has become well entrenched in the literature, and some not wholly apt analogies drawn with the much more recent history of areas like the southern part of the United States.

As in America – though for very different reasons – the supply of slaves became increasingly finite. Not only could slaves achieve freedom but, as the wars of conquest gradually drew to a close, so the potential market dwindled. Britain, noted for its export of slaves before the Roman invasion, was in AD 43 one of the last acquisitions; but there is little evidence to show that it continued to contribute to the servile pool. Thus originates a hypothesis that envisages the onset of a decline in Italian agriculture because the human materials to run the capitalist estates started to disappear. By the time of the emperor Trajan, who took office in AD 98, methods of production had to diversify, it is argued, so as to take account of a system that no longer worked. Come the time of Antoninus Pius, who ruled from AD 138 to 161, the crisis had fully matured, resulting in the abandonment of many of the major villas and in the creation of a new system. This, it is claimed, explains why at Ostia the layers of the mid-second century AD onwards contain for the most part not objects made on Italian soil, but imports: glass, vessels, tableware, marble and fragments of jars which held wine and oil. This 'crisis' was to usher in a period when the land in Italy was to be worked again by smallholders who became increasingly tied by legislation – aimed at restoring the profitability of Italian agriculture – to farming their small and ineffective plots, so that in the end they were to have much in common with the serfs of the Middle Ages.[12]

Here we are summarising what, in modern parlance, would be called one of the prevalent 'models' representing the agrarian history of a critical period in the Roman history of Italy, a matter that we shall return to again later. Embodied in it are overt assumptions that capitalistic farming is bad (and hence relevant to the preoccupations of modern society in Western Europe), and that the Roman experience is an effective demonstration of this. Not surprisingly, these ideas have provoked all manner of reaction, ranging from scrupulous reassessments of the ancient authors to detailed examination of the role and history of the peasant smallholder. Was he really so eclipsed by the rise of slave-run *latifundia*, as the ancient sources suggest?[13]

The archaeological evidence compiled in recent years has come to figure with increasing prominence in these debates. Sometimes it has been pressed into service, so as to buttress some of the existing ideas; but, more often than

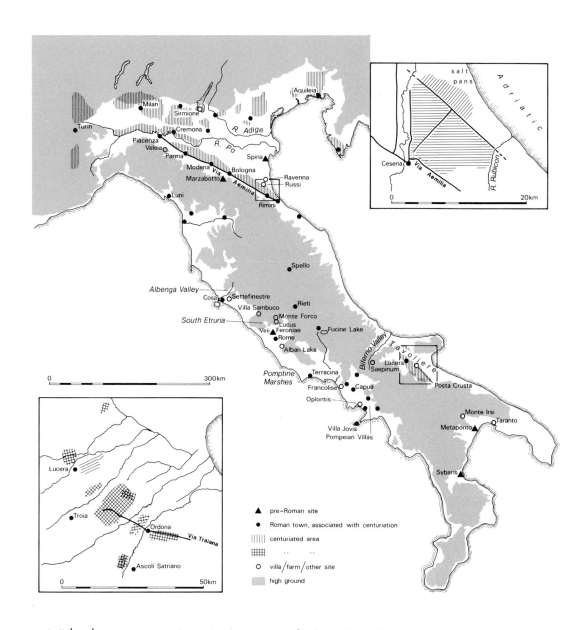

Map showing areas of Roman centuriation, land reclamation and the villas and farms mentioned in the text. The insets show centuriation in the Tavoliere (bottom left) and in the Cesena area of the Po Valley (top right).

not, it has been seen as an important new area of information. Reconnaissance from the air, which has been so conspicuously successful in Britain and parts of France and Germany, has on the whole been employed comparatively little in Italy. This is partly because over much of the peninsula crop- and soil-marks do not register ancient features well, often because of the prevalence of unsuitable cover, such as olives and vines. However, there are some dramatic exceptions. Photographs taken during the Second World War of the great flat plain of northern Apulia, the Tavoliere, revealed an extraordinary pattern of sites and field systems. Many were settlements of prehistoric date, while others belonged to the medieval period: however, it was the extraordinary detail of the Roman landscape which was perhaps the most striking component of these discoveries.[14]

Immediately obvious was the existence of a number of areas where the land had been divided up into grids of square fields, a system that is known as centuriation. This is a subject to which we must return later on, but it will be helpful to say a few words about it now. Centuriated lands are commonly found in the vicinity of the colonies, where there was a need to divide up the surrounding territory on a very extensive scale in order to allocate a parcel to each colonist. This must commonly have been carried out when the settlement was founded, but it was also a practice that was continued into Augustan times, if not later. The grid was created by laying out a chequer-board pattern of roads, the squares usually having sides of 20 *actus*, the equivalent of 710 metres. One *actus* was made up of 120 Roman feet, and the unit square measurement was a *iugerum*, made up of 1×2 *actus*. Land allocations were normally expressed in terms of *iugera*; however, a further unit was a *heredium*, namely 2 *iugera*, and 100 *heredia* equalled a *centuria* – hence the name centuriation (or, in Latin, *limitatio*, from which we derive our word 'limits').[15]

Like any unfamiliar system of measurement, all this sounds rather complicated, but it helps to illustrate the development of a sophisticated school of land surveyors. They were called *agrimensores*, 'measurers of the fields', or *gromatici* (named after the *groma*, their principal surveying instrument). Their job was a thoroughly important one, for it was to change the face of quite large parts of the Italian countryside. Naturally, practical considerations such as the lie of the land and the existence of rivers often intervened, forcing modifications to the blueprint, like the use of non-standard sizes of block; but it is the overall size of this landscape planning that cannot fail to impress.

The revelation of these field systems in the Apulian Tavoliere was a triumph of aerial photography; however, there was also much more to be seen of these buried traces of Roman activity. In particular, there were the farms, often lying within rectangular ditched enclosures, each with its own carefully aligned approach road. Some of the enclosures were of quite considerable size – one measured as much as 150×45 metres – and it can hardly be doubted that these mark the sites of the rural smallholdings of the colonists, quite probably those of nearby Lucera. But what was even more remarkable were some astonishing crop-marks, which demonstrate some of the agricultural activity. These include parallel rows of pits, carefully aligned with the roads, and neatly and systematically laid out. One group, for example, contains thirty-six rows, each with about thirty pits, and there is no difficulty, both on modern analogy and by reference to the ancient writers on agriculture, in identifying this as an olive plantation. On the other side of the road is a rather different arrangement, in that the rows here consist of a series of continuous trenches; this is entirely consistent with the most

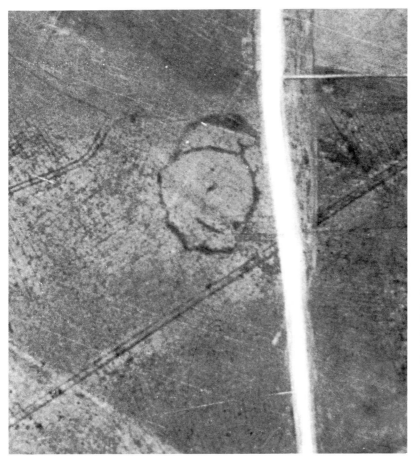

Aerial photography in the flat Tavoliere of northern Apulia here reveals two superimposed enclosures of a Neolithic farm (centre), as well as a buried Roman-period landscape. Visible are the parallel ditches of a Roman road; the regularly laid-out pits for olive trees (left); and parallel trenches for vines (right). The white vertical stripe is a modern road.

efficacious way of planting vines, a practice that is carried on down to the present day.[16]

The startling degree of detail shown on these photographs, which were promptly published by the principal discoverer, J. S. P. Bradford, was followed up in the post-war years by a programme of field walking and excavation. Of this we shall have more to say later, when we look in greater depth at the history and economy of this remarkable landscape. Northern Apulia, however, is by no means the only centuriated landscape to have been mapped from the air in Italy, although nowhere else is the detail so fine. Much of the Po Plain, with its host of new Roman towns and its flat terrain, was divided up into regular parcels of land, the major divisions of which still in places survive as modern field boundaries. These were first clearly defined by Italian archaeologists using aerial photographs taken in the 1930s, the Roman grid of fields becoming obvious as a result of the added perspective gained from height. As in the Tavoliere, the photographs disclosed the remarkable way in which the Romans shaped the landscape to suit their particular needs, a comment both on the strength of their position, and upon

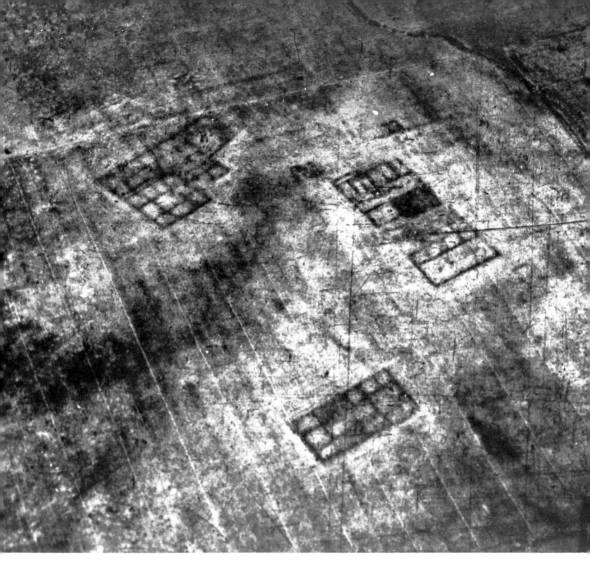

A Roman villa revealed by differential crop growth in the Tavoliere of Apulia. The three buildings may represent the *pars urbana* (residence) and the *pars rustica* and *pars fructuaria*, the working and storage areas, as described by Varro.

the determination that they brought to the planning of their towns and the adjoining territory.[17]

In Northern Europe archaeologists went on to develop aerial photography as a vital technique in the identification of new sites, and in the plotting of older landscapes. In Italy there was to be important work on the observation of known sites and on the major features, particularly ancient roads, of the contryside; but a rather different, and ultimately very influential line of research, emerged in the post-war years, namely field-survey.[18] Today this has become a rather sophisticated matter, but in earlier days it was very much the case of recording what was visible on the surface of ploughed fields, or concealed in olive groves or woodland. There were many pioneering figures in this work, but special prominence will always go to two. One was Thomas Ashby, Director of the British School at Rome from 1906 to 1925, who devoted most of his lifetime to the meticulous recording of the antiquities of Rome and particularly its environs, the Roman Campagna. Many were sites – villas, temples, roads and the like – which have now been damaged or destroyed, making Ashby's work irreplaceable.

Moreover, he was highly influential in shaping the development of the Italian school of topographical studies, the fruits of which are now to be found in dozens of regional studies under the title of *Forma Italiae*.[19]

The other main pioneer of field-survey was John Ward-Perkins, Director of the British School at Rome from 1946 to 1974. In the early 1950s, land reform schemes were resulting in the breaking-up of huge amounts of long-standing pasture, and thus the destruction of an enormous amount of archaeological information. In the southern part of Etruria (and later on elsewhere) Ward-Perkins set in train a programme of ground reconnaissance which, over twenty years or more, covered in detail some 1,000 square kilometres of the area to the north of Rome. The results were extraordinary. Something in the order of two thousand sites came to light; the evolution of the road network, from its inception in Etruscan times through to the post-medieval period, was worked out, and, as knowledge advanced concerning the date of the different sorts of pottery that were picked up, often in huge quantities, so an increasingly elaborate picture could be drawn of the history of settlement in the region – not least for the Roman episode. Happily, the success of the South Etruria survey soon inspired others to carry out similiar work elsewhere. Today the Italian peninsula is being worked by archaeologists as never before, now aided by batteries of specialists, such as soil scientists, experts on environmental evidence and scholars with a detailed knowledge of the pottery.[20]

The quantity of information that is emerging is prodigious, with projects in Molise, the area of Cosa, Campania, Apulia, the regions of Gubbio and Luni and many more. Not only can we begin to say a good deal about various landscapes in pre-Roman, classical and medieval times, but we can also measure the results against the written record, a comparison that often reveals quite unexpected discrepancies. Hand-in-hand with this there has also been excavation. Until the early 1960s our picture of rural settlement was very much dominated by the villas in the Pompeii area (discussed briefly above), sites which had mainly been investigated with the imperfect techniques of the last century. 'There was not a single villa which had been systematically excavated in accordance with the standards long accepted in many of the Roman provinces', as Ward-Perkins was later to write. This was in his introduction to the report on a trail-setting investigation of a pair of villas in the vicinity of the village of Francolise, in the Ager Falernus, to the north of Naples.[21]

The Francolise villas, known as Posto and San Rocco, turned out to provide highly important insights into the social and economic history of the late Republican and early Imperial periods of this region. Both were in existence by about 80 BC, and saw progressive modifications over the next two centuries or so. Neither outlasted the end of the second century AD, although Posto was reoccupied in late Roman times. Both were working farms, Posto at a modest level, while San Rocco was to acquire an elegant residence, the *domus*, once the owner had become well-to-do.[22]

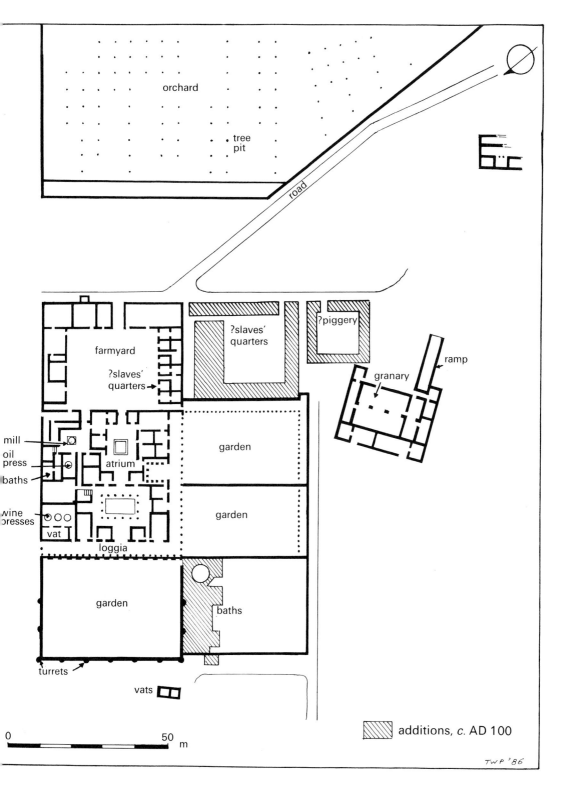

orchard

tree
pit

road

?slaves'
quarters

?piggery

ramp

farmyard

?slaves'
quarters →

granary

mill

oil
press

atrium

garden

baths

wine
presses

garden

vat

loggia

garden

baths

turrets

vats

additions, c. AD 100

0   50
           m

TWP '86

Since the Francolise excavations the investigation of villas and farms has progressed immeasurably, sometimes within the context of field-survey programmes, in other cases as independent projects. They have ranged from peasant smallholdings, as at Monte Forco, to the large establishments like the Villa of the Volusii at Lucus Feroniae, both in the Ager Capenas, to the north of Rome.[23] Objectives have varied. Some have sought to work out a hierarchy of rural sites, others have been concerned to define the character of a *villa rustica* in areas other than Campania, and many have been concerned with the reconstruction of the economy as reflected by the botanical evidence and the animal bones.[24] Fundamental to modern approaches is the notion that the villa as we know it from our literary sources, and from the Pompeian evidence, in fact manifests wide regional variation.

However, probably the most influential project has been the investigation, recently concluded, of a magnificently preserved villa at Settefinestre. This site lies some 140 kilometres to the north-west of Rome, close to the coastal colony of Cosa, which was founded in 273 BC. This is a region that has been extensively surveyed over the last decade or so. Sites of the third century BC are on the whole elusive, and may have been erased by later agriculture. Traces of centuriation are known, however, and it is thought likely that each colonist was given 6 *iugera* of land (1.5 hectares), barely enough for a living. Cosa's population was supplemented by an additional thousand colonists in 197 BC, and there is evidence to suggest that it was at this time that roads, and probably full centuriation, were extended up the Albenga Valley to the north-east.[25]

During the second century BC significant changes began to occur. By this time some individual colonists were no doubt beginning to become wealthy, as is suggested by the construction of more elaborate houses in the town itself. In the countryside, too, more substantial buildings make an appearance, if we can judge from the one excavated site, at Giardino Vecchio. This was a building some 25 metres square with some rooms grouped around a court. These included living quarters with cemented floors and plastered walls, working and storage areas, and facilities for making wine. Perhaps the farmer had already begun to specialise in what was to become one of the major cash-crops of the late Republic. The farm did not, however, outlive the end of the first century BC, and may well have been abandoned a generation or two earlier. The excavators conjecture that this can be directly related to the rise of the large villa estate, run by slaves.[26]

Certainly, the results of this field-survey and the excavation of the Settefinestre villa do support this conclusion. As at Francolise, large villas make their appearance in the first few decades of the first century BC. Settefinestre itself was probably built around 75 BC, a time when land was being widely redistributed through confiscations in the wake of Sulla's victory over the followers of Marius. Nero's ancestors, the Domitii Ahenobarbi, who owned lands in the Cosa area, may well have acquired them at this time.

The façade of the Giardino villa in the region of Cosa, where the wall is embellished with miniature towers, resembling the wall of a town. First century BC.

Unquestionably, the Settefinestre villa was very grand indeed. Perched on a low hill overlooking a fertile valley and only four kilometres from Cosa, it still conserves a magnificent façade; this stands nearly five metres high, and is embellished by miniature round turrets. From a distance it looks exactly like a fortified town wall, an assertion in architecture of the owner's power and wealth. Curiously, two other villas in the Cosa region have similar turreted walls, although the style is not found elsewhere, except on some funerary monuments in Campania.[27] This wall, in fact, revetted a terrace with an ornamental garden of a sort that has been thoroughly investigated in recent years, which contained a series of underground vaulted basements.[28] At a higher level was the *domus*, the main residence. This was laid out as a perfect square with sides measuring 150 Roman feet (44.35 metres). It followed the usual pattern of rich houses, so that the entrance passage led into a hall, or *atrium*, with a central pool, and with reception rooms and bedrooms around. Beyond this was a peristyle court, surrounded by other rooms, leading into a great loggia that ran the whole length of the *domus*. Situated high above the valley, it commands quite splendid views.

The great majority of the rooms were decorated with sumptuous mosaics, mainly in polychrome, and the walls rendered with plaster, which was painted in the so-called Second Pompeian Style, including architectural views, carried out to a high standard. On one corner of the main residence, however, there was also a separate working quarter, together with a small bath-suite and a typically Roman communal lavatory, seating twenty people. The industrial installations included an oil-press and vats for storing oil, as well as a complex for the manufacture of wine. The bases of three presses were found, and in addition many of the fittings. Next door was a vat room, where the grapes were trodden. In the centre was a large plug-hole, allowing the grape juice to drain through to containers below.

The emphasis upon wine production is of great interest, matching the evidence from the Campanian villas. Moreover, it is possible to make some rough guesses at the size of the production, since there are about a dozen large villas known in Cosa's territory, suggesting estates of about 500 *iugera* (125 hectares). Using figures cited by the ancient authors, this would mean that an estate like that of Settefinestre was producing in excess of 1.2 million litres of wine a year, a very sizeable amount. By way of comparison, a great modern French château like Meursault in Burgundy farms 40 hectares and has in its cellars some 500,000 bottles and 2,000 huge casks. What is of even greater interest is the fact that there are some grounds for supposing that the Settefinestre estate may have been owned by a well-known senatorial family, the Sestii; it is recorded that they possessed lands in the Ager Cosanus, and in the same area (especially from the town of Cosa and its port) have been found large numbers of wine amphora handles stamped SES. These handles have an interesting distribution, for they show that the containers were shipped up the north-west coast of Italy, into southern France and north-east Spain, and far up the Rhône Valley. The market for Cosanus wine was indeed widespread.[29]

So far we have concentrated upon the main block at Settefinestre. The site was, however, much more extensive. There were three other great walled gardens, as well as the main *pars rustica*, with the farm buildings. Here was a farmyard surrounded by buildings, some of which would seem to have been for storage, while others would have been suitable for slaves. Another structure contained twenty-seven separate rooms with concrete floors and a trough in each corner, arranged around a yard. The doorways were provided with emplacements for hatches, and it is thought that the complex comprised a series of pigsties. There was also a barn, and a large walled enclosure, either containing an orchard or used for penning in stock.

The remarkable picture evinced by these excavations is testimony of just how much can be learned from methodical and scientific investigation. It is satisfactory, too, that something can also be said about the later history of the site; namely, an extensive refurbishment of the *domus*, with many new mosaics and wall-paintings, in the late first century AD and, it is thought, a drastic running-down in the production of wine and oil soon afterwards. There may have been a swing towards the growing of cereals, although this is far from certain. What is clear is that within the next half century the villa was abandoned, so that by the 160s and 170s it was gradually crumbling into ruins.

The history of the villa estate at Settefinestre can in some respects be compared with those of the Francolise villas in northern Campania, which we referred to briefly above. All three came into being within a few decades of each other, and each was abandoned during the second half of the second century AD. However, there are also significant differences. At the outset neither Francolise villa was particularly grand or extensive: Posto consisted of half a dozen rooms and an attached farmyard, while San Rocco, although it had a *domus* and a separate farm, was nevertheless far from luxurious. Around 30 BC new building work was put in hand at both sites. Posto remained relatively modest, with a residential area suited much more to a bailiff than a well-to-do owner seeking a pleasant occasional sojourn in the countryside. San Rocco, on the other hand, was considerably enlarged, and drastically remodelled. The focus of the *domus* became a peristyle court, open to the skies. There were porticoes on two sides affording fine views, mosaics in almost every room, and, in order to provide water for the complex, new cisterns were built with a total capacity of no less than 1.1 million litres. There was also a walled garden and, of course, the *pars rustica*. Unfortunately, we can say little about the overall economic emphasis of the farm at this stage, but later on two substantial presses for making olive-oil were installed, together with the appropriate vats, and it is likely that this was a prime area of specialisation from the beginning of the farm's history — especially as the Posto villa was also in the main a producer of oil.[30]

It has been conjectured that this upturn in the fortunes of these two villas might be connnected with Octavian's victory at Actium in 31 BC; for Augustus, as he was later to be known, assigned centuriated land to the veterans whom he settled at Cales (modern Calvi). But more plausible is the idea that these fairly rich estates were bought up by his supporters, confident in both their investment and their future. The chronology is right, and the idea is appealing, but totally lacking in proof. Whatever the truth of such a hypothesis, however, it is clear that for the time being the estates did well. Bath-houses were installed about AD 50 at both San Rocco and Posto, and at San Rocco modern oil-presses and a couple of brick or tile kilns were built. One has the impression that the owners were capable men with an eye both for comfort and for profit: hence, perhaps, the diversification of activity on the farm into the manufacture of bricks and tiles at a time when these were starting to be of much greater importance in the building trade. It recalls, too,

Map showing the location of the most noted wines of Roman Italy. They cluster mainly in the areas of the great villa estates, and exclude many important regions of today, such as Chianti, Soave and Valpolicella.

the running-down of wine production at Settefinestre a few decades later, a period when Italy began increasingly to import foodstuffs from abroad, particularly France, Spain and North Africa. There must have been consequences for the balance-sheets of individual estates, and it is instructive to see them reflected in the material remains.[31]

We have selected these villas for particular attention, since the excavations of them have proved to be milestones in the study of the countryside of central Italy. They help us to demonstrate that comfortable farmhouses, as well as luxurious country houses with attached farms, were in existence by the early first century BC, but had slipped into decline, in some areas at least, by the later second century AD. The emphasis upon the production of wine and oil, both excellent investments, is also in accord with other sources of evidence. It is not for nothing that, when we plot on a map the location of Italy's most noted Roman wines, they show a remarkable grouping in southern Etruria, Latium and Campania, precisely the areas where these villas that we have been considering are situated. Interestingly, the map does not pick out some of the modern regions producing famous Italian wines, such as Chianti, or the Soaves and Valpolicellas of the Verona region – a comment, no doubt, on the way in which success in more recent Italian history has tended to verge towards the north and away from the south.

To be sure, in Roman times parts of the far south appear never to have really prospered. Taranto, for example, was an unpopular posting for retired veterans (sent there by both C. Gracchus and Nero) and, according to Horace, was merely a quiet country retreat, suitable for a tired business man.[32] Perhaps the Greek influence in this former colony of Sparta was as strong as it seems to have been in Naples, which retained its Greek institutions and language down into the period of the late Empire.[33]

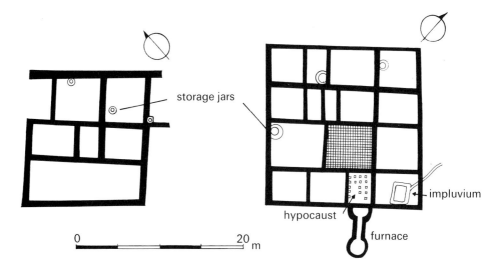

storage jars

hypocaust

impluvium

furnace

Two farms in the Metapontine countryside of southern Italy, not far from Taranto. Ponte Fabrizio (left) dates to the fourth century BC and San Biagio (right) to the third–fourth centuries AD, thus displaying a remarkable conservatism of architectural tradition.

Nevertheless, Greek ideas and practices did play a significant part in the shaping of Italy's Roman landscape. It is instructive to look at the district of Metaponto, a region of flat coastal plain tucked into one corner of the Gulf of Taranto. Metaponto was a Greek colony, founded around the middle of the seventh century BC. Famous in its day (Pythagoras was buried there), it went into decline after the Second Punic War. Survey of the area around the city has revealed a remarkable picture of rural life and the way in which it was organised. Particularly striking are two systems of land divisions with strips separated by what seem to be roads, marked by side ditches. Each block measures 325 × 205 metres, and the systems cover altogether several hundred square kilometres. Current thinking is that these boundaries, one set of which extend the axes of the street grid of Metaponto, were laid out as early as the middle of the sixth century BC.[34] Within these field systems were the sites of the farms and of the nearby cemeteries. They are, in effect, the precursors of small villas like those at Posto and San Rocco, and some scholars have been tempted to see the Roman villa as a development from the Greek farm, and centuriation as a logical progression from Greek land divisions at sites like Metaponto. Certainly, the ground-plans of some early Roman farmsteads are remarkably similar to examples in Greece: the Villa Sambuco in the Tolfa Hills to the north-west of Rome, for instance, finds close parallels both at Posta Crusta, near Foggia in Apulia, and with a farmhouse near Olynthos, in north-eastern Greece.[35] Indeed, in the Metaponto area the form of the farmhouse, once established, seems to have remained extraordinarily standard throughout the Hellenistic and Roman periods, in terms of both the plan and the building techniques – mud brick upon stone foundations. This is an argument which we could pursue much further, but without any hope at this stage in the investigation of reaching any certain conclusions. What matters for our purposes is that in areas like the Metapontine lowlands there was a rural landscape which in some respects anticipates what was to follow in many parts of the peninsula.

At one of these Metapontine sites an enlightened policy of environmental sampling, combined with rich preservation of organic material under waterlogged conditions, has shed a great deal of light upon the economic history of the region. The site in question is a religious sanctuary, Pizzica Pantanello, a status which might well bias the sample; however, the deposits (which fill a reservoir) do seem to reflect local agricultural activity. During the heyday of the city of Metaponto the main crops seem to have been olives, figs and vines. Even the willow and poplar supports for the vines were found. Some cereals were grown, including wheat and barley, and it is ears of barley which appear upon the Greek coins of Metaponto. By the end of the fourth century BC, however, a considerable change had taken place in that the cultivation of cereals and vegetables expanded vastly, at the expense of vines and olives. The excavators interpret this as a sign of greater specialisation in the economy, and perhaps as a response to the increasingly unsettled conditions of the time, but it will need much more evidence to sustain – or to refute – that conclusion. They also suggest, on the basis of the plant remains and the animal bones, that the Roman annexation of the region brought about a profound economic change: that the arable land very largely gave way to pasture, devoted in the main to the grazing of sheep and goats. At the same time the number of farms declined very sharply and, after a brief reverse in the late Republic, continued to dwindle throughout the period of the Empire.[36]

All this is fascinating stuff, not least because it would appear to provide a close match with the conclusions reached by historians using documentary sources: that in the wake of the Hannibalic Wars, from the second century BC onwards, large parts of the south were turned over to sheep ranches, staffed mainly by slave labour. Perhaps, indeed, the fit is just too neat, although it does seem to find support from some other excavations and field-surveys. Not enough ground has been looked at, or published, to make for any sort of certainty, but it is striking to see how our samples from the south-east in particular consistently seem to record a sharp drop in the number of rural sites from the third and second centuries BC. In the valley of the River Bradano, for example, which flows into the sea at Metaponto, the overall scale of the depopulation has been described as 'massive', and not dissimilar results have been reported from elsewhere in the region. Despite the archaeologists' reluctance to be seen to be proving the historians' judgements – better that the archaeological evidence should speak for itself – the case for a switch from arable to pasture, and all that this implies, does seem to carry weight. Yet an excavation at Monte Irsi, in the upper reaches of the Bradano Valley, showed that it was pigs, not sheep, that became more important in the early Roman period at this site, and that occupation continued well into Imperial times. It leaves one with the uneasy feeling that generalisations of any sort may well be premature, and that in the end the story of even one part of a valley could well be very different from that of another.[37]

In fact, there is now a good deal of evidence to suggest that matters are much more complicated than they seemed even ten years ago. Until that time the principal source of evidence came from a massive, long-term investigation of some 1,000 square kilomteres in the region to the north of Rome, south Etruria. As we mentioned earlier, two thousand sites of all periods were recorded. Many were revealed during the great programme of land reform that, from 1950 onwards, brought huge areas of pasture under the plough, often for the first time. In the process, many were also to be effectively erased from the landscape, adding urgency to the project.

In the early years of the South Etruria survey analysis of the data was hampered by a lack of detailed knowledge about the dates of the pottery that was picked up in great abundance. Over the last twenty years or so this situation has been transformed, so that changes in the density and type of sites can be worked out with ever-increasing precision. As a result we can now say a good deal about the way in which man's use of the landscape changed. It is really very striking, for example, to see the way in which the Roman conquest of the region brought about the demise of almost every pre-existing town (Nepi, Sutri and Veii, which lapsed into relative obscurity, are the principal exceptions). Moreover, in the countryside there was a dramatic increase in the number of farms, reaching a peak in the time of Augustus at the turn of the millennium, to be followed by a gradual decline. These farms seem to divide into several broad classes. At the lowest end of the scale were very small sites, best equated with what Varro and Columella call a *tugurium*, a peasant's cottage or hut; in the middle rank were medium-sized establishments of modest architectural pretensions, perhaps a *casa* or smallholding; and at the upper end were the villas, ranging from the comfortable but ordinary place to rather grand complexes, with luxuries such as fine mosaics and a bath-suite in the owner's residence.[38]

Very few of these sites have been properly excavated, and we cannot yet say much about them. However, there are some clues. For example, at Monte Forco, in the Ager Capenas, a small farmstead has been investigated, and is shown to have been built in the Augustan period. It was a modest little house, only 10.95 × 5.15 metres in size, with a farmyard outside, and an estate that was probably no bigger than 2.5 hectares. Perhaps its owner was a retired veteran, some of whom may have been settled here under Caesar,[39] or a veteran's son. Similarly, at Crocicchie, on the Via Clodia, there was a

small house and a separate building, perhaps a barn, constructed again in early Imperial times. Two centuries later a simple bath-house was added on, suggesting that these smallholders were gradually becoming more wealthy. No doubt they, and most others in the region, grew cereals, including wheat, barley and millet, as well as vines and olives. There may have been specialisation, but a mixed economy (including livestock) is likely at most farms.[40]

A mosaic floor, decorated with dolphins, in the bath-house of a small villa at Crocicchie, to the north-west of Rome. Third century AD.

Some landowners, on the other hand, did diversify their activities. Pottery and tile kilns are known from a number of sites, and at Monte Aguzzo, in the Ager Veientanus, and at Monte Maggiore, in the Ager Faliscus, outcrops of the basalt (*selce*) that was used to pave the roads were extensively quarried; the well-appointed houses of those who profited from this are to be found all around the quarries, and one wonders whether T. Humanius Stabilio, who paid for a bridge over a stream in the depths of the northern Ager Veientanus, not far from one of the quarries, might have been one of them.[41]

Grander villas are also known. One has only to stop at the last *Autostrada* service station before reaching Rome to visit the amazingly rich villas of the senatorial family, the Volusii. Here is both a fine residence and a *villa rustica*, lying within the suburbs of the town of Lucus Feroniae; the villa platform is bigger even than the town's forum. Several emperors owned estates in southern Etruria, and the remains of what were clearly very large and well-to-do complexes have been identified at a considerable number of sites, some with conspicuously well-preserved remains.[42]

The interpretation of this vast body of information from South Etruria is, however, rather problematic and continues to provoke a good deal of controversy. In part, this stems from the temptation of regarding the results as typical of Italy as a whole, a view that is readily dispelled by a visit to the area today. Everywhere there are the smart country cottages, the service roads, the shops and the restaurants that the weekender, escaping from Rome, requires – a situation that cannot have been too different in classical times. Increasingly, it is only in the backwoods that 'traditional', rustic ways of life are preserved, a feature that can also be read into archaeological evidence, as far as we can understand it. The picture from South Etruria is more a mirror of what was happening in Rome itself than in the rest of the peninsula. The steady rise in rural settlement during the later Republic, the peak in early Imperial times, and the slow decline thereafter, all broadly fit the history of the capital city in Roman times.

The other feature about the survey which has puzzled scholars is the abundance of evidence for smallholders in late Republican and Imperial times. This was a period when, as we have seen, the literary evidence suggests that large slave-run estates were prevalent, ousting the peasant farmer. Whilst the archaeological evidence tells us little about patterns of landowning in South Etruria – only a series of inscriptions could do that – there nevertheless seems to be little doubt that there were a good many small farmers in the region, alongside those who owned very big estates. Moreover, many of these smallholders seem to have retained their farms well into Imperial times, as at the Crocicchie site. This recalls figures from land registers like that for Ligures Baebiani, a town near Circello, twenty-five kilometres to the north of Benevento. Here an inscription dating to the early second century AD shows that 21.3 per cent of the land was in the hands of just 3.5 per cent of landowners (the wealthiest possessed 11.2 per cent), while the poorest 14 per cent of landowners owned 3.6 per cent – very much the smallholders attested archaeologically in South Etruria. Indeed, it would seem that only in the late Roman period, when the number of sites declined sharply, do the large villas come to manage most of the landscape.[43]

The fact of the matter is that the free peasant farmer did survive in many areas, although his traces are conspicuous neither in the ancient literature nor in the archaeolgical record. If we take as an example the area around Rosia, which lies some fifteen kilometres to the south-west of Siena, survey work has so far revealed only one large Roman villa in an area of some twenty square kilometres; the likely presumption, therefore, is that the land was being farmed mainly by smallholders who lived in slight buildings which are now exceedingly hard to find.[44] Still clearer is the evidence that has been recovered by a large-scale project of ground prospection in the areas to the east and north-east of the Roman colony of Cosa. We have already described the palatial villa at Settefinestre, which is thought to have been the base of a substantial slave-run estate. This is just one of a series of such villas within a ten-kilometre arc of the walls of Cosa, and here there seems little doubt that from the first century BC or before the land was largely in the hands of very rich magnates. To the north-east stretches the great Albenga Valley, along whose length were three Roman towns, all colonies: namely, Talamone, on the coast; Heba; and, much higher up, Saturnia. As with Cosa's territory, this landscape was originally divided up into centuriated squares, but it was to develop in a rather different way. In the lower and central part of the valley villas and farms are interspersed, although with a heavier concentration of large sites towards the coast. In the higher reaches the villas tend to cluster around the town of Saturnia, with many more outlying farms. By and large, then, the rich snapped up the prime locations, while the small farmers worked the more remote, less convenient, and no doubt less profitable areas.[45]

That said, even the villas were probably nothing like as splendid as that at Settefinestre: the majority are probably best seen as large, comfortable farmhouses rather than stately country mansions. Increasingly, this type of site is being properly investigated in all parts of the peninsula, and we shall be able to say much more about them in a few years. One recently excavated example is to be found less than fifteen kilometres from the centre of Rome, between the Via Gabina and the Via Prenestina, to the east of the city. Known simply as site 11, the villa probably originated in the third century BC. Before long there were three ranges of rooms, arranged around a courtyard, with a walled garden or yard on one side. Painted plaster was used to decorate the residential part, and the impression is of a fairly well-to-do villa. Early in the Imperial period the house was enlarged, the main building now covering some 25 × 30 metres, and an *atrium* was put in. This lent a fashionable air to the place and, as a further sign of prosperity, in the early second century AD a bath-house and a pool in the garden were added. Somewhat later facilities for the manufacture of oil were installed in one corner of the house; this is an interesting development, which might be taken to suggest that the owner had decided to invest in a product that was by now being imported on a vast scale, particularly from North Africa. If so, it can hardly have been a successful venture, for by the mid-third century the villa had begun to collapse into ruins, and the site became a haunt for squatters.[46]

The demise of this villa in the mid-Imperial period follows, as we have seen, an often repeated pattern, and we shall try to determine the reasons and extent of it in chapter 7. Meanwhile, the Via Gabina site furnishes a useful example of a medium-sized villa in western-central Italy, a type of site with some urban-like sophistication and an emphasis upon the production of wine and oil that seems to have been especially common in this region of the peninsula. Elsewhere in Italy, however, recent work is beginning to suggest that the villas and farms were rather different from those in the area of Campania and Etruria. One region currently under investigation is in the great Biferno Valley of Molise, which runs down into the sea near Tèrmoli on the Adriatic coast. The Biferno River rises high in the Apennine Mountains and traverses more than eighty kilometres as it winds its way towards the sea; it is not, therefore, surprising that over this diverse terrain the Roman farming pattern manifests considerable variation. In the lower part of the valley modestly sized villas turned out to be fairly common, totally contradicting the historical evidence, which implies very little Romanisation of the region and a heavy concentration on sheep-farming. In fact, there appears to have been extensive cultivation of vines, olives and cereals, as well as a mixed stock economy – cattle and pigs feature as prominently in the collections of animal bones as sheep. On the other hand, the villa buildings tend to be much less grand than their counterparts on the Tyrrhenian side of the country; at Matrice, for instance, a large complex to the north-east of Campobasso, it was the austerity of the architecture and internal decorations that most impressed the excavators, rather than the luxurious nature of the building. Very possibly, as they suggest, the owner lived in the nearby town of Fagifulae (modern Montagnano), which lies just five kilometres away – a pattern of farm ownership which may well have been as common in classical Italy as it is in many areas today.[47]

The atrium of a comfortably appointed town-house situated by the forum (background) at Saepinum. Sheep passing through the forum on their way to summer pastures no doubt discommoded the town's inhabitants.

In the upper reaches of the valley the pattern changes. The villas are mainly replaced by more homely farmsteads, and the vines and olives give way to the cultivation of vegetables and cereals – as befit the different soils and climatic regime. Moreover, the raising of sheep was of particular importance, and involved an intricate system of transhumance networks. Transhumance has played – and continues to do – a vital role in the management of the pastoral economy, and special drove-roads, *tratturi*, that linked the summer and the winter pastures seem to have originated far into antiquity.[48] These drove-roads, together with the upland farms, serve to underline the importance of sheep in the Roman economy. Here was the source of lamb (which figures often in our one surviving Roman cookery book), milk, cheese and particularly wool. Cloth and textiles were high-price items in antiquity, although they were manufactured in many towns. Pompeii, for example, has yielded a great deal of evidence for the production of cloth, particularly from the first century BC onwards. Some of the larger houses were converted into premises for manufacturing and dyeing the goods, and some affluent cloth-merchants, like Marcus Vecilius Verecundus, advertised their activities by means of a painted shop-front. The size of the dividends may be measured by the fact that these fullers had their own corporation centre, named after their patroness, Eumachia. It lay on one side of the forum and was the most imposing building there after the basilica.[49]

It is particularly good that Pompeii has produced so much conclusive evidence for the importance of wool production, since it helps to underline how multi-faceted the agrarian economy of Roman Italy must have been. As more and more so-called 'backwater' areas like the Biferno Valley of Molise are investigated, so we shall be able to gain a more balanced view to set against the picture derived largely from the villas of the western part of central Italy.

So far we have dwelt only in passing upon another important aspect of the rural landscape, namely centuriation. With the vast network of new colonies that were created during the Republican period, the allocation of land to the settlers became of prime importance. Individual *coloni* were assigned parcels of land, the amount varying both with the status of the settlement and, no doubt, with the availability of suitable terrain. Some of these allocations were very small, barely enough to earn a living from;[50] but one often reads of plots of 50 or more *iugera* (13 hectares), which would have been quite sufficient for an adequate income. Careful mapping was, of course, a vital prerequisite, and a corps of surveyors – and appropriate manuals, setting out the necessary guidelines – soon came into existence. Whether the land was to be divided into squares (centuriation, *limitatio*), rectangular strips (*strigae* and *scamna*) or irregular areas (*subseciva*, 'land cut away by a line'), it all had to be carefully marked out, and boundary stones had to be set up. Hyginus Gromaticus, writing in Trajan's day (AD 98–117), tells us that 'many founders of colonies looked to suitability of terrain, and set up their *decumanus maximus* and *cardo maximus* [the main axes] where they were

The Porta Ventura at Spello (ancient Hispellum), a gate set flush with the wall. It dates to the Augustan period (27 BC – AD 14).

going to make the most of the assignation of land ... [These] were set up on the best soil, as in the territory of Hispellum in Umbria'. Hispellum (modern Spello), which lies to the south of Assisi, is indeed situated on good land, being on one side of the valley of the River Topino, and it is fascinating to see how place-names like Perticani (from *pertica*, 'a surveyor's rod') and Limiti (from *limites*, 'paths') survive down to this day – as do traces of the centuriation.[51]

The work of the land-surveyors was, in fact, widespread, extending over many parts of Italy (and elsewhere). Their tasks were manifold since, the fieldwork apart, they also had to keep registers, supervise the lottery with which the land was allocated, and settle the inevitable disputes. Some idea of the scale of their work may be gained from the estimate of one modern scholar that in the decade at the beginning of the second century BC no less than a million *iugera* of land (252,000 hectares) was handed out to 100,000 families.[52]

The origins of what was to become a great civil service department are obscure; but we do know that the Greeks developed carefully worked out schemes of land management, and Etruscan practice is likely to have played its part too; the Roman unit of measurement, the *actus*, may derive from the Etruscan word *acnua*. But the fact of the matter is that from the sixth and fifth centuries BC many of the more sophisticated city states of the Mediterranean were evolving precise ideas of planning, urban and rural, and Rome had a fund of common knowledge and experience upon which to draw. When the colony of Tarracina Anxur was founded in 329 BC each of the three hundred settlers was given 2 *iugera* of land, just half a hectare; today something of the rectangular plots can still be traced in the layout of modern farm-tracks on the flat ground to the north-west of the present-day town of Terracina. Although we cannot be certain about the date of these field systems, these may be one of the very early examples of Roman landscape planning, and there seems little doubt that it was Latium and Campania, where Rome first expanded, that the initial experiments in land allotments began.

However, it is in northern Apulia, and over vast tracts of the Po Valley, that centuriation is most conspicuously represented. In the Apulian Tavoliere aerial photography and excavation have revealed a complex sequence. To the east of Lucera, a colony founded in 314 BC, the early system consists of a series of parallel roads, lacking cross-divisions; to the north, though, there is a regular grid, covering some twenty-five square kilometres, with individual plots measuring 20 × 20 *actus* (710 metres), or 200 *iugera* (50 hectares). Elsewhere in the Tavoliere there are also units of 16 × 16 *actus*, and to the south-west of Foggia is a huge centuriated area measuring some 20 × 10 kilometres. Interestingly, in one part a second phase of field divisions on a different orientation has been imposed over the primary scheme, a phenomenon also repeated elsewhere. Here, therefore, there may be a reflection in the archaeological record of the work of later land commissioners: the Gracchan reforms, for instance, are well reflected by boundary stones attesting to their work.

Many farmers may well have lived in the towns, and travelled on a daily basis to their fields; this is a time-honoured practice, still current today, as anyone who has travelled into a Tavoliere town at dusk, passing cart after cart, will know. This must be the explanation for the almost total lack of Roman sites in the countryside around Troia (ancient Aecae). In other areas, however, aerial photography has revealed the location and layout of the farms with extraordinary clarity. A few are quite elaborate, with a residence and working and storage areas; but the great majority are much simpler: a ditched enclosure approached by a drove-road, and a modest house. At Masseria Nocelli, eight kilometres to the south-east of Lucera, to take an excavated instance, the principal building measured only 10 × 15 metres, and was a very simple structure (although it was provided with a double-action vacuum water pump, invented according to Vitruvius by one Ctesibius). Water must have been a problem in this dry landscape but the farmer, nevertheless, seems to have prospered. Founded in the late second century BC, the site may have been developed as a consequence of the Gracchan land reforms. The animal bones suggest that pigs provided the main source of meat, while cattle were kept for ploughing and for hauling carts, and sheep (the most numerous animal) for wool and cheese. Some cereals were grown, but vines and olives were also produced in abundance. This much is very clear on the aerial photographs, where the lines of pits for the olive trees and the parallel trenches for the vines are revealed with quite extraordinary clarity. No doubt the farmer was able to secure a good profit from these crops, underlining the point that he was working not merely to subsist but to make money from his land. Even so, he cannot have been very successful, for his buildings remained simple and were eventually abandoned in the first century AD. Although he invested extensively in vines and olives, as recommended by the ancient agronomists, he was unable to attain the great profitability of so many farmers on the western side of the peninsula. Roman Apulia may not have been given over entirely to sheep ranches, as many ancient – and some modern – sources would have us believe; but the state-conceived land allocations, however much they favoured mixed agriculture, do not seem to have been entirely successful either.[53]

In the Po Valley, on the other hand, the Roman development turned this once marshy region into one of the very prosperous parts of Italy. Strabo tells us precisely this, and lists some of the rich variety of produce: millet, acorns for feeding pigs, wine stored in wooden jars 'larger than houses', wool of all qualities, and even pitch. Cereals, as Pliny reminds us, were of particular importance, adding that after grapes and corn the turnip cabbage (*rapum*) was 'the most profitable harvest of all for the land that lies across the Po'. Flax and lucerne were also grown, the latter being a valuable feed-crop for stock and a useful fertiliser of the land. Just as today, the Po Valley towns of antiquity were thriving places, which benefited hugely from the fertile land with which they were surrounded.[54]

The way in which the Roman surveyors and engineers brought this land under control in the early days of colonisation can still hardly fail to impress. The key was the Via Aemilia, a great road that stretched for nearly three hundred kilometres along the north-eastern side of the Apennine Mountains. It was built by the consul Marcus Aemilius Lepidus in 187 BC, so as to link the many colonies along this route, such as Rimini, Cesena, Bologna, Parma and Piacenza. Much of the vast area of centuriated land to be found in the Po Valley is aligned upon the Via Aemilia, a measure of the careful planning that lay behind the enterprise. Naturally, the orientation of individual territories varied, as the road changed alignment; but the regularity of the overall system is its most remarkable characteristic.[55]

Mosaic, dating to the early second century AD, in the villa at Russi, near Ravenna.

Most of the individual units measure 20 × 20 *actus*, an area of 200 *iugera*, or one century. They form part of territories that were often huge: at Parma, for instance, the centuriation covers an area of 180,000 *iugera* (45,000 hectares). These figures are rather hard to square with Livy's observation that the original 2,000 colonists sent to Parma were awarded just 8 *iugera* apiece, amounting to less than 10 per cent of the total centuriated land. However, we know that reinforcements were sent to Parma in the late first century BC, and it is likely that what we see in the region is a centuriated landscape representing many more than one phase of development.

Other allotments were much more generous. The *coloni* at Bologna, Bononia, received 50 or 70 *iugera*, and at Aquileia, founded in 181 BC, settlers received 50, 100 or 140 *iugera*, according to rank — a way, no doubt, of tempting more influential citizens to this unattractive area. What we still know little of, however, are details of the farms that grew up in these great centuriated landscapes. The sites are certainly there to be found. In the area to the north of Modena, for example, a great many small villas and farms, some with mosaics, have recently been revealed by field-survey. Most seem to have come into existence by the late first century BC, but yield few finds later than about AD 200.[56] Perhaps the villa near Russi, a few kilometres to the south-west of Ravenna, originated as the allotment of a *colonus*. Built in the Augustan period, it was a spacious but hardly luxurious structure, where the residential area (which had some pleasant if unspectacular mosaics) lay almost cheek by jowl with a granary, barn and other 'working' rooms. The property was several times improved and extended during its four or five centuries of existence — the improvements included the building of a separate bath-house — and it is easy to imagine the site as the enterprise of a veteran soldier, turned farmer, whose heirs became comparatively wealthy as time went by.[57]

Even though one could have journeyed several hundred kilometres through centuriated flatlands, divided up — as today — into ditched, fertile properties, the northern part of Italy is not without its more mountainous parts. In the Apennine Mountains especially centuriation was all but impossible, and land was divided up in more conventional ways. Many of the upland valleys were, in fact, extremely fertile, as the twenty-five-kilometre drive from Piacenza through the hills to the small Roman town of Velleia will readily show. Perched on the side of a hill, Velleia was surrounded by good farmland. It is particularly fortunate that in 1747 a bronze tablet came to light in the basilica recording a remarkable donation by the emperor Trajan. Dating to the early second century AD, the tablet tells how Trajan deposited over one million sesterces, to be used as mortgages: the idea was to promote agricultural development of the region, and at the same time to provide food for three hundred poor children from the interest on the loans, rated at 5 per cent. It emerges that the average estate amounted to about 130 *iugera* (33 hectares), and that the real profit lay in pasture for stock and in timber.[58]

This welfare scheme, the *alimenta*, for the support of uncared-for children is a further remarkable instance of the way in which Roman ideals were to permeate all aspects of life in Italy. It seems to have originated on a private basis in the mid-first century AD, and was taken up as a major state scheme by first the emperor Nerva (AD 96–8) and then by Trajan (AD 98–117). Inscriptions recording alimentary awards are known from most parts of the peninsula, and have been variously interpreted. The idea that they were intended to help the small farmer has been long rejected, but the notion that they were intended to stem population decline which, in turn, might effect recruitment to the legions seems far-fetched. In short, we do not know why the *alimenta* was instituted, although the surviving documents are of particular interest in that they provide absolute values of estates, and help to plot patterns of purchase. For Velleia, for example, the figures have been used to show that, of 323 farms owned in the period of Augustus' principate, these devolved to just 52 properties within the period of a century. To many this has seemed good evidence to support the idea of the growth of large estates concentrated in the hands of the exclusive few. Certainly, this was a process that was commonplace in antiquity, particularly in areas where military veterans were settled. Soldiers were not by experience or by inclination well suited to the life of the farmer. This is why, as Tacitus explains, the drafts of ex-soldiers to the depopulated colonies of Taranto and Anzio were not a success. Similarly, when land was awarded to Sulla's veterans in the territory of Praeneste it was quickly reformed into much larger estates: rural life may well not have suited them, especially with Rome and its attractions only a short trip away.[59]

The archaeological evidence is here of the greatest interest. The pattern is not wholly consistent from one region to another, but most of the field-surveys seem to show a general decline in the number of sites from the second century AD onwards. In the Faliscan area of southern Etruria, for example, there is a 22 per cent drop during the second century, 40 per cent more are abandoned by AD 300, and within a century that figure is halved again. Whilst we cannot attach too much accuracy to these percentages (data gathered from field-survey is useful only as a general guide), the overall trend is likely to be correct. Moreover, it is one that can be traced in many other parts of the peninsula, implying a gradual but far-reaching transformation of the rural landscape.

Any attempt to interpret these figures is full of pitfalls, for the archaeological evidence does not tell us about land-ownership. Documents like the Velleia tablet are valuable, since they do indicate a trend towards the creation of fewer, larger estates; but this may not be universal, and other factors such as falling populations may be at work. What is certain is that by the late Roman period the number of smallholders had declined drastically and, in all probability, a good deal of land had gone out of cultivation.

These are matters, however, that we shall return to later, when we review the very different world of late antiquity in Italy. Meanwhile, we have tried to open a few windows, through which we can gain glimpses of Italy's varied agrarian history. It is a story full of diversity, but made remarkable by the sheer scale of the transformation of the countryside. Whatever the economic and social implications of the Roman 'villa system' – and here the debate has hardly begun – it is nevertheless astonishing that a casual stroll in anywhere but the most mountainous areas can bring to light the remains of what is recognisably a Roman villa or farm. No-one can ever guess how many villas there may have been, but it is their very ubiquity which most vividly underlines the huge wealth and success of Roman Italy.

FURTHER READING

General works include K. D. White, *Roman farming* (1970); A. G. McKay, *Houses, villas and palaces in the Roman world* (1975); J. Percival, *The Roman villa* (1976); J. J. Rossiter, *Roman farm buildings in Italy* (1978); J. M. Frayn, *Subsistence farming in Roman Italy* (1979) and *Sheep-rearing and the wool trade in Italy* (1984). See also A. Giardina and A. Schiavone (eds), *Società romana e produzione schiavistica* (1981); and J. Kolendo, *L'agricoltura nell'Italia romana* (1979). On labour see P. D. A. Garnsey in *Proc. Cambridge Phil. Soc.* 25 (1979), 1ff. and (ed.), *Non-slave labour in the Graeco-Roman world* (1981); and D. W. Rathbone in *JRS* 73 (1983), 160–8. For wine and wealth, N. Purcell in *JRS* 75 (1985), 1–19; for property, M. I. Finley (ed.), *Studies in Roman property* (1976); for the *alimenta*, R. P. Duncan-Jones, *Economy of the Roman empire* (1982). For centuriation, J. S. P. Bradford, *Ancient landscapes* (1957); F. Castagnoli, *Le ricerche sui resti della centuriazione* (1958); P. Tozzi, *Saggi di topografia storica* (1974); O. A. W. Dilke, *The Roman land surveyors* (1971); R. Bussi (ed.), *Misurare la terra* (2 vols, 1983); and G. D. B. Jones in *Arch. Classica* 32 (1980), 85ff. Regional studies include J. H. D'Arms, *Romans on the Bay of Naples* (1970); T. W. Potter, *The changing landscape of south Etruria* (1979); A. Carandini (ed.), *La romanizzazione dell'Etruria: il territorio di Vulci* (1985); for Molise, G. Barker *et al.* in *PBSR* 46 (1978), 35ff.; J. Carter, *The territory of Metaponto* (1983). See also K. S. Painter (ed.), *Roman villas in Italy* (1980). Major site reports are listed in the bibliography and include Buccino (Dyson 1983), Francolise (Cotton 1979 and Cotton and Métraux 1985), M. Irsi (Small 1977), Russi (Mansuelli 1962), Settefinestre (Carandini 1985), Villa of the Volusii (Moretti and Moretti 1977). For Pompeian villas, see also Jashemski 1979 and Kockel 1985.

—6—

ROADS, AQUEDUCTS AND CANALS

Appius Claudius laid together stones smoothed, levelled and shaped at the corners, without mortar or any other bonding material, to form such a compact and cohesive whole that anyone who saw them did not believe that they were separate stones, side by side, but an unbroken surface. And despite the length of time that elapsed and the number of vehicles that, day after day, passed over them, their structure is no way broken, nor did they lose their smoothness.

Thus wrote Procopius in the sixth century AD about the Via Appia, a highway first conceived in 312 BC, nearly a millennium before.[1] The builder of the first 132 miles, from Rome to Capua, was Appius Claudius, a censor, one of the high-ranking magistrates. His achievements are aptly summed up in a panegyric inscribed upon a marble slab and displayed in the Forum of Augustus in Rome: 'He conquered many Samnite cities. He destroyed the Sabine and Etruscan armies. He refused to make peace with King Pyrrhus. During his censorship, he built the Via Appia.'[2] Road-building, then, rated as an achievement to be matched with the greatest military and diplomatic successes, a verdict that is often echoed today: for it is hard not to be impressed with the vast network of communications that the Romans laid down, linking all parts of a huge empire. Moreover, in Italy, the motorways apart, one is so often travelling along a road that was first brought into being by Roman engineers. Even many of the ancient names survive, such as the Via Flaminia, the Via Appia and Via Latina, underlining how very fundamental was the Roman contribution to Italy's communications.

It is a further common assertion that all roads led to Rome, a notion derived in part from the great 'Golden Milestone' that Augustus set up at one end of the Forum in 20 BC. It was, in fact, a stone column, embellished with plaques in gilt bronze, which recorded the distances to all the main cities of the Empire, as measured from Rome.[3] However, it would be truer to say that Rome was the hub, from which radiated outwards this great road network – a series of spokes which were gradually extended as more and more territory came within the Republic's orbit.

We should not of course forget that the Romans learnt an enormous amount about the techniques of road-building from their neighbours, the Etruscans. With the formation of the city-states of Etruria in the early centuries of the first millennium BC the creation of routes of communication became increasingly important. Tracks served initially; but once wheeled vehicles, attested in graves from the later eighth century BC, came into widespread use, so the need for properly constructed roads became more pressing. The chief difficulty derived from the tangled volcanic terrain of Etruria, much of which is seamed by deep, steep-sided ravines. Fortunately, much of the rock is fairly soft, and can be broken up with a pickaxe. Thus, it became a feasible proposition to dig cuttings which enabled roads to be constructed at a suitable incline and width.[4]

Some of these Etruscan road cuttings still survive, particularly around centres which escaped later development. The most dramatic comprise great incisions, 20 or 30 metres deep, occasionally retaining traces of the wheel-ruts at the base. Moreover, in south-eastern Etruria it has proved possible to reconstruct a large part of the overall network, revealing a web of roads and

The Via Amerina to the south of Nepi, in southern Etruria. It is paved with basaltic *selce*.

tracks that connected both the major and the minor centres. By the time that the Roman armies came to annexe the region – the chief Etruscan centre, Veii, fell to them in 396 BC – there was a very serviceable network of communications. The only real bars were tracts of dense forest like the Ciminian, which separated central and southern Etruria. When in 310 BC the soldiers of Q. Fabius carried out a plundering expedition to the north of Ciminus, they found the forest 'pathless and terrifying' and, so Livy tells us, had to cut their way through.[5]

The existence of this road network was important in that it both facilitated conquest, a point that the Romans can hardly have missed, and provided a convenient model demonstrating what could be achieved. It is particularly instructive to look at the Latin colony of Nepi, which was founded early in the fourth century BC. Here we can see how an inconvenient, long-established cross-country route was soon replaced by a much more direct line. Called the Via Amerina, it had little of the sophisticated engineering or, indeed, the straightness of line of many of its successors; but it is a fine illustration of the Roman determination to create a new order of things, seen here in an early experimental form.[6]

Many of the first roads must have been like the one to Nepi: namely, direct links with newly founded colonies and other nearby towns with which ties were developed. The Via Ostiensis, which led to the maritime colony of Ostia (founded in the fourth century BC), must have been one such; another was the Via Praenestina, which headed eastwards to the important centre at Praeneste (modern Palestrina). One indication of the early date of these roads is the fact that they came to be known only by their destinations. Soon, however, roads were to take their name from the censor who, with the Senate's approval, initiated the project. One of the first was Appius Claudius, who was heralded – as we have seen – as the builder of the first stretch of the great Appian Way.

The Appian Way is famous for many reasons: for the magnificent and well-known length on the outskirts of Rome; for its role as a major highway in many wars of antiquity; and not least for a famous journey undertaken by the poet Horace in 37 BC.[7]

The road that Horace knew was far longer than in Appius Claudius' day. Originally it took the traveller along the coastal plain south-west of Rome to the important town of Capua and the rich lands of Campania, a total of 211 kilometres. Around 288 BC it was extended south-eastwards into the mountains to Benevento and thence down to Venosa, and within forty years it had been taken as far as the main south Adriatic port of Brindisi (Roman Brundisium) – a distance of some 370 kilometres. Horace came from Apulia, and he journeyed to Brindisi in company with Virgil and Maecenas and others. His story, full of quips and asides, provides a fascinating insight into travelling conditions of the time.

The journey was to take Horace and his companions fifteen days; but, he notes, 'the Appian Way is less tiring for those not in a hurry', and, in any case, 'by reason of the water, which was frightful, my stomach and I were on hostile terms'. There were to be stops at Ariccia and Forum Appii (which 'swarmed with sailors and knavish tavern-keepers'), and then they took the canal overnight through the Pomptine Marshes, a much easier option than the road. Mosquitoes and the chirping of marshland frogs kept sleep away, but they eventually landed at a shrine to the goddess Feronia, and set off, probably in a carriage, to Terracina. At that time the Via Appia had to climb the steep hill to the sanctuary of Jupiter Anxur, perched above the town (later, Trajan put in a great cutting beside the sea). It was to be a slow ascent over a distance of three Roman miles. Then it was on to Fondi and Formia, where they put up, 'weary indeed', at a villa owned by a brother-in-law of Maecenas.

Villa at Licenza, in the hills east of Tivoli. It has been claimed as Horace's Sabine farm, given to him by his patron, Maecenas, in 33 BC.

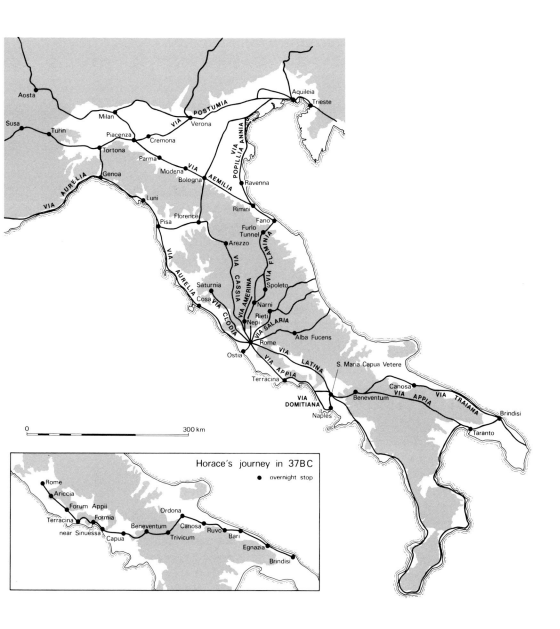

Some of the principal Roman roads of Italy. The inset shows the route taken by Horace and his companions to Brindisi in 37 BC.

At Sinuessa, on the coast near Mondragone, the party was joined by Virgil, Varius and Plotius and, riding on mules, they set off for a *mansio*, or official posting station, by the crossing of the River Savone. The road now led to Capua, and turning eastwards they moved up into the hills to Caudium, where they enjoyed a merry evening at a villa owned by Cocceius. Perhaps it was a good thing that the next stage was only a short one, to Benevento; this is a town magnificently situated in the Apennine Mountains, where their host nearly set the inn on fire in cooking thrushes for them.

They now turned off the Appia, taking an easier route down into Apulia.

129

It was a slow journey, as it is today, necessitating an unplanned halt at a villa en route. But henceforth it was downhill, riding in light carriages, probably to Ordona (Roman Herdonia), to the south of Foggia in the Tavoliere plain. Here the local bread was 'quite magnificent', a reflection no doubt of the fine farmland of this fertile region. But heavy rain impeded their progress, and the road deteriorated, so that there were frequent stops at Canosa, Ruvo di Puglia and then at the 'little fishing port of Bari'. Finally they arrived first at Gnathia (modern Egnazia) and then at Brindisi – 'the end of this long tale and this long journey'.

Horace's story is well worth recounting in detail, if only for the vivid insight that it casts upon the nature of travel at this period, albeit by a group of well-to-do people within Roman society.[8] Transporting goods by road must have been commensurately slower and more difficult,[9] although it is easy to see how armies could exploit the road network to great advantage. Certainly, Rome realised at an early stage the military importance of a system of rapid communications that linked her with the colonies. Thus the Via Appia was to be just the first of a series of long-distance highways that reached out into all parts of the peninsula.

Such roads were of course expensive: Diodorus Siculus claims that Appius bankrupted the state treasury in building his road.[10] Moreover, it needed paving, a very costly job. The grey volcanic basalt (*selce*, or in Latin *silex*), which was eventually to be used on so many highways as well as on town streets, was employed sparingly in this early period. Livy tells us that the short stretch of the Appia from the Temple of Mars in Rome to Bovillae was paved in *silex* in 294 BC; but this was a rarity.[11] A gravel surface was normally employed as, later, it was to be in many parts of the Empire.

A number of other major roads can also be dated to the third century BC or even before. The Via Valeria, which connected Rome with its colony of Alba Fucens, founded in 303 BC high in the Apennine Mountains, is certainly of great antiquity. It may well have originated as a track used by shepherds taking their flocks into the uplands to graze on the summer pastures. Similarly, the Via Salaria, which led to the hill town of Rieti (Roman Reate), enshrines in its name what must have been a very old-established route in the salt trade. The Tiber mouth was a major centre of production of this commodity, which, whether used as a preservation for foodstuffs or as an ingredient in the processing of animal hides, was of vital importance in the ancient economy, and it is interesting to see this reflected in the name of one of the major roads leading out of Rome. Finally, the Via Latina must also have come into use at a very early stage. Passing through the country of the Latini, down the Sacco and Liri valleys into Campania, it is likely to mark out a route established with the Etruscan expansion southwards in the sixth– seventh centuries BC. As Strabo reminds us, it remained a much frequented alternative to the Via Appia (which it eventually joined at Casilinum, near Capua), used by the armies of both Pyrrhus and Hannibal.[12]

For none of these roads is there any wholly certain evidence for the date at which they were made Roman public rights-of-way; but it is a fair guess to suppose that they had been long established by the end of the third century BC. If so, it was nevertheless the period from about 220 BC onwards that witnessed the most striking changes. Finance had a great deal to do with this. The successful wars in the east yielded huge amounts of wealth for the treasury, and the money therefore became available for a great many public works. At the same time trade was expanding, bringing in still more revenue, which was again to Italy's advantage.

The earliest major road of what may be considered the second main phase of construction was the Via Flaminia.[13] Begun in 220 BC as the initiative of the censor Gaius Flaminius, it was to provide the primary line of communication across the Apennine Mountains to Rimini on the Adriatic coast. This opened up the whole of the Po Plain, underlining the road's military role. Indeed, it was to retain this military importance for much of its history, both as a line of march to and from Rome, and as a road which connected a series of strategically significant towns. Narni, for example, was defended by the troops of Vitellius against those of Vespasian in the course of the wars of AD 69 – the 'Year of the Four Emperors'.

The course of the road is well established. It headed northwards from Rome up the western side of the Tiber Valley (following an old Etruscan route) and, once across the river, near Otricoli, it struck off north-eastwards into Umbria. At Narni, it divided into two, one route running up through Terni and Spoleto, and the other through Carseoli and Bevagna. Which is the older is disputed, but Spoletium was founded as a colony in 241 BC and must lie on an early road. The two routes converge again beyond Foligno, and head off into the Apennine Mountains along a twisting but not difficult course before descending to Fossombrone (Roman Forum Semproni). This town lies at the mouth of the famous Furlo Gorge, where an outcrop was pierced by a tunnel, nearly 40 metres in length and over 5 metres wide. Dated by an inscription to the reign of Vespasian (AD 69–79), it is still in use today, and succeeds an older and smaller tunnel.[14] From here on the road follows one of the many valleys that drain down into the Adriatic, in this case that of the Metauro River, which flows into the sea at Fano. Fanum Fortunae, made a colony under Augustus, probably originated as an early trade centre, and was famous for its temple of Fortune; but it clearly had major strategic significance as a junction between the principal road to Rome and traffic along the Adriatic coast.[15] Even so, the Flaminia did not stop here, but carried on northwards as far as Rimini. This occupied a vital position which controlled access into the Po Plain, and had been a Latin colony since 268 BC. A further advantage was the presence of a fine harbour, and it was logical to terminate the road at so critical a point.

Much of Gaius Flaminius' road was ingeniously constructed, steering a carefully worked-out route through countryside that is often difficult and tangled. Technically, it represents a considerable achievement, and it is interesting here to look again at the Via Amerina, the road that led from

Rome to Nepi. In 241 BC the Romans annexed the territory adjacent to Nepi, the Ager Faliscus, and forcibly moved the inhabitants of the chief Faliscan city, Falerii (modern Civita Castellana), to a new site. This was called Falerii Novi, and was positioned more or less due north of Nepi. The Via Amerina was duly extended from Nepi to Falerii Novi (and eventually beyond), and we may reasonably suppose that what we see on the ground today is the road as laid out in the later third century BC.[16] If so, the traces are particularly interesting, since the new stretch of road is characterised both by the choice of a bold, straight line, and by the construction of carefully graded cuttings to facilitate the crossing of valleys. Still more striking, however, is the use of masonry bridges with arches that span the rivers. If these bridges are original features, then they must be some of the earliest examples known to us. As Livy tells us, it was not until 174 BC that the censors, Flaccus and Albinus, put out contracts for the building of bridges 'in many places', to be coupled with resurfacing of the roads in gravel (and, inside Rome, with basalt *selce*).[17] The work in the Via Amerina could pre-date this major programme by several decades, and might well represent a piece of early experimentation. Equally, given an abundance of *selce* outcrops in the vicinity of the road, it is also possible that the paving that is still today conspicuous in many places on the ground was laid at that time.

These thoughts lie very much in the realm of conjecture; what is known for certain is that the construction of the Amerina and the Flaminia was a harbinger of a massive programme of road construction during the second century BC — work that was to transform Italy's network of communications.[18] The list of new roads is a long and impressive one, although it has a

The Roman bridge at Ponte di Nona, which still carries the Via Praenestina. It was probably built in the first century BC. The development of masonry bridges revolutionised road-building.

pronounced bias towards the north where so many new colonies were being founded. The peer was undoubtedly the Via Aemilia. Laid out in 187 BC by the consul M. Aemilius Lepidus, it ran from Rimini to Piacenza, along the western edge of the Po Plain. As Livy points out, its primary purpose was military, for it passed through the territory of the warlike Boii (defeated in 191 BC) and ran close by the region of the fiercely anti-Roman Ligures, whom Aemilius had just defeated.[19] Significantly, it was his army that built the road, a practice that was later to become standard. Together with the foundation of colonies along its route, such as Bologna, Parma and Modena, it helped to secure Rome's position in the region and, in time, played an important part in the diffusion of Roman 'culture' across the Po Plain.[20] The road became the main base line for the great schemes of centuriated land division, and was itself eventually extended so as to reach almost every major city of Cisalpine Gaul (as it came to be known), as well as Susa (Roman Segusium) in the far north-west, the gateway to the Mont Cénis pass over the Alps, Aosta (Roman Augusta Praetoria), strategically placed at the foot of the Col of Great St Bernard, and Aquileia, the once-huge city to the west of Trieste, founded in 181 BC. A generation later, in 148 BC, a great highway was built to facilitate east–west communications between Aquileia and Genoa by way of Piacenza, Cremona and Verona. One can only imagine the huge impact that the vast works of engineering must have made upon the local populations. This was further reinforced by the Via Popillia Annia, which ran along the coastal dunes from Rimini to Aquileia, today's SS 309 and 14, the 'Strada Romea'. Built in 132–1 BC, it served both to link the two great cities and also as a further base-line for the programme of land allocation.

There are many ways in which these roads of the later Republic disclose a certain ruthlessness of design. Veii, for example, Rome's long-time Etruscan rival, was completely bypassed by the new road network, and duly lapsed first into obscurity (Martial mentions the place, but only to comment on its dreadful wine), and ultimately into desertion.[21] Similarly, the Via Aurelia, which ran up the western seaboard of central and northern Italy, is typified by its directness of line which, rather like its modern namesake, left on one side all but the most important cities. We do not know exactly when it was built in this form, but it was certainly before 109 BC, when an extension as far as Genoa, called the Via Aemilia Scauri after its builder, was laid out. This was closely tied up with the fact that between 121 and 118 BC Rome had acquired substantial holdings in southern France, soon to become the province of Gallia Narbonensis. Here, then, was the beginning of much longer-distance communications, matched in the east by the construction of a road that was to run all the way to Byzantium (modern Istanbul), the Via Egnatia of 130 BC. This was the start of a vision that was truly empire-wise, so that by the time of Diocletian in the late third century AD there were 373 major highways through the provinces, covering 85,000 kilometres.[22]

One immensely significant figure in the history of road development was

C. Sempronius Gracchus, whose land reforms were of such importance in Roman Italy's agrarian history. Appian tells us that 'he had great roads built the length and breadth of Italy', while Plutarch describes his law of 123 BC, which provided for resurfacing and, where necessary, the building of bridges, embankments, kerbstones and milestones.[23] Milestones were to become of some importance. Rather like coins, they afforded a splendid opportunity for some suitably phrased words of publicity and advertising, and the magistrates, censors and, later, the emperors who erected them rarely missed this opportunity. Around six hundred are known from Italy, the earliest being of 249 BC.[24] The majority date from the later second century BC, however, and were placed every Roman mile (1,480 metres). Apart from the censor or emperor responsible for the work, they recorded the distance from the town at the beginning of the road, normally Rome itself. Details of renovations and repairs were also often added, making them highly valuable historical documents: thus an example found in the bed of the River Reno, not far from Bologna, and dating to 2 BC, reads: 'The Emperor, Caesar Augustus, Pontifex Maximus, in his XIII consulate, in his XXII year of tribunician power, saw to it that the Via Aemilia was restored from Rimini to the river Trebbia. Mile 79'.[25]

Upkeep and modernisation of the roads was, of course, as pressing a problem as it is today. Public funds were normally used, although local authorities and private landowners had on occasion to foot the bill. Under Augustus a board of officials, the *curatores viae*, was set up to manage the state highways, developing an administrative system of the later Republic. Augustus was also responsible for establishing a proper postal service. It was based upon a network of official stations, distributed along the main roads. Here there would be inns (*mansiones*), and changes of horse and carriage for the messengers, who travelled on average about eighty kilometres a day. The costs of these stations were borne locally, a considerable hardship; eventually the emperor Nerva remitted these charges on the towns of Italy (although not on those in the provinces), and transferred them to the state. This was suitably commemorated on a coin of Nerva issued in AD 97; the legend read VEHICULATIONE ITALIAE REMISSA, 'the [cost of] transportation in Italy is remitted', and on the coin's reverse were shown two mules, peacefully grazing.[26]

The creation of a formal postal service rather aptly sums up the importance of the role that roads had come to play both within Italy and beyond. They must rank as one of the great achievements of the Republic. However, when Augustus was formally proclaimed emperor in 27 BC, he inherited a network of largely unpaved roads, which undoubtedly needed attention. For example, a recently investigated section through the Via Cassia, to the north of Rome, showed that the original road was only just over 2 metres wide within its drainage ditches, with a simple gravel bed. This was almost certainly the surface laid in 154 BC, when the highway seems to have been constructed. It was subsequently enlarged, but still with a gravel

Part of the Ponte d'Augusto, the great Augustan bridge at Narni, which carried the Via Flaminia over the valley of the Nar. The bridge is over 30 metres high and 160 metres long.

surface, and it was not until the time of Augustus that it was paved with blocks of basaltic *selce*.[27] If the achievement of the Republic was to create the network, then it was the task of the Empire to upgrade and improve them.

Augustus, as so often, led the way. As he proudly proclaims in his autobiography: 'in my seventh consulship [27 BC], I restored the Via Flaminia from the city [of Rome] as far as Rimini, together with all the bridges excepting the Mulvian and the Minuscian'.[28] Traces of his work are still abundant. A huge viaduct over the valley of the River Treia, some forty-five kilometres to the north of Rome, is even now there to be seen, as is the magnificent bridge over the gorge at Narni; 30 metres high, it has a span of 160 metres and was made of concrete faced with blocks of white travertine. Today the express train between Rome, Perugia and the north still passes beneath one of the arches.[29]

Left The arch of Augustus, at Rimini (ancient Ariminum), built in 27 BC. Also the town's main gate, it marks the end of the Via Flaminia, and commemorates the emperor's achievement in refurbishing the road in that year. There was a comparable monument at the beginning of the Via Flaminia in Rome.

Below The bridge at Rimini completed by the emperor Tiberius in AD 21. It carried the Via Aemilia over the River Marecchia, whence it headed north-westwards up the Po Plain.

The work on the Via Flaminia was fittingly commemorated by the construction of two arches, one at each end of the road. That at Rimini still stands, the oldest extant example of its kind; it dates to 29 BC. Cassius Dio tells us that both arches carried statues of Augustus, a reminder of the power and authority that was invested in him. Similarly impressive is the great bridge over the River Marecchia, dedicated in AD 22, which takes the Via Aemilia out of Rimini. Wherever one travelled in Augustan Italy, building work initiated by the emperor, or by others close to him (particularly his lifelong friend Agrippa), would have been going on. New Alpine routes were opened or improved, including the Great St Bernard and the Brenner. Some of the engineering here was truly spectacular. At Donnaz, for example, some distance to the south-east of Aosta, the road builders have hewn out of the rock a stretch of over 220 metres, an astonishing feat. In addition, a major route from Aquileia into what is now Yugoslavia was opened; the Via Aemilia was renovated; and other major roads, like the Via Cassia, may well have been paved at this time.[30] Moreover, private landowners were also active. Some had to contribute to the upkeep of state roads, where they crossed their land; but many more were busy improving the private country roads which were so important in linking the towns with the rural estates.

It is especially impressive to see the large number of roads that were

paved with basalt (mainly, so far as we can tell, in the first century AD); or to read inscriptions like that built into a small bridge in the countryside to the north of Rome, recording how T. Humanius Stabilio constructed the bridge *in privato trasientibus*, 'at his own expense for those who crossed it'.[31] Fortunes were undoubtedly made by those who exploited the basaltic *selce* deposits, as the large number of rich villas around a quarry at Monte Maggiore, in southern Etruria, quite clearly shows; they even built themselves a long, paved haul-road, connecting the quarry with the Via Flaminia, another mark of their success.[32]

Most country roads, however, remained as simple *strade bianche*, those white tracks of today's Italian countryside, dusty in summer, and furrowed and skiddy in winter. Excavation of one small paved road in southern Etruria, dating to the first century AD, turned out to cover innumerable deep ruts of an earlier track cut into the bedrock by iron-tyred wheels; transport cannot have been easy, even at the best of times.[33]

Maintenance of the main highways was a problem that dogged all later emperors. Augustus, Vespasian, Trajan and Hadrian carried out work on the Via Flaminia over a period of some 160 years, and for many of the main highways a special *curator* − a man of high-placed senatorial rank − was appointed to oversee its maintenance. Some new roads were built, like Domitian's route of AD 95 along the Campanian coast from Sinuessa (modern Mondragone) to Puteoli, or Trajan's much easier course for the Via Appia, between Benevento and Brindisi, which was opened in AD 109. The poet Statius has left us an account of the building of the Via Domitiana. As so often, it was the successor to a series of country tracks, in themselves of no little use to the contractors. The picture is of myriad groups of workmen: those digging the ditches that both drained and defined the course of the highway; men clearing the surrounding land; other laying the make-up and preparing the surface: 'Oh, how many gangs are working at the same time,' he exclaims. At the end of the day was a solid paved road, 4 to 4.5 metres wide, impressive enough in its creation to excite the admiration of a celebrated Neapolitan poet.[34]

No less impressive was Trajan's work on the Via Appia at Terracina. We have already referred to Horace's long climb up to the temple of Jupiter Anxur, built on the headland of Pesco Montano, high above the town. In AD 109 the headland was cut back so that the road could pass in front of it, more or less at sea-level. The cutting is 36 metres deep, and the achievement is proclaimed by a series of depth measurements, carved into the rock every ten Roman feet: the lowest reads CXX (120 Roman feet). A triumphal arch was built at the base of the cutting, no doubt with a suitably phrased inscription to commemorate the work. Not surprisingly, it led to the development of a major new suburb on the lower ground, a clear indication of the way in which roads tended to shape the pattern of settlement growth.

These great public works, involving the use of huge squads of men, still serve as a reminder of the immense resources that Rome was able to deploy.

Trajan's cutting, the Pesco Montano, of AD 109 at Terracina for the Via Appia; depth measurements are carved into the rock.

Still more to the point, they show how a great state, given supreme authority at the centre, could impose its will over a vast geographical area. The Roman roads of Italy – and later of the Empire – were to play a crucial role in disseminating 'Romanisation' and thereby a form of cultural homogeneity: but in the last analysis it was only the huge power of Rome that made this possible.

The significance of the road network is well brought out by a series of itineraries, which record the main highways, the settlements along them and the distances.[35] Probably the best known is the Peutinger Table, a medieval copy of a map of the third century AD, acquired by Count Peutinger of Augsburg in the early sixteenth century. The map was designed to help the traveller plot his route, and his stops, along the major highways. The roads are drawn up in parallel lines. There is some topographical detail, particularly rivers and mountains, and different symbols are used to denote the various types of settlement or building – temples, spas, granaries, ports and the like. Even the names of quite minor settlements are marked, as are the better-known features like the Crypta Neapolitana. This was a remarkable road tunnel, 705 metres in length, which was constructed to ease the difficulties of journeying between Naples and Pozzuoli and was still in use until recently, something of its character comes down to us in a letter written by the philosopher, Seneca, to his friend Lucilius (57, 1–2):

Nothing is longer than that tunnel, nothing is darker than those torches which do not allow us to see among the shadows, but only to see the shadows. Apart from that, even if there were light, the dust will hide it; and, if the dust is annoying in the open, what will it be like there, where it whirls about on itself and, trapped without an air-hole, falls back on those who have raised it?

The Peutinger Table is by no means the only road-book to come down to us. There is, for example, the Antonine Itinerary, a series of road-maps that seem to have been drawn up originally for the emperor Caracalla in the early third century, although there are some revisions made a century or so later. There are also objects that list road routes, particularly the four Vicarello silver goblets.[36] Dating to the early Imperial period, they were found at Aquae Apollinares (modern Vicarello), a spa by Lake Bracciano, just to the north of Rome, where Apollo was worshipped as a god of healing. They list a route from Cadiz (ancient Gades), in Spain, down to Rome. Interestingly, they take the traveller along the Via Aemilia through Turin and Piacenza to Rimini, and then down the Via Flaminia. This is known to have been the preferred route rather than the much shorter Via Aurelia, in part no doubt because it traversed less marshy and malarial countryside.[37]

Not only are the road books and itineraries a mine of topographical and place-name information, but they also rather neatly sum up the way in which the network in effect fossilised from the mid-second century AD onwards. Just as Hadrian, who died in AD 138, was the Empire's last town-builder, so the main task of road-building was in effect accomplished by the end of his day. It was, however, a task well done: something to be marvelled at in late antiquity and, even in our day, something to admire as we travel the very same routes that were laid out in Roman times.

Aqueducts and the water supply

'The Romans had the best foresight in those matters which the Greeks made but little account of, such as the construction of roads and aqueducts and sewers'. So wrote Strabo (5.3.8), and his thoughts were echoed by Pliny, who claimed that of Rome's water supply 'there was nothing more wonderful in the whole world'.[38] It is a verdict that has often been reiterated, especially in the light of magnificent aqueducts like those of Segovia (Spain), the Pont du

A *cuniculus* or drainage tunnel, under excavation at Tuscania; the technique was developed by the Etruscans.

Gard (France) and Aspendos (Turkey).[39] However, it is often forgotten that, as with roads, the Romans learnt a very great deal about hydraulic engineering from the Etruscans and the Greeks.

From as least as early as the fifth century BC there had been experimentation, particularly in southern Etruria, with underground tunnels, known as *cuniculi*. These served a variety of purposes. They were used to drain boggy land by collecting surface water in vertical shafts and diverting it in a horizontal tunnel into another valley: one remarkable system near Veii, the Fosso degli Olmetti *cuniculus*, extends for no less than 5.6 kilometres.[40] They were also employed by the road-builders; as an instance we might cite the Pietra Pertusa road, which linked Veii with the Tiber Valley. Along its course it crossed no fewer than four valleys that were drained with *cuniculi* and then entered an enormous tunnel cut through a high ridge: this was constructed at a depth of 40 metres below ground-level, was over 2 metres wide and extended for a length of 300 metres, a major feat of engineering. Within Veii itself tunnels were used both for drainage and to collect water in large tanks, while some distance to the north, at a small site today called Ponte del Ponte, there are the remains of what seems to be a pre-Roman aqueduct. The water was collected from a spring, and channelled in a *cuniculus*. This opened into a solid masonry aqueduct, 10 metres high, which spanned a small gorge, 30 metres wide. Whereas Roman engineers would have constructed an arch for the stream beneath to pass through the aqueduct, here another *cuniculus* was built on one side of the valley, an indication of its early date. A further tunnel was then cut to take the water down to the settlement, 100 metres away.[41]

These remarkable structures vividly demonstrate how accomplished the Etruscan engineers became in the control of water. They were undoubtedly responsible for the Cloaca Maxima, which drained Rome's Forum area, and may well have designed the forty-five kilometres of *cuniculi* that are known from the Alban Hills. We can also see them at work in the north: at the extraordinary city of canals at Spina, on the Adriatic, and at the valley site of Marzabotto, not far from Bologna. Here covered drains running down the centre of the streets were in use from an early stage of the town's history, which belongs predominantly to the fifth and fourth centuries BC.[42]

The Romans thus had a fund of experience – and local examples – on which to draw, aided by two important inventions. These were first the arch, a Greek innovation but little used by them; and secondly the discovery of the properties of concrete. This probably occurred in the second half of the third century BC, but concrete came into widespread use in the following century. However, there was to be no overnight revolution in the development of hydraulic engineering; rather as the network of major highways remained largely unpaved until early Imperial times, so the system of aqueducts – so far as we know – was mainly a creation of the post-Republican age.

There are, of course, exceptions, of which Rome itself is the most notable.[43] The city was eventually to be served by eleven aqueducts, built over a period of more than five hundred years. The two oldest were the Appia (constructed, like the Via Appia, by the censor Appius Claudius, in 312 BC), and the Anio Vetus of 272 BC. Significantly, both used tunnels with vertical shafts, in the Etruscan manner; but the Anio Vetus also employed short lengths of arch, signalling the way forward. The major breakthrough, however, was made with the construction of the Aqua Marcia, completed in 144 BC. Eventually capable of delivering over 800 million litres of water a day, it tapped springs in the hills to the east of Tivoli, more than fifty kilometres from Rome (where some of the arches can still be seen). It made use of long bridges but, most significantly, the *specus* or channel was made watertight by cement, and covered over with slabs. This meant that the water could be forced upwards, being under pressure, on the 'inverted siphon' principle. Most aqueducts in antiquity relied quite simply on a gradual downhill slope (the magnificently surveyed Aqua Alexandriana of AD 226, for example, had an average fall of just 43 cm per kilometre over its 22-kilometre length); but, although not widely employed in Italy, the principles of moving water under pressure, usually in lead pipes, were understood, and are mentioned (not very correctly) by the architect Vitruvius.[44] One of the problems was finance. We know the Aqua Marcia cost the huge sum of 180 million sesterces, and this meant that, wherever possible, cheaper expedients were sought. Even so, it was the munificence of one L. Betilienus Varus, a local magnate, that paid for another exceptionally early aqueduct, that of Alatri, which lies some seventy kilometres to the east of Rome. Built around 100 BC, it tapped a source twelve kilometres to the north of the town. This involved crossing the deep gorge of the River Cosa, which it did by means of a bridge with two tiers of arches; but it also involved using the inverted siphon principle, since at one point the *specus* lay at a depth of over 100 metres below the level of the receiving tank.[45]

Just one other aqueduct was built for Rome before the days of Augustus and Agrippa, namely the Aqua Tepula of 125 BC. Nevertheless, the advantages must already have been manifest, notwithstanding the enormous difficulties and costs of constructing the aqueducts, and the constant problem of their maintenance. However, we must be wary of misinterpreting the role of the aqueduct. From a modern standpoint, it would be easy to assume that they were envisaged as convenient sources of drinking water, which would also serve to flush out the sewers, and thus help with sanitation. This, however, would be far from the truth. The point is well made by the water towers at Pompeii, which lay at the end of the aqueduct system. The water was distributed by three pipes, each higher than the other. The lowest – and, therefore, the fullest – fed the public fountains; the middle the public baths; and only the highest the private houses. In other words, the ordinary town-dweller was least well served by the aqueducts, for they were intended much more for public display than for private convenience.

In fact, it seems likely that the development of aqueducts, scores of which are attested in Italy, is closely linked with the way in which baths – public and private – came to be adopted as a regular part of Roman life. Baths seem to have been a Campanian innovation. The Stabian baths in Pompeii, themselves dating to the second century BC, have been shown to overlie a still older complex, with an exercise space and a row of hip-baths, laid out as early as the fourth century BC. The notion of the baths being a type of recreational club was thus established from the outset, although the inspiration probably lies in the small-scale but communal bath-houses of the Greek world. However, it was not until about 20 BC that Agrippa laid out the first public baths in Rome, setting a precedent that was followed by many of the emperors, both in Rome (such as those of Caracalla and Diocletian) and in the provinces.[46] Agrippa's baths stood close to where the Pantheon now lies, but little survives of them. They were amongst a huge building programme of the time, prompting Augustus' famous boast about finding Rome a city of brick and leaving it one of marble.

Agrippa's work on Rome's water supply was particularly important. He built no fewer than 700 basins, 500 fountains and 130 distribution points, and also 3 new aqueducts: the Julia (33 BC), the Virgo (19 BC) and the

Alsientina (2 BC). It was the Aqua Virgo that fed his baths (and still supplies the Trevi fountain). In addition, he restored the four older aqueducts and the sewers (which he is reputed to have explored in a boat).[47]

No less remarkable is the scale on which water was provided for other Italian cities and towns. Hitherto most places had relied solely on cisterns and wells for their water supply, so that in a town like Cosa every house had its own reservoir.[48] From the time of Augustus onwards aqueducts were constructed for most towns of any consequence, and some, like Terracina, were provided with two or three. By the second century AD the existence of aqueducts, and running water, must have seemed almost standard.

Naturally, many were fairly simple in design, so as to offset the huge costs. But even comparatively modest towns, such as Lucus Feroniae (fifteen kilometres to the north-east of Rome), or the once renowned Etruscan city at Vulci – in Roman times a fairly ordinary *municipium* – had aqueducts capable of delivering over three million litres of water a day. Moreover, some could be very grand. Conspicuous traces still exist of Minturnae's splendid aqueduct, an Augustan gift to the colony, while that at Venafrum, also of Augustan date, stretched for over thirty kilometres. Much of its channel ran underground, but *cippi*, or boundary stones, were set up to mark out its course (a strip 8 Roman feet wide), and there survive copies of the regulations for its use and maintenance. The peer of Augustan aqueducts, however, must be the enormous Serino system. This took waters that rose in

A section of the eleven-kilometre-long aqueduct that served Minturnae, in Campania. It was built in *opus reticulatum* (diamond-shaped reticulate work), at the expense of the emperor Augustus.

The Porta Maggiore at Rome, built by Claudius to carry his two aqueducts (on top of the gate) over the Via Praenestina and the Via Labicana. In front is the extraordinary late Republican tomb of the baker Eurysaces.

the hills above Avellino, in Campania, and over its ninety-six-kilometre length fed the towns of Naples and Pozzuoli, with branches to Nola, Cumae, Pompeii, Atella (near modern Aversa), Acerrae, Baia and Misenum.[49]

At least sixteen Augustan aqueducts are known, a measure of the importance that was attached to them. Later there were to be even more magnificent structures, like the two that were finished under the emperor Claudius for Rome: one, the Aqua Claudia (completed in AD 47), extended for seventy-four kilometres, and the other, the Anio Novus (AD 38–52), for

Public latrines at Ostia. Roman hydraulic engineers greatly improved hygiene in many towns. Note the fine reticulate work behind.

no less than ninety-five kilometres. It is the longest of all aqueducts and the loftiest; some of its arches are more than 33 metres high. The famous Porta Maggiore in Rome was built to carry the aqueducts over the Via Praenestina and the Via Labicana.

Augustus established a board of *curatores aquarum* to supervise the aqueducts, a job that was held by a one-time governor of Britain, Frontinus, in AD 97–8. He has left us a long treatise on Rome's water supply, including the estimate that in his day 44 per cent of the total delivery was piped to private houses.[50] However true this may have been, it is important not to exaggerate the effectiveness of the aqueducts. Our sources are full of references to repairs, and it is clear that some aqueducts did not work at all well. The Aqua Claudia, for example, which was completed in AD 52, was the subject of major repairs in AD 71 after being out of action for nine years, and was being further mended in AD 80–1 by the emperor Titus.[51] Similarly, a detailed recent study of an aqueduct which served the very important town at Cherchel in North Africa has revealed a story of poor design, shoddy construction and numerous attempts to patch it up and make it work.[52] No doubt much the same was true of many Italian examples, and one is left with the impression that in some towns (particularly after private patronage dwindled from the late second century AD onwards) the aqueducts may not have functioned very often. Rome may have been in a rather better position,

146

for in the early fourth century it had no fewer than 11 large baths, 856 smaller baths, 1,352 public water cisterns and 144 public lavatories to supply – and Imperial patronage to help; but this may have been the exception to the rule.[53]

Many towns, of course, took other measures. Ostia, for example, received an aqueduct under the early Empire, and very soon afterwards new public baths were constructed. However, many private houses retained their own wells, and many public baths, like that of Neptune, had their own reservoir; wheels were sometimes employed to help draw up the water.[54] Such practices seem not to have been uncommon. When, for instance, the great general Belisarius laid siege to Naples in 536, he straightway cut the aqueduct; but this discommoded the inhabitants not at all, since they in any case used wells. Indeed, we could dwell at much greater length on the fascinating subject of the highly effective systems of water storage and distribution – and the baths and fountains themselves, public and private – that the inhabitants of Italy's towns and countryside evolved. Whether one thinks of great bathing establishments like the Baths of Trajan near Civitavecchia (Roman Centumcellae), or the modest bath-house of the little villa at Crocicchie near Rome, it is their very ubiquity that impresses. Moreover, there is a sufficiency of evidence to show that in some areas at least baths, fountains and aqueducts did continue to function into late antiquity. Rutilius, for example, writing in the early fifth century AD, provides an admiring account of the Baths of Trajan near Civitavecchia,[55] and we hear of both fourth- and fifth-century repairs to aqueducts. For example, the Ostrogoth Theoderic, King of Italy between 493 and 526, repaired the aqueducts of Verona, Parma and Ravenna. Ravenna he made his capital, and it is recorded that the aqueduct, which he restored in 502–3, had been out of action for a very long period.[56]

Aqueducts, then, remained as important symbols of Romanised civilisation; as structures worthy of patronage, public and private; and as costly and sometimes ineffective ways of transporting water. Their patrons were on the whole more concerned with the fountains and baths that they supplied than with practical hygiene, and it was the decline of patronage that led eventually to their desuetude. The Church, soon to become the power in the land, was not interested in such frivolous diversions as attending the baths: 'Baths are for the needs of the body, not for the titillation of the mind', as Gregory the Great, Pope from 590 to 604, crisply observed.[57] It is somewhat ironic, for some of his successors, like Sixtus v, were moved to imitate the aqueducts of Roman times by building their own. They may well have agreed with Edward Gibbon's verdict, that aqueducts 'rank among the noblest monuments to Roman genius and power'.

Canals and drainage

If the Roman roads and aqueducts of Italy continue to inspire awe and admiration, then hardly less impressive are the many drainage and water transport schemes that were implemented. Land reclamation and irrigation had of course been practised in some areas, such as Egypt and the Near East, for thousands of years. Canal-building was a well-established technique, and some spectacular examples are known: for example that of the Assyrian King Sennacherib, which ran for eighty kilometres from the uplands to his capital of Nineveh. Dated by inscriptions to 691 BC, it was stone-built, water-proofed with a form of concrete and was in places over 20 metres wide. It included sluice-gates and viaducts in its design, and was apparently intended both as a source of drinking water and for irrigation.[58]

In Italy both the Greeks and Etruscans carried out schemes of land reclamation and water management. We are told, for instance, that in 444 BC the people of the Greek city of Selinus, on the southern coast of Sicily, invited Empedocles to check an epidemic. This he did by draining the marshy ground in the valleys that flanked the town.[59] Similar schemes were carried out in the territories of Metapontum and Heraclea, both of which lie on the coast within Italy's southern instep. However, these were followed by the construction of a series of dykes, which both drained the land and divided it up into regular fields. Here, if anywhere, must be seen the germs of the ideas of centuriation, discussed above (p. 101).

The Etruscans, as we saw earlier, devised a system of *cuniculi* to reclaim the marshy land in the valleys; but it is at Spina that their skills in hydraulic engineering are best exemplified. A town situated on a tributary mouth of the River Po, and founded about 540 BC, its central feature was a great canal 15–20 metres wide, which linked the sea with the river. Furthermore, the entire settlement was divided up into a grid of regular blocks, along the lines of many Greek cities of southern Italy and elsewhere; however, at Spina the 'streets' were laid out not as roads, but as canals, rather like medieval Venice. The houses were built on sand-bars, supported by wooden piles, and the success of this inventively designed city is to be measured by the enormously rich contents of the graves in the cemeteries.[60]

The early hydraulic schemes, however enterprisingly conceived, were nevertheless on a comparatively small scale. On the other hand, once Rome began to expand its territory, matters became very different. From the second century BC onwards, in particular, there were both the financial resources and the manpower to undertake vast projects of a sort that are only possible with a strong central government. Moreover, as the network of settlements expanded, so the need for more land became pressing. Huge areas of marginal terrain, such as the Po Plain, had to be brought into cultivation, and investors were not slow to appreciate the possibilities of a good profit. The point is well brought out by Suetonius' account of the draining of the Fucine Lake, a great basin nearly twenty kilometres across, high in the Apennines of central Italy. The project was eventually undertaken by the emperor Claudius, after being considered a number of times before and rejected as impracticable. 'Claudius', Suetonius writes, 'undertook the scheme as much for profit as for glory: a group of businessmen had offered to shoulder the expense if he rewarded them the reclaimed land.' He then goes on to give an idea of the huge cost of the project: 'the outlet took eleven years to dig, even though 30,000 men were kept continuously at work; it was three miles long and his engineers had to level part of the hill and tunnel through the remainder'. It did not, in fact, work very well – the outlet became frequently choked – but it does illustrate the extraordinary lengths to which the Romans were prepared to go.[61]

Even so, the beginnings were small. Rome itself was particularly prone to flooding, and it fell to the Etruscan overlords, Tarquinius the Elder and Servius Tullius (c. 616–535 BC), to drain the low-lying ground later to be occupied by the Forum. They also built the great sewer, the Cloaca Maxima, initiating a scheme of tunnels some of which, so Strabo tells us, 'were in certain places large enough for even wagons loaded with hay to pass through'.[62] But the Tiber still caused problems, and in the third century BC it was embanked in stone. Nevertheless, it continued to require constant maintenance, and it is a telling comment on the declining standards of the early medieval period when one reads in the *Lives of the Popes* of a great flood in AD 791: all of the lower part of Rome was inundated for three days, after the water had broken through the Flaminian gate, and Pope Hadrian had to organise a ferry system of punts along what is now the Via del Corso to supply people stranded in their houses.[63]

Outside Rome it was not long before ambitious projects were being put in hand. Livy tells us how, as early as the fourth century BC, a 1.8-kilometre tunnel and a 24-kilometre canal were cut to lower the water-level of the Alban Lake; while towards the beginning of the third century BC the consul M. Curius Dentatus made an 800-metre channel to drain part of Lake Velinus. This was an upland basin bordering the town of Reate (modern Rieti), and the land (which was to be divided up by centuriation) was badly needed by the colonists.[64]

The creation of new farmland became, in fact, a prime objective in many regions. Very often the new towns were located close to low-lying coastal flats and valleys. These were in themselves unhealthy (as Vitruvius was careful to stress) but, once drained, proved fertile and highly profitable for agriculture. This was the case with the wetlands around the River Clanis, near the colony of Liternum in Campania, drained in the second century BC; and it also prompted many attempts to bring under control the huge Pomptine Marshes to the south-west of Rome.[65] The first attempts were made in 160 BC, and Caesar, Augustus, Nero and even, at the end of the fifth century AD, Theoderic all initiated schemes to drain the region; but in the end it required the technology and resources of the present century to achieve complete success.

In the vast Po Valley, on the other hand, a massive effort at land reclamation was attended with just rewards. The huge project is supposed to have been begun by the Etruscans; the first Roman work was put in hand in 109 BC by M. Aemilius Scaurus. It was necessitated by the rapid gowth of

The so-called Porta Augusta at Perugia. It in fact dates to the third or second century BC, illustrating the emergence of engineering skills on a massive scale.

colonies in the region, all of which required land that could be divided up by centuriation. It was no easy task. Every year the spring melt of the mountain snows brought down vast quantities of water and silt into the plain below, far more than the sluggish rivers could cope with. The silt clogged the outlets into the sea and the water topped the banks, flooding large parts of the interior. This is why cities like Ravenna, which once stood on the Adriatic coast, now lie stranded far inland, separated from the sea by mud-flats of quite recent formation.[66]

For Ravenna the solution was a canal that linked the city with the estuary of the River Po. It was constructed by Augustus, who wanted to make the city the base of the Adriatic fleet, with a port at Classis, a suburb on the coast. It was a shrewd move, for Ravenna was to become something of a boom town and, from AD 404, an imperial capital of great magnificence. Elsewhere in the Po Valley, other measures to alleviate flooding were taken. Two inscriptions show, for example, that the River Adige, which divides the territories of Padua and Ferrara, was canalised to make it more efficient, and the same is no doubt true of some of the other rivers.[67] These were used in combination with a clever system of canals and dykes, which both drained the land and provided a very efficient system of communications. The fertile landscape of today's Po Valley cannot have looked so different in antiquity, when the region became renowned for the bounty of its crops.

Canals are known from other parts of Italy, like the one providing an alternative route to the Via Appia through the Pomptine Marshes, built by M. Cornelius Cethegus in 160 BC; or Nero's scheme to build a ship-canal

between Lake Avernus, to the north-west of Naples, and Ostia. In Suetonius'
words, it was to be '160 miles long, and broad enough for two quinqueremes
[war galleys] to pass. Prisoners from every part of the empire were ordered
to be transported to Italy for this task, even those convicted of capital crimes
receiving no other punishment but this.'[68] The idea was to bypass the Tiber
mouth, where silting made constant difficulties for shipping. The plan was
never completed, but it well illustrates the grandeur of some of the projects
envisaged. Most drainage works were, however, much more mundane: what
mattered was the regular maintenance of the ditches and dykes that kept the
water-table low in the many flatlands around the peninsula. Once let slip, it
was only a question of time before the ground again became waterlogged
and malarial, suited neither for cultivation nor for settlement. When in AD 15
we hear of a vigorous debate in the senate about proposed flood-abatement
schemes and their consequences, good and bad, it is a clear reflection of the
importance of such measures in the day-to-day life of the country.[69] In late
antiquity, however, when the local authorities could no longer cope with
these problems, the absence of flood-prevention schemes was to cut away
one of the underpinnings of Italian agriculture, and thus the main support
system of the very towns themselves.

FURTHER READING

For roads, R. Chevallier, *Roman roads* (1976) is generally useful, as is T. Pekáry, *Untersuchungen
zu den römischen Reichstrassen* (1968), discussed by P. Wiseman in his 'important 'Roman
Republican road building', *PBSR* 38 (1970), 122–52. See also D. Sterpos, *The Roman road in
Italy* (1970); F. Castagnoli *et al., La Via Aurelia* (1968); F. Castagnoli, *Via Appia* (1956); T.
Ashby and R. A. L. Fell, 'The Via Flaminia', *JRS* 11 (1921), 125–90; M. W. Frederiksen and J. B.
Ward-Perkins, 'The ancient road systems . . . of the Ager Faliscus', *PBSR* 25 (1957), 67–203.
For travel, see L. Casson, *Travel in the ancient world* (1974).

For aqueducts see T. Ashby, *The aqueducts of ancient Rome* (1935); E. B. Van Deman, *The
building of the Roman aqueducts* (1934). For the Aqua Alexandriana, J. B. Ward-Perkins and A.
Kahane, *PBSR* 40 (1972), 122ff. For Augustan aqueducts, see L. J. F. Keppie, *Colonisation and
veteran settlement in Italy* (1983); and for late Roman aqueducts, B. Ward-Perkins, *From classical
antiquity to the Middle Ages* (1984). For pre-Roman antecedents see J. B. Ward-Perkins in
Hommages à Albert Grenier, Collection Latomus 58 (1962), 1636ff. For canals and drainage, see
R. J. Forbes, *Irrigation and drainage* (1955); and T. W. Potter, in *The evolution of marshland
landscapes*, ed. R. T. Rowley (1981), 1–19. For *cuniculi* see S. Judson and A. Kahane in *PBSR* 31
(1963), 74–99.

—7—

THE BALANCE
OF TRADE

An area which has witnessed particularly vigorous debate in recent years is that of the Roman economy. Much of it stems from the application of modern ideological concepts, most notably Marxist thought, to the interpretation of the ancient world. Roman Italy has taken a prominent place in the discussion, principally because of the role that slave-labour played in the evolution of the agricultural and industrial economy of the country. As one of our most eminent ancient historians of today has observed: 'in Rome and Italy, from early in the third century BC to the third century AD, slavery effectively replaced other forms of dependent labour'.[1]

As we tried to show earlier, not all scholars would entirely agree with this assessment; nevertheless, the figures are telling, for it has been estimated that, out of a total population for Roman Italy at the end of the first century BC of between 6 and 7.5 million, no fewer than 2 to 3 million were of servile status.[2] Quite large numbers worked in the towns. There may, for example, have been as many as 400,000 in Rome, out of about 1,000,000 inhabitants.[3] Of these, a high proportion were owned privately by individual citizens, and of course by the emperor; but many more were the property of the state. We know, for instance, that 700 alone worked on the sewers and the water-supply systems in Rome in the late first century AD.[4]

These are, of course, maximum figures, calculated for the period when the population is likely to have been at its height, about the time of Augustus, but they provide a rough order of magnitude. Moreover, although there were more than four hundred towns of importance in Roman Italy, it is clear from the ancient authors that there were also huge numbers of slaves who worked on the country estates. These villas clustered primarily in the fertile lands of Campania, Latium and the coastal part of Etruria, and came into being mainly during the later second and first centuries BC. A number may have replaced smaller, family-run farms; but many more were completely new foundations, like the great Settefinestre villa, in the territory of Cosa on the coast of Etruria, described earlier.

Precisely how the slave-run estate evolved is a much debated matter, particularly whether it can be claimed as a Roman innovation; but the historical context is clear. There were fortunes to be made in the wars of conquest, and the best investment was in land – property holdings were essential for those who aspired to public office or even military service. Moreover, Italy's own internal upheavals also brought possibilities of acquisition. Large-scale confiscations followed Hannibal's invasion in the late third century BC, once those unwise enough to support him had been identified; just as the Social War and its aftermath brought riches to some and poverty or worse to others.[5] The ownership of land and of slaves meant social respectability, and there was no shortage of opportunity for those able to snap up a quick bargain. When the Aegean island of Delos was made a free port in 166 BC, as a rival to all-too-successful Rhodes, ten thousand slaves could change hands in a day, according to Strabo; no surprise, therefore, that the Romans soon had their own market-place on this diminutive island, the so-called Agora of the Italians.[6]

We need not reiterate the way in which villa estates became common-place in many parts of the peninsula during the late Republic – even though the great slave estates, to our knowledge, belong mainly to western-central Italy. Their diffusion coincides with what both archaeologists and historians regard as a period of steep population increase, of both slaves and free-born. One scholar, for example, calculates that there was a rise of nearly 30 per cent – some 2 million people – in Italy between about 225 BC and the time of Augustus, a reasoned guess that is entirely endorsed by the results of work on the ground, especially field-survey.[7] Many were concentrated in the towns – one consequence of the creation of the large estates, which dispossessed many smallholders. This in turn created particular problems, since feeding a city the size of Rome was well beyond the capacity of the surrounding countryside: hence the beginnings of a massive import of foodstuffs from Sicily, North Africa, Egypt and elsewhere.

Generally, however, we can suppose that the level of production, both in agriculture and in manufactured goods, went up sharply. Let us concentrate upon farming first, since this is where the bulk of the wealth lay. Two factors are immediately obvious. One is that an enormous amount of extra land came into cultivation during the late Republic in most parts of the peninsula. This is implicit in the literary evidence and is verified by almost all of the field-surveys, with the particular exception of some areas of southern Italy. Even in densely occupied regions, like south-eastern Etruria, the number of sites of late Republican date is more than double that of the early to mid-Republic.[8] Secondly, this huge expansion in settlement was facilitated by – and greatly benefited from – the massive programmes of land improvement that so characterise this period, especially in areas like the Po Valley.[9] In combination, these two factors alone must have ensured a much larger farming surplus than before.

In addition, there were improvements both in farming techniques and in the equipment that was used. The manuals of Cato, Columella, Varro and the rest are full of good advice about crop rotation, manuring, irrigation, estate management and much more, while the tools themselves became increasingly efficient. Iron implements like a more effective spade, hoes with several tines and a variety of sickles and bill-hooks became more readily available, and no doubt made their unspectacular but nevertheless considerable contribution.[10] However, perhaps the most significant change was the introduction of slave-run farms which specialised in the production of particular crops sold for cash, rather than in an all-round 'subsistence' economy. The crops varied, largely according to the environment and conditions. With intensive labour there was money to be made from orchards, with apples, pears, peaches and nuts – Italy was famous for its almonds, hazelnuts and walnuts – and, with luck, exotic birds and poultry, for the dinner tables of the rich, could also be profitable. Varro tells of the huge gains made from the sale of 5,000 fieldfares (a type of thrush), at three *denarii* apiece, raised on his aunt's farm in the Sabine hill country; 'to make a haul like this', he adds, 'you'll need a banquet, or somebody's triumph . . . or club dinners – which are now so frequent that they cause the price of provisions to go soaring up'.[11]

Varro's comments were published in 37 BC, when Italy's fortunes, despite the political upheavals, were approaching their height. Most of his readers, however, probably put their money into other cash-crops, in particular wine and, to a lesser extent, olives. Wine, and its production and export, occupies a central place in discussions of the economy of Roman Italy.[12] This is in part because it earned for many of those who invested in vines huge profits, at any rate for a time; but it is also a subject that is highly susceptible to archaeological analysis through the surviving remains. Both the presses and storage tanks have been often identified on the villa sites and, increasingly, the vine-trenches themselves are now coming to light.[13] But the most useful indices for the ancient wine trade are the containers in which the liquid was carried, namely amphorae. Amphorae are large pottery containers that were used in antiquity for shipping commodities such as wine, oil and garum, the piquant sauce made from pickled fish which was the gentleman's relish of the ancient world. Many amphorae bear name-stamps on their handles, probably those of the manufacturer, and some retain traces of painted inscriptions; these may record shippers, contents and date. Fortunately, the style of amphora shapes changed throughout antiquity, allowing an approximate division into chronological periods; moreover, detailed study of the pottery fabrics, particularly the microscopic examination of the mineral inclusions in the clay, can tell us where the amphora was manufactured. Given enough amphorae, and a meticulous examination of the fragments – a tedious task, often involving thousand upon thousand of

Italian Dressel 1 wine amphora from Welwyn Garden City in England, a clear instance of long-distance trade. *c.* 30–10 BC. *(British Museum)*

pottery sherds – some very useful statistics about trade in antiquity can be built up.[14]

Whilst the main types of amphorae were classified long ago, principally by the German scholar Dressel, the accumulation of figures concerning the form, origin, contents and distribution of amphorae is much more recent.[15] Moreover, the classification has become much more refined, as archaeology begins to grapple with the material evidence of a highly complex industry. Even so, certain patterns about trade in antiquity are beginning to emerge, which become continually more interesting – and more controversial.

Much of the evidence derives from the excavation of sites where the amphorae are found in closely dated layers: these help to provide a century-by-century picture of what was being marketed.[16] But much more informative are the shipwrecks which litter the coast of much of the Mediterranean. These present an extraordinarily interesting picture both of the cargoes and of the changing balance of trade. Some of the most thoroughly investigated wrecks come from the southern coast of France and north-western Italy, using techniques (particularly the aqualung) evolved during the Second World War. One wreck, explored by Nino Lamboglia – a great pioneer of Roman pottery studies in Italy – lay offshore from Albenga.[17] This was a large merchant vessel, probably of some 450 tonnes, which may well have been carrying as many as 10,000 amphorae when it foundered at the beginning of the first century BC: this would be the equivalent of about 250,000 litres of wine. Another, at the Madrague de Giens, not far from Toulon, is still being explored.[18] However, it is already clear that the ship, which sank about 60–50 BC, was some 30 to 35 metres in length, weighed between 300 and 400 tonnes and had on board between 5,000 and 8,000 amphorae, stacked in three or four levels. These amphorae were of a more-or-less standard shape, known to archaeologists as Dressel Form 1. These were Italian wine carriers, and in this case seem from the stamps on the handles to have come from the estates of P. Veveius Papus. This name has been tracked down to the Fondi–Terracina area of Campania, a region celebrated in antiquity for a *grand vin* known as Caecuban.

The cargo of the Madrague vessel consisted, therefore, principally of fine-quality wine, destined perhaps for the great port of Marseilles and the cities of southern Gaul. But it also included grapes, probably preserved in *defrutum*, a syrupy liquid that resulted from the boiling down of must, the grape juice;

Underwater photograph of the shipwreck at the Madrague de Giens, off the southern French coast. Most of the cargo comprised Dressel 1 Italian wine amphorae.
c. 60–50 BC.

and many pottery vessels – cups, dishes, bowls and lids. A considerable number of these were 'black-glaze', a distinctive type of pottery produced both in Campania and in many other centres in the Italian peninsula. Easily recognised by its shiny black-coated surface, this was the principal table-ware for much of the period of the Republic, and it was widely exported, a matter that we shall return to later on.[19]

These wrecks are just two of a huge number that have been identified in this region over the last forty years. Statistics are available for 103 Roman wrecks along the southern French coast, and the figures are very instructive. Just nine came to grief prior to the second century BC, and only thirty-three post-date the reign of Augustus. No fewer than fifty-four, however, sank in the second and first centuries BC, and the great majority had sailed from Italian ports, bearing goods and commodities produced in Italy. They reflect an extraordinary boom in the export market of later Republican Italy.[20]

Most of the wine carried in the Dressel 1 amphorae (which contained on average about twenty-four litres) originated in the vineyards of Campania, Latium and Etruria – the great volcanic belt of western-central Italy. This was the region where most of the famous Italian *crus* were produced. Campania was especially noted. This was the home of Falernian, a celebrated vintage described by Martial as 'immortal', of Caecuban, and many more. They remind us that the qualities of different wines were a much discussed matter in antiquity. Most were drunk young, but some were aged longer – perhaps ten or fifteen years, as is occasionally recorded in painted inscriptions on the amphorae. Indeed, a vintage wine like Opimian, named after a consul of 121 BC, was reputedly still being drunk more than a century later.[21]

Wine drinking, therefore, was a serious matter as far as the connoisseur was concerned. However, the ancient agronomists, in advising the landowner, were particularly concerned that his investment should be both efficiently managed and as profitable as possible. Only Columella, writing in the first century AD, provides much in the way of figures; but these, in company with other evidence, suggests that the return on investment may have been in the range of 7–10 per cent, rather than the 5–6 per cent normally realised on agricultural produce.[22] No wonder that the percipient landowner thought it worth his while to put money into vines.

The export trade seems to have begun early, particularly in Campania. The wine was initially carried in amphorae of a type known as Graeco-Italic; but around 150 BC the Dressel 1 amphora was evolved for shipping Italian wine, and other goods too. As wreck cargoes show, these included grapes and olives, apparently preserved in *defrutum* syrup. Figs were also exported, underlining the fact that a great deal of trade was in perishable commodities which are only preserved under exceptional circumstances: the amphorae are in effect mere trail-markers of activity that has left little trace in the archaeological record.[23]

The invention of the Dressel 1 amphorae presaged an enormous expansion both of production and in the markets. Whereas pre-Roman 'trade' was largely a matter of the exchange of rare and costly gifts amongst members of a ruling élite, in the years of the mid- to late Republic there began to evolve a rather different sort of economy.[24] It can be documented not only by the dramatic rise in the number of shipwrecks, with its implications of much more sea-traffic, but also in the huge numbers of amphorae that are found. At Châlon-sur-Saône, for example, a nineteenth-century scholar estimated that 24,000 Dressel 1 amphorae had been recovered from dredging of the river, and that the deposit probably still contained a further 200,000–500,000 more! Similarly, around Toulouse it is said that so many intact amphorae were buried in the ground 'that they almost prevent the earth from being fertile'. Even in remote Brittany Dressel 1 amphorae have now been found on no fewer than fifty-five sites.[25]

Most historians correlate this evidence for a dramatic rise in trade with the growth of the great slave-staffed villas, distributed along the Tyrrhenian belt of western-central Italy. Many were built around the first quarter of the first century BC, to be rapidly developed as successful commercial enterprises. The Settefinestre villa, in the territory of Cosa, is thought, for example, to have been producing as many as 4,260 amphorae of wine a year.[26] That much of this was exported is beyond doubt, and it must be this villa or one near it that was shipping Dressel 1 amphorae stamped SES on the handles. These stamps are particularly common in the town and port of Cosa, and must surely represent an abbreviation of the name P. Sestius, a magnate who is known to have owned land near Cosa. More importantly, these SES stamps have also turned up in many other contexts. They occur in five shipwrecks along the coasts of southern France and north-western Italy, as well as on many sites on the land in this area. However, the most telling feature of their distribution is the way in which they penetrate right up into central Gaul, especially via the Rhône Valley: here is dramatic confirmation that the agents of P. Sestius were selling his wine in the markets of southern and central France – and, no doubt, doing very well out of it.[27]

The overall distribution of the Dressel 1 amphorae is still more instructive, for it helps to pick out the main market areas as they were in the first century BC. In Italy they are found mainly on sites that were easily accessible from the coast but rarely inland, a reflection both of the high costs of land transport and of the gradual pace at which the interior was becoming Romanised. Similarly, there are comparatively few in the east Mediterranean, where the Greek world had for long had a distinguished wine industry. In the west, on the other hand, they turn up everywhere. At Cherchel in coastal Algeria, for example, at least thirty per cent of the wine derived from Italy, and in parts of Gaul and Spain the figure is very much higher. Eventually the market even extended to south-eastern Britain, where the local chieftains had gold, silver and iron, cattle and corn, slaves and even hunting dogs to exchange.[28]

The Gauls were particularly enamoured of Italian wine. It has been estimated recently that as many as forty million amphorae may have been shipped to Gaul during the first century BC and, while the army must have

A relief showing wine, contained in a great skin, being taken into town on a cart. Third century AD. (Unprovenanced, *British Museum*)

consumed a good deal, so too did the Gallic nobility. As Diodorus wrote: 'they gulped down what the merchants bring them quite undiluted … becoming so drunk that they fall asleep or lose their wits. Many Italian merchants … consequently regard the Gauls' taste for wine as a godsend. They take the wine to them by ship up the navigable rivers or by chariot travelling overland, and it fetches incredible prices.'[29]

Diodorus goes on to add that in return for one amphora of wine the merchant received one slave – a highly advantageous deal when, in Italy, a slave cost the minimum equivalent of sixty amphorae.[30] Fortunately for the traders, the exchange of gifts of wine had become a well-established and prestigious custom in Celtic society, and the Romans were more than content to cater for this taste and make fortunes out of it. Moreover, there were other commodities much needed in Italy that the Gauls could provide. Most notable of these were metal ores. The extraction of gold, silver, copper and lead in the south-west of France was well under way by about 100 BC, and this is a region notably rich in amphorae, while large-scale iron-working in the same area, and elsewhere, also seems to witness a dramatic upsurge from about 60 BC, if not before. It is inconceivable that a considerable quantity of these metals did not go to Italy, along with items like Gallic hams, which were particularly coveted for the dinner table.[31]

What the evidence points to, therefore, is the evolution of a complex economy, based partly on direct exchange of goods and partly on money. The word 'money' derives from the fact that Rome's mint was originally placed in the temple of the Goddess Juno Moneta. The city had been minting coins officially since 289 BC, but it was not until the late third century BC that the silver *denarius* and a wide range of bronze denominations became well established. Nevertheless, many other cities in Italy, especially the Greek foundations, continued to strike coins, so that purchases involving money must have been fraught with complications. Even so, by the late Republic transactions in coin were no doubt commonplace in Italy, not least because soldiers were normally paid in this way. Indeed, it is significant to see just how many coin-hoards were buried in Italy in the second and first centuries BC; very large numbers of coins were concealed during times of national or foreign strife, and it is easy to imagine the soldier who was called up for duty, or the threatened well-to-do, putting their cash into what was – and sometimes still is – regarded as the safest bank, namely the ground.[32]

All too little is known about how the markets in Italy itself were organised, although there are some clues. Very often they took place in conjunction with a religious festival, as at the town of Lucus Feroniae, which lay on one side of the Tiber Valley, to the north-east of Rome. The town took its name from the goddess Feronia, a deity venerated at the site from at least as early as the third century BC. Every year there was a great festival, which drew people from all quarters: Latin, Faliscan, Etruscan and Sabine. It was a chance not only to participate in and witness the religious ceremonies (including a bare-footed walk through heaps of embers and ashes), but also to buy and exchange all manner of goods.

Fairs and markets must, indeed, have been commonplace in both town and, in more sparsely inhabited areas, in the countryside too. As today, they were often staggered, so that traders could travel on from one to another. This is illustrated by a splendid calendar, which lists the markets between Capua and Rome: peg-holes are provided so that the market of the day could be appropriately signed. As at Lucus Feroniae, many may have been held in conjunction with religious ceremonies, for commerce and the gods were closely bound up; this is clear, for example, from inscriptions dedicated by merchants to Jupiter Nundinarius and Mercurius Nundinator, *nundinae* being the Latin for the market-day.[33]

The emergence of these local markets was a prerequisite in the development of larger-scale commercial enterprise. Hand-in-hand with the spread of colonies they provided the ways and means for the dissemination of goods and produce. Even so, longer-distance trade seems to have begun early. It can be well measured by the type of pottery referred to earlier, known as 'black-glaze' or sometimes as 'Campanian'. These vessels, produced from about 300 BC, especially in Campania, and intended as a cheap substitute for vases of metal, are the generally undistinguished heirs to a rich tradition of Greek pottery manufacture in Italy. Their importance lies in the fact that they were made on an enormous scale and traded very widely. Already by the early third century BC dishes and cups, known from their decoration as products of the 'atelier des petites estampilles', were being sold to markets all over western-central Italy, as well as to southern France, Corsica, Sardinia, Sicily, Spain and Tunisia, foreshadowing the trade of later centuries. Then from about 200 BC the industry expanded hugely, particularly in the size of its sales to Gaul and to Spain. Before long there were also attractive drinking cups made with rather different fabrics, from kilns in central Italy, and, much more rarely, elaborate vessels, often based on forms fashionable in the Hellenistic east. Some of these were occasionally signed by the potter; at Cales in Campania the dumps of wasters from these vessels cover a huge area. Everything, therefore, points to the development of mass-production, designed, it is often conjectured, to exploit a glut of unskilled labour, especially slaves. Let us again recall the founding of the Aegean island of Delos as a free port in 166 BC, with its huge throughput of people sold into bondage.[34]

During the first century BC the black-glaze vessels were being manufactured in a much wider series of centres, and became progressively less attractive. However, they now begin to turn up in the inland sites of Italy, hallmarking, in an archaeological sense, the spread of Romanisation that followed the end of the Social War. They also continued to be exported on a huge scale, the pottery vessels normally being used to fill spaces in the ships between more bulky goods, such as amphorae. Although low-cost and fairly trivial items in themselves, the black-glaze pots provide vivid testimony to a huge expansion both of production and of trade — and of a reorganisation of the industry to meet these demands.[35]

This commercial expansion in Italy seems to have reached its peak in the late first century BC and the early decades of the first century AD. It was a period which saw not only a still greater increase in output, but also a diversification in industry. Never before had Italy produced such a variety of goods: silver, bronze, glass, pottery and much more. There were also a number of other important changes. One was the adoption of a new form of amphora, known as the Dressel 2–4, which soon ousted the old Dressel 1 design. Based on a prototype evolved on the Greek island of Kos, the new shape was lighter and held more wine — on average 27.5 litres as opposed to 24 — which may explain why it became popular. Before long other provinces were also manufacturing the type, especially Spain; although no-one can have foreseen it in the halcyon days of the Augustan age, it was a harbinger of commercial competition from the provinces which was ultimately to spell out disaster to Italy's economy. But this is to jump ahead, for many of the industries that came to be established within the country in the later first century BC were to produce goods of a high order of quality.[36]

One was a pottery industry which, in ancient terms, was to have a world-wide impact. Around 50 BC craftsmen in Arezzo, a former Etruscan city with a long tradition of manufacturing, began to imitate the shapes of black-glaze, but with a finish in red. At first it was marketed only locally, but within twenty years it had begun to circulate more widely. By 15 BC they had adopted a series of vessels, mostly plain but with others highly decorated in figured relief, whose prototypes largely derived from the Hellenistic east. The ware, today known as Arretine (from Arretium, the Roman name for Arezzo), is immediately recognisable by its bright red, glossy finish and, in

Mould used for the manufacture of decorated Arretine bowls in the factory of M. Perennius at Arezzo. A lion hunt is shown. *(British Museum)*

its day, was to find its way to places as far afield as southern India and Britain. The names on the vessels show that the majority of craftsmen were slaves or freedmen, who themselves originated in the Greek east. Here they had learnt suitable techniques of production, including mass-production by means of moulds, and large-scale firings in kilns. Before long some ninety firms had been established at Arezzo, each with on average between ten and fifteen artisans – mainly slaves – although the largest enterprises numbered about sixty.[37]

The Arretine products soon became a popular table-ware, and Roman proprietors like M. Perennius Tigranus (who, with his principal artisan, Bargathes, was responsible for some of the finest and most influential styles) clearly did immensely well. The natural sequel was the setting up of branch workshops, so as to cut transport costs. Cn. Ateius, for example, is known to have started a workshop at Pisa, and also at Lyon in France; here he could exploit the markets of Gaul, especially the new military bases in the Rhineland. Arretine imitations, 'Italian sigillata', was also produced at Puteoli in Campania and doubtless at more so far unidentified centres in Italy. Other potters were not slow to follow. Relief-decorated cups, attractively coloured, were made by firms like those of Aco and Sarius in the Po Valley and at Lyon; and in France rival concerns producing a ware akin to Arretine and Italian sigillata started at Lezoux, near Clermont Ferrand, and at La Graufesenque, near Millau, in Languedoc. Ultimately, they were completely to eclipse their Italian progenitors.

Productivity also embraced many other areas. Wine was produced in Apulia and widely exported, especially across the Adriatic and into the Aegean to islands like Delos. Both wine and oil were shipped from Apulia up to the Po Valley, even though this region itself produced both commodities. Olive-oil from Istria – the peninsula that extends southwards into the Adriatic from Trieste – was famous, but the archaeological evidence, in the form of Dressel 6 amphorae, proves unexpectedly large-scale manufacture of wine in the Po Valley. The names on the amphorae show that some eminent individuals invested in this area, like Appius Caludius Pulcher, consul in 38 BC, and C. Laecanius Bassus, a member of a distinguished family of the first century AD. Their potteries at Pola also made tiles, pipes and storage jars or *dolia*, reflecting a commercial interest even by people of high senatorial status, who traditionally did not involve themselves with petty industry.[38]

It would be easy to exaggerate the role of mass-production in this period of Roman Italy, for most firms remained very small, and a large number of items were produced to individual order. Furniture is a good instance, and could command astronomical prices.[39] Nevertheless, there were industries where the output was enormous. Efficient lighting, to take one example, could well be regarded as a prerequisite of civilised life, and all the evidence points to a well-organised system of lamp manufacture, using olive-oil as a fuel. At the top end of the market were lamps fashioned by craftsmen, employing relatively expensive materials such as bronze; but the majority

Left The base of a terracotta lamp stamped by the maker, Fortis. Late first to early second century AD. *(British Museum)*

Right The Portland Vase. *(British Museum)*

bought mass-produced items, made of terracotta. From the second century BC the use of moulds enormously increased output, and it was not long before Italian lamps were being exported. Some were plain but others had quite elaborate figured decoration. By about 20 BC certain firms began stamping their products, particularly those based in the Po Valley. Thus we can trace how a highly successful manufacturer such as Fortis, who had workshops in north and in central Italy, also established branches in the provinces: in Gaul, Germany, Yugoslavia and probably elsewhere. Sometimes popular designs led to unauthorised imitation, which can provide difficulties in interpreting the pattern of production; but lamps do occur in wrecks, like the hundred figured Italian lamps recorded from a ship that foundered in the Balearics in the AD 40s, presumably on its way from Italy to Spain.[40]

The standardisation of lamps and pottery vessels is to some extent matched by another industry which developed remarkably in this period, that of glass production. Glass had been known since about 1500 BC, and in Hellenistic times centres like Alexandria, in Egypt, made exquisite vessels for the privileged few. But it was not until around the middle of the first century BC that glass-makers, probably in Syria or nearby, stumbled upon a new technique that made possible mass-production: the art of glass-blowing, especially into a mould. Once introduced into Italy, glass manufacture soon established itself as a major industry, with applications in many fields. The vogue for luxury items, such as the Portland Vase, an Augustan work of

near-peerless beauty, continued and expanded; this is a blown amphora, with superimposed layers of glass of two different colours, opaque white and blue, where the craftsman has partially cut away the outside surface so as to set two figured scenes (perhaps the marriage of Peleus and Thetis) against the dark-blue ground. Cast vessels, often in polychrome, were also popular for the more expensive items, and were widely exported; many sought to imitate the rarer materials such as agate and fluorspar. However, it was a fairly standardised series of mould-blown vessels that really revolutionised the market. Quick and cheap to make, they appealed for their elegance, for their colour and fine decoration, and even for their lack of smell and taste: were they not so fragile, observes Petronius' outrageously *nouveau riche* character, Trimalchio, he would prefer them to cups of gold.[41]

Glass vessels were also practical in that they could be used to store and transport perfumes, unguent oils for the baths, and foodstuffs – and even the cremated ashes of one's forebears. It was a highly versatile material, and not suprisingly glass-works sprang up rapidly both in Italy and in the provinces. Aquileia, in the north-east, was to be one very important centre, and others are known in Rome and Puteoli; but they must have become commonplace as the techniques – and the popularity of the product – became widespread in the last decades of the first century BC.

The explosion in the size and range of the manufacturing industries, considerably aided by the availability of cheap, often servile, labour, can therefore be traced in many fields. We might add the quarrying of stone, particularly the fine white marble of Carrara, so favoured by Michelangelo. The nearby town of Luni, made a colony by Augustus, was to prosper enormously from handling the marble and shipping it out through its port. Under the Empire quarries (like mines) largely became imperially owned, but there was always money to be made by those who took up the contracts and handled the material. Indeed, Carrara marble, whether used in buildings or (to a lesser extent) for costly objects such as decorated sarcophagi, became an extremely popular commodity, not least in Rome itself.[42] Similarly, many magnates found it lucrative to exploit the clay beds on their estates, and manufacture bricks and tiles. This was a practice of long standing in the south of Italy, and it gradually spread northwards during the first century BC. However, it was the great fire in Rome of AD 64 that spurred on this form of investment, following an unprecedented demand for less flammable building-materials. This explains why so many tile kilns were constructed on villa estates at this time, and it is particularly useful that many owners found it convenient to stamp their products, and eventually often included a consular date. It can now be seen that the Tiber Valley brick-yards did particularly well in this business (which, perhaps surprisingly, involved overseas trade to cities like Carthage), and it is an instructive comment on the profitability of the enterprise that brick production became an imperial monopoly in the early third century AD[43]

The balance-sheet that we have been drawing up for the time of the late

Republic and early Empire so far comes out firmly in favour of Rome and large parts of Italy. However, this must be set against some losses. Of prime significance is the *annona*, the supply of corn, in particular to the city of Rome. The subject is a complex one, reflecting inevitable vicissitudes of supply and demand, and a multitude of legislative action. Boiled down to essentials, the *annona* meant that from 300 BC, if not before, Rome was unable to provide a sufficiency of grain for its population. Bad harvests, combined with speculation in the market, exacerbated the situation, and it became necessary for the authorities to step in. The solution was two-fold. In the first place, it was essential to ensure a supply, which was achieved – although in an up-and-down fashion – by importing the grain through the port at Ostia. Initially much of it came from Sicily and Sardinia; later Egypt and parts of North Africa became the prime producers. Secondly, prices had to be controlled. Laws to ensure this were not passed before the last quarter of the second century BC; but the sequel was the implementation of a free hand-out which, if the numbers receiving it were soon restricted (150,000 in 57 BC), was nevertheless an early and important act of state social intervention – albeit for good political reasons. Augustus himself took over the responsibility for the corn supply in 22 BC following an acute famine, and raised the number of free recipients to 200,000. Thereafter an increasingly elaborate bureaucracy emerged, and a special procurator was appointed under Claudius to manage the supply. Similar arrangements prevailed in other Italian towns, emphasising the huge importance that the *annona* came to acquire.[44]

Much of the grain from Egypt was shipped by a special fleet which sailed from Alexandria to Pozzuoli in the Bay of Naples, which, during the Republic, was a much safer harbour than that at Ostia. Claudius attempted to remedy this by constructing a new all-weather harbour some three kilometres to the north of Ostia. It was a huge task, which involved the

A grave sculpture showing L. Ampudius Philomasus, a corn merchant, and his wife and daughter. From Porta Capena, Rome. *(British Museum)*

Entrance to the warehouse, the Horrea Epagathiana, at Ostia. Mid-second century AD.

building of two great moles that jutted into the sea, with an artificial island between. It did not really work, and Tacitus records a huge loss of shipping that sank in rough weather.[45] This is why the emperor Trajan (AD 97–117) ordered the construction of a land-locked inner basin, linked with the Tiber by a canal, the Fossa Traiana. More than 200 metres across, the hexagonal shape of the harbour can often be picked out when flying into Rome's Leonardo da Vinci airport. Within a short space of time houses and storage facilities were being built around it, reflecting the growth of a prosperous and thriving community. Indeed, Portus, as the harbour-town came to be known, eventually was completely to eclipse Ostia, which, within two centuries, had been stripped of its municipal rights.[46]

Nevertheless, Ostia in the early Imperial period was a busy and bustling commercial town, full of great warehouses for storing the grain and other goods that came through its port. These were then shipped up the Tiber in barges into Rome itself. One has only to visit the Piazzale delle Corporazioni, to the north of the theatre in Ostia, to appreciate the point. Here is a square surrounded by more than sixty offices, representing commercial associations from all over the ancient world – Alexandria, Carthage, Marseilles and many other major cities. Each is identified by a mosaic floor in the arcade around the piazza where the trade-mark of the company is displayed, together with an appropriate inscription. Whilst corn-merchants predominate, cheek-by-jowl are customs officials, dockers, salvage crews and shipbuilders, a Lloyds of antiquity that must have been a continual hubbub of noisy argument and debate.[47]

Many of the merchants may well have been from Spain, for another commodity that Rome imported in huge quantities was olive-oil from regions like the Guadalquivir Valley to the north of Málaga. This is graphically attested by a huge dump of broken Spanish oil amphorae close to the Tiber at Monte Testaccio, not far from the Ostian Gate in Rome. It takes its name from the Latin word for potsherds, *testae*. It has a circumference of nearly one kilometre, and calculations suggest that it represents an importing to Rome of four million kilos of oil, carried in some 55,000 amphorae, every year.[48]

The growth of the Spanish oil trade with Italy, which became increasingly marked from the later first century AD, is symptomatic, however, of a much wider phenomenon. If, the corn trade apart, Rome and the richer parts of Italy had shown a net profit under the later Republic, then quite early in Imperial times the balance began to tip the other way. That said, it is not an easy subject to quantify, and different regions responded to the changing emphases in the economy in very variable ways. Moreover, the totting-up of figures in the balance-book is doubly complicated by the fact that many goods (particularly grain) came to Rome in the form of taxes and rents: Sicily, for instance, contributed a tithe of its wheat harvest in the first century BC, amounting to about thirty million litres of grain, probably between 5 and 10 per cent of what the city of Rome needed under the Empire. The grain supply was further increased as individual rulers bought up land, as in North Africa, which gave a good yield of cereals.[49]

Taxes, therefore, can help to distort the overall picture, and render it difficult to search for a more general picture. Nevertheless, there are some clear indications. For example, the best quality red-gloss figured table-ware made at Arezzo went largely out of production by about AD 50 (although some plain wares continued to be made rather longer). They were partly replaced by an indifferently made ware known as 'late Italian sigillata', produced in Pisa, Puteoli and elsewhere, but more particularly by imports from the south of Gaul, the so-called 'samian ware'. Indeed, by the middle of the second century even the Italian red wares were no longer being produced, and it is remarkable that, thereafter, no high-quality table-ware was ever again produced in Italy down to the end of antiquity. It is ironic that the Gallic industries, which were initiated by Italian potters, should in turn start to capture the home market; but the evidence is unmistakable, even including a case of Gaulish vessels that still awaited unpacking when the eruption of Vesuvius overwhelmed Pompeii in AD 79.[50]

Another important development in Gaul was the establishment of new vineyards, many of which, such as Bordeaux and Burgundy, were to develop into the famous *crus* of today. Slowly the markets that Italian wine-growers had monopolised began to fall away. A famous edict of Domitian, issued in AD 92, ordered that there should be no new vineyards in Italy, and that half of those in the provinces should be uprooted: the production of grapes and wine was getting out of hand, and putting into jeopardy other areas of agricultural production.[51] Spain, too, was creating a great surplus in olive-oil, garum, salted fish and even pots, both of Arretine Italian sigillata type and other forms of vessel. However, the most significant development was the emergence in North Africa – especially in what is now Tunisia – of production centres for a new style of table-ware that we call African red-slip pottery, as well as olive-oil. The vast areas of olive plantations that one can see today in Tunisia – for example, to the west of Sfax, where they provide an unending vista – very much had their counterpart in Roman times. Trade with Italy began slowly, in about AD 60, and seems from the distribution of the pottery and the amphorae to have been particularly directed at the centres on the western side of the country; but before long a huge market had come into being.[52]

Much fascinating current work is going on in Italy to define and explain this apparent upheaval in the system of economic checks and balances. At Ostia, for instance, a careful excavation in the 1960s and 1970s of the Baths of the Swimmer, built in the reign of Domitian (AD 81–96), has sought to trace the decline of Italian products in some detail. The finds in the layers in the baths suggest that here, at any rate, Spanish oil and wine dominated the market in the first half of the second century AD but that by about AD 200 Africa had achieved a monopoly, certainly in oil. Italian products, by contrast, accounted for virtually nothing. These conclusions have, however, provoked great controversy, particularly if one tries to generalise from the results of the excavation of a tiny part of one site, itself a single town out of a total of more than four hundred in peninsular Italy.[53] What does seem clear, however, is that the amphora (the Dressel 2–4) that was made to ship Italian wine throughout the first century AD went out of production in the early second century. This has suggested to many that Italian wine production, at any rate for export, very largely came to an end. Moreover, this seemed to be corroborated at villa sites like Settefinestre, where excavation suggests that the cultivation of vines largely gave way to cereal production at this time and that, within a matter of decades, the site had been abandoned. Many other villas, especially in coastal Etruria and Campania, appear to show a similar pattern and, as these are precisely the areas where villas with large slave-gangs predominated, it was a natural conclusion to argue that it was the collapse of the 'slave mode of production' that brought about this decay. Furthermore, scholars point out, the use of slaves was much more restricted in provinces like Gaul and Spain, leading to an altogether healthier situation.

All this is heady stuff, not least because of its Marxist overtones. Inevitably, reaction has set in. Some have attempted to identify amphora types that replaced the Dressel 2–4; others have argued that wooden barrels were used instead of jars; and the literary and epigraphic evidence has been pressed into service to demonstrate continued production of wine in Italy in the second and third centuries AD – perhaps mainly cheap stuff for home consumption, bearing in mind that Cato allowed the equivalent of a bottle of wine per day for each slave.[57] Moreover, as excavation and fieldwork proceeds in other parts of the peninsula, we can see that, for every villa that was abandoned, others carried on. Latium has new farms being built in the second and third centuries AD; in parts of the south many villas survive into the fourth and fifth centuries AD; and in the Adriatic provinces many sites in the countryside are still being occupied in late Roman times. So the picture can hardly be called clear-cut.[55]

Let us try to sum up. There are great dangers in applying modern economic theories (consciously or unconsciously) to the ancient world, for the economy was never manipulated in anything like the same way as it is today. Nor have we been tempted to delve into complex questions like the nature and effect of the money supply, a fascinating issue which is beginning to come into focus, but only slowly.[56] Moreover, we must recognise our evidence for what it is: highly patchy and very partial, making it imprudent to draw more than tentative conclusions. Nevertheless, it would be otiose not to recognise some clearly spelt-out trends: that many parts of Italy achieved an extraordinary diversity of production in late Republican times; that trade, especially in the west Mediterranean, reached a peak in the Augustan age; and that Gaul, Spain and, most impressively, North Africa were the heirs to Italy's greatness from quite early on in the Imperial period. On the other hand, there is a regional diversity to this picture that at present escapes very precise definition, but which in time may well call for radical reinterpretation. Historians have not hitherto been laggardly in deciphering those patterns; but, if the archaeological evidence that we have cited is any guide, then we shall look forward to continued, and exciting, debate, which will refine – and perhaps transform – these tentative conclusions about the balance of trade in the very first international state.

Further reading

Apart from standard works (like M. Rostovtzeff, *Social and economic history*, M. I. Finley, *The ancient economy*, R. P. Duncan-Jones, *Economy of the Roman empire*), see particularly: P. D. A. Garnsey *et al.*, *Trade in the ancient economy* (1983); J. H. D'Arms and E. C. Kopff (eds), *The seaborne commerce of ancient Rome* (1980); A. Giardina and A. Schiavone (eds), *Società romana e produzione schiavistica* (1981); J. H. D'Arms, *Commerce and social standing in ancient Rome* (1981); and K. Hopkins, *Conquerors and slaves* (1978), and his 'Taxes and trade', *JRS* 70 (1980), 101–25. For Ostia, see Carandini *et al.*, in *Studi Miscellanei* (vols 13, 16, 21, 23; 1968–77); and also their *Settefinestre. Una villa schiavistica in Etruria romana* (1985). For amphorae, see J. J. Paterson, 'Salvation from the sea', *JRS* 72 (1982), 146–57; N. Purcell, 'Wine and wealth', *JRS* 75 (1985), 1–19; E. Rodriguez-Almeida, *Il Monte Testaccio* (1984); and now D. Peacock and J. Williams, *Amphorae and the Roman economy* (1986). For shipwrecks, see A. Parker in K. Muckelroy (ed.), *Archaeology under water* (1980), 50ff. Other important works include D. Peacock, *Pottery in the Roman world* (1982); J. W. Hayes, *Late Roman pottery* (1972, supplement 1980); D. M. Bailey, *Catalogue of lamps in the British Museum II: Roman lamps made in Italy* (1980); and W. V. Harris, 'Roman terracotta lamps: the organisation of an industry', *JRS* 70 (1980), 126–45.

—8—

GODS AND THEIR TEMPLES

T here was a grove below the Aventine, dark with the shade of oaks, and when you saw it you would say 'There is a deity there'. (Ovid, *Fasti* III, 295–6)

Religion permeated almost every walk and corner of ancient life, so much so that, from our modern, much more secular standpoint, the attitudes of antiquity can seem quite unreal. There were, of course, sceptics, just as today. It was quite permissible to poke fun at Hercules who, although the divine founder of Herculaneum, could nevertheless be shown drunkenly urinating in a celebrated statue found in the House of the Stags in the town. Similarly, there was Hannibal's reaction to divination, normally a matter of great importance: when told that he could not begin a battle because the entrails were unfavourable, he is said to have retorted: 'Do you put more faith in a slice of veal than in an old general?' Nevertheless, in their different ways most people did pay respect to religion, and it coloured many aspects of their lives. One of the numerous festivals in the Roman calendar was the Lemuria, a time in May when ghosts from the family, particularly of those who had died young, might return to haunt their kin. Ovid tells how every householder rose at midnight and walked through his domain, spitting out nine black beans and proclaiming: 'with these I ransom me and mine'. The ghosts then ate the beans and, while looking well away, the householder washed his hands, beat a gong and cried nine times: 'ancestral ghosts, depart!' As a modern historian comments: 'it is difficult to imagine Livy or Horace or Agrippa solemnly getting out of bed and going through this ritual. And yet they probably did – at least in a modified form'.[1]

For most Romans, in fact, religion was primarily a question of establishing the right sort of relationship with the gods. It was in many ways a rather unemotional business, attended by very precisely defined rituals, often revolving around festivals fixed by long tradition in the annual calendar. As the consul Q. Marcius Philippus is said to have remarked: 'the gods look kindly upon the scrupulous observance of religious rites, which have brought our country to its peak'.[2] We have a good deal of information about these rituals, both from ancient literature and from inscriptions. Ovid, for example – the Augustan poet best known for his *Metamorphoses* and for his elegies about love – also wrote about the calendar; this was a long poem known as the *Fasti*, with a book for each month. Only the first six books survive, covering January to June, but in combination with official calendars, inscribed on stone, and the remarks of other writers, they give us a fairly clear idea of the religious festivals of the year. These are conspicuous both for their frequency – 115 days of the year are marked out for some reason or another, irresistibly bringing to mind the profusion of public holidays in Italy today – and for the complex mix of tradition: for Roman religion was, above all, a blend of many elements, rustic and urban, Italic and Etruscan, Roman and Greek.

During the period of the Republic, these different strands slowly came together, and the dates of the festivals soon became enshrined in the official calendar (which in 46 BC took on substantially the same monthly divisions as today). Despite the secular overtones that many of the religious occasions came to acquire, there is a sense of belief and purpose behind the inscriptions and in the buildings and other remains that immediately separates our modern world from that of antiquity. Let us briefly refer to some of the important dates in the calendar, as it was about the time of Augustus.

The year opened, appropriately enough, with the installation in Rome of the new consuls, a magnificent event described for us by Ovid.[3] It was a popular occasion, watched by many people as the procession wound its path up the Sacred Way to the temple of Jupiter on the Capitol, the seat of Rome's patron deity. Here white bulls were sacrificed in front of a huge throng, the vows were made and the new consuls sat on their official chairs in front of the crowd, before descending the hill to attend a congregation of senate. This was just one of the many great state occasions in the Roman year, and it is not difficult for those who have been in Rome for a contemporary celebration to visualise the colourful scene. Some time later – the date was not precisely fixed – there was a chance for jollification after the Compitalia, a festival marked by sacrifices at shrines placed at boundaries and crossroads. It was in origin an agricultural ceremony to propitiate the *lar*, or spirit that presided over each farm, and it is striking to see how the traditions of the countryside became incorporated into the life of the towns, to which so many rural folk migrated.

More sombre was the Parentalia, a time in February when it was customary to honour the dead, particularly parents. This was the moment to place food offerings at the tomb to satisfy the restless spirits, the *Manes*, who, Ovid tells us, could spread death and destruction if not thus placated. It is a custom almost as old as man himself, and the cemeteries would have been awash with offerings brought by the relatives, a tradition that has hardly died in parts of Italy today. By contrast, the Lupercalia, which took place at the same time in the heart of Rome, was a hugely popular and wild occasion, which acquired a reputation for considerable impropriety. The deity involved is unknown, but its formal purpose was the purification of the city. Its culmination was a race by two teams of near-naked young men from the Palatine to the Forum, watched by huge crowds. It survived until AD 494, when it was replaced with the festival of the Purification of the Virgin Mary, one of the many direct links between the worlds of paganism and Christianity.

March originally marked the beginning of the New Year, and was appropriately devoted to Mars – *optimus, maximus*, the greatest and the best. Mars coupled the protection of the growth of crops with his patronage of war, both vital matters in the early days of the Republic. Neither much concerned the ordinary Roman of later centuries, but the festival lived on, not least on 14 March, when there were horse-races in the Campus Martius in Rome – a legacy, perhaps, of the cavalry action of former times. The following day was the festival of Anna Perenna, a goddess of obscure origin; in Ovid's day this was the occasion of a great picnic on the outskirts of Rome: the poet pictures the old man, full of good wine, helping the tipsy old wife home, a day well spent if not religiously inspiring.

April was also a time when it was customary to honour the gods and goddesses whose role in Rome's legendary history remained as folk-memories. The Feriae Latinae, for example, was a joint festival of the Romans and the Latins, held in the Alban Hills, where the city of Alba Longa (modern Castel Gandolfo) had once been the leading city of Latium. It was attended by the consuls and many other leading figures, and its importance is reflected in the fact that it was still being held as late as the third century AD. The other major festivals of April were less serious in concept, but of no less interest. One, the Parilia, honoured two shepherd-deities, and evidently related to remote agricultural traditions; but in Rome it came to be identified with the city's birthday, and even Ovid himself, who was not of a religious disposition, took part in the celebrations (which included leaping over a bonfire). Another was the Floralia, again a very ancient cult connected with springtime flowering; from the third century BC, on the instruction of the oracle contained in Rome's Sibylline Books, an annual games was held, and there were somewhat lewd performances in the theatres – precisely the sort of thing that was later to attract the wrath of early Christians like St Augustine.[4]

Long-established festivals also brought colour to the month of May, like the ritual of leading a bull, a sheep and a pig around the fields, so as to purify the growing crops; the animals were then sacrificed to Ceres. As Virgil remarks: 'no-one should take a sickle to the ripe grain until he has crowned his head with a garland of oak and danced an impromptu dance of thanks to Ceres'.[5] In Rome the ceremony came to mean little, but the idea was perpetuated in taking a census, when the people to be counted were grouped

The theatre at Spoleto, of late Augustan date. Theatres were largely used for ceremonies of religious inspiration.

together, while a bull, a sheep and a pig were led around them before being sacrificed to Mars. Augustus records performing three such *lustra* for a total of 13,233,000 Roman citizens, bringing back 'many exemplary practices of our ancestors which were disappearing in our time':[6] one can well imagine the curiosity that this provoked but, as we shall see, it was very much in accord with the spirit of his time.

During the summer months there were many festivals: to Vesta, whose shrine in the Forum, cared for by the Vestal Virgins, represented the heart of Roman family life; to Fortuna, when there was a splendid fête with many boats on the Tiber, which even slaves were allowed to attend; and to Apollo, Diana, Jupiter and Hercules. Hercules was particularly popular in the business world, largely because of his reputation as a smart, and perhaps unscrupulous, dealer. Many traders made dedications to him, including one L. Munius from Rieti, who offered a tenth of his profits to the god, provided that the god helped him to get the sum right.[7] The remark, however naive, is touching, and at a stroke reminds us of the meaning of faith. How interesting that he might have been one of those flourishing merchants – his inscription dates to the early first century BC – whose fortunes we traced in the previous chapter. As he came from Sabine country, perhaps on 21 August he sometimes went to the Circus Maximus in Rome to participate in the festival of the god Consus. According to tradition it was when the Sabines were watching the games in honour of Consus, the god of grain storage, that the Romans were able to carry out the Rape of the Sabine women, while their men were preoccupied with the events before them. If he had attended the festival L. Munius would have no doubt enjoyed the spectacle, initiated with a sacrifice, which was overseen by the priest of Quirinus and the Vestal Virgins and followed by horse-racing. Ovid advised watching the pretty girls, not the horses; but the occasion was no doubt splendid.

The autumn and winter brought many more festivals, including that of Bona Dea, the 'good goddess'. This was a cult that was exclusive to women, who met in early December at the house of the chief pontiff to make the sacrifice of a sow. Bona Dea was related to Faunus, an early Latin deity of nature and the countryside; fertility seems to have been at the heart of the ritual and men were rigidly excluded. The Saturnalia, on the other hand, was everybody's feast, the pagan precursor of Christmas, the god Saturn standing for the good times of before, which might again return.

At first sight the variety of these festivals and the sheer number of deities is bewildering, the more so because we have touched only on some major occasions. This is to leave aside, for example, important gods like the *lares*, who guarded the house (where there was always a shrine), and the *penates*, who protected the domestic supplies (from *penus*, a store house). Moreover, from Augustan times onwards other divinities were to achieve popularity, and one religion, Christianity, was ultimately to become – officially, at any rate – supreme. This underlines the fact that Roman religion was above all eclectic – all but the most barbaric practices were tolerated – so that it came

7 Arretine vase showing the seasons, made by Cn. Ateius in *c.* 10 BC. It lacks its base. Found at Capua. *(British Museum)*

to be a complex amalgam where deities could change their nature and both rise and decline in popularity.

The roots of Roman religion are complex, but it is clear that it developed very much in parallel with the Latin and Italic parts of the peninsula. This applies both to the emergence of deities with personalised characteristics, such as Mars (a national Italic god also known as Mamers and Mavors, and the origin of tribal names like Marsi and Marrucini), and to the creation of formalised ritual. In AD 1444, at Gubbio (ancient Iguvium), in Umbria, nine inscribed bronze tablets were found.[8] Written in Umbrian and dating to between about 200 and 89 BC, the texts record the proceedings and rituals of a brotherhood of priests, the *frater atiieriur*, in Latin the Fratres Atiedii. The rituals include the purification of the city, with a sacrifice to the triad of Jupiter Grabovius, Mars Grabovius and Vofionus Grabovius (the equivalent of the Roman triad of Jupiter, Mars and Quirinus, an ancient Sabine deity worshipped on the Quirinal Hill in Rome); the purification of the people of Iguvium, where there was a procession that went three times around them, recalling the census *lustrum* of Rome; a procession through the fields to the grove of Jupiter; and sacrifices in the event of unfavourable auspices to ensure the retention of good and the rejection of evil.

These tablets, together with others, like one from Agnone (which contains a remarkable list of seventeen Samnite deities with altars at the sacred grove there), cast an enormous amount of light upon early religious practices in Italy.[9] It is clear that many sanctuaries initially consisted of no more than an open-air grove, in Latin a *lucus* or *nemus*, where the tablets were displayed on a tree. One of the most famous was close to modern Nemi (the name is a direct survival of *nemus*), situated on the side of a lake in the Alban Hills, to the south of Rome.[10] Here was the sanctuary of Diana Nemorensis, presided over by a strange priest–king, the Rex Nemorensis, who, in Strabo's words, was a 'run-away slave who has slain with his own hand the man previously consecrated to that office' – a contest initiated by violating the grove with the plucking of a branch.[11] The sanctuary began very early and was a religious centre for cities of the Latin League; when the king Servius Tullius founded an altar to Diana on the Aventine Hill in Rome in about 550 BC it was with a clear political motive – to show, in Livy's words, that 'Rome, by common consent, was the capital city'.[12] The sanctuary at Nemi remained popular, however, particularly amongst women, who associated her with childbirth and healing and who paid their honours with great processions.[13]

The archaeological evidence from Nemi shows that the first temple on the site was built in the late fourth century BC, lending architectural permanence to the sacred place. From then on it expanded. The temple was rebuilt in the second century BC, and later a theatre was added, reminding us that theatres were often constructed for religious ceremonies rather than for entertainment. Many votive objects – statuettes, feet, hands and the like – were dedicated by people suffering from particular maladies, a cult practice that

A bronze tablet from Agnone, in southern-central Italy. Inscribed in the Italic tongue, Oscan, it concerns the statues of various deities. *c.* 300–100 BC. *(British Museum)*

we shall review further below. There was further building work in the first and early second centuries AD, attesting to the wealth and fame of one of the best-known sanctuaries of central Italy – and the starting point for the very great modern work of anthropology, Sir James Frazer's *The Golden Bough*, first published in 1890.

Another very important early Latian sanctuary lay twenty-eight kilometres to the south of Rome at Lavinium (modern Pratica di Mare). Traditionally founded by Aeneas, that weary fugitive from the Trojan Wars, it was recognised in antiquity as the seat of the cult of the Penates (the guardians of the stores) that later was to become of such significance in Roman religion. We also know that Castor and Pollux were worshipped there by 500 BC, as well as many other deities that became popular at Rome; thus, given that Lavinium had strong contacts with the Greek world too, it may well have played a crucial role in transmitting Hellenic ideas to Rome. The sanctuary seems to have been huge, and contained a notable series of thirteen altars arranged in a line, apparently for open-air worship. They were built over a long period, from the sixth to the second centuries BC; this, coupled with the temples (including one to Zeus' wife Hera), suggests that here was a site of great importance in shaping some of the early religious traditions of Rome itself.[14]

Sanctuaries like Nemi and Lavinium, or Pietrabbondante for the Samnites, doubtless played a major role in formulating early religious traditions, and so, too, did the Etruscans. They also had a centre where, for a time, their league of cities met annually at the festival of the goddess Voltumna; it is said to have been near Volsinii, probably to be identified.with modern Orvieto, but the site has not been found.[15] Religion dominated Etruscan life, and they developed particular expertise in the art of divination. As the emperor Claudius, an early and passionate Etruscologist, is said to have remarked: 'It often happened that when the [Roman] State fell upon evil days, the Etruscan soothsayers were summoned to Rome, and ceremonies were revived and thereafter faithfully observed.'[16]

Many Etruscan cults and deities were of extreme antiquity, but they also absorbed a great many ideas from the Greeks, both in southern Italy and in Etruria itself. We know, for example, that there was a Greek trading centre in the sixth century BC at Gravisca, the port of Tarquinia, where Hera, Aphrodite and Apollo were worshipped, and the Etruscans continued later to venerate Aphrodite, whom they identified with their own goddess, Turan. They also learnt from the Greeks to fashion deities in human form, and to build temples in which to house the cult statues. The architecture from the first reflected both their own individuality of approach and the materials to hand – brown volcanic *tufo* stone, wood and clay: wonderful figures (especially on the roof) and other decorative elements in terracotta were to be their substitute for the marble that was so much more readily available to Greek craftsmen.

Elaborately decorated temples were being built by the Etruscans from about 550 BC. This included Rome, where the Tarquin kings constructed a great temple to Jupiter Optimus Maximus on the Capitoline Hill. Dedicated on 13 September in the first year of the Republic, 509 BC, it was the finest achievement of Etruscan Rome. Raised on a high podium in the Etruscan manner, it had three cult rooms or *cellae*. The central one was occupied by Jupiter, with a wonderful statue made by Vulca, a celebrated Etruscan craftsman from the city of Veii (subsequently Rome's deadliest enemy). The figure wore a gold-embroidered purple toga, later to be adopted by Roman generals celebrating a triumphant victory. On either side were rooms for the goddesses Juno and Minerva, making up the celebrated Roman Capitoline triad. The pediment was also elaborately decorated and was crowned with another terracotta figure of Jupiter, also made by Vulca, shown in a chariot drawn by four horses and holding a sceptre and thunderbolt.[17]

The impact of this magnificent edifice can easily be imagined. Jupiter became the official state god of the city and, in time, the Capitoline triad was to symbolise Rome in many parts of the Empire, especially in the colonies of the west. Moreover, many of the architectural characteristics of the Etruscan style of temple persisted into Imperial times. As Dionysius observed, when the Capitoline temple was rebuilt in 69 BC after a fire had destroyed its by then very old predecessor: 'it was erected upon the same foundations and differed in nothing but the costliness of the materials'.[18] In practice this meant the use of a high plinth, so that the temple towered above one, as with

The lofty Capitolium in the forum at Ostia, dedicated to Jupiter, Juno and Minerva. *c.* AD 120–30.

the still later Capitolium of Ostia, which dates to Hadrian's reign; an orientation designed so that the temple should be seen face on rather than from the side, so as to focus attention on the altar which was placed in front of the building; and a deep porch (*pronaos*), supported by columns – a striking contrast with Greek temples like the Parthenon in Athens where the *cella* is completely surrounded by columns.

Greek influence did, of course, make itself strongly felt. One of the temples still visible in the Largo Argentina, in the heart of Rome, has a Greek-style colonnade around three sides, whilst another has columns on all four sides (as is the case in a pair of further examples in the nearby Forum Holitorum). Others, like the so-called temple of Fortuna Virilis, on the east bank of the Tiber, incorporate the columns into the walls of the *cella*, a manifestly hybrid arrangement; it belongs to the second century BC. The Greek architectural orders also came into widespread use, and the decorative elements strongly reflected Hellenistic traditions. Indeed, the circular temple of Hercules Victor in Rome's Forum Boarium (a design with a long history in Greece) has features, amongst them the use of Pentelic marble, which suggest that the craftsmen may have been Greek. It is one of a series of highly elegant round temples which culminate, architecturally speaking, in the astonishing building that is Hadrian's Pantheon in Rome.[19]

Despite this Greek influence, in the new colonies the design of many of the temples remained firmly rooted in Etruscan tradition. This is well illustrated at Cosa, where the principal religious focus was placed on a high hill in the southern corner of the town, a suitably eminent position. Initially there was a temple to Jupiter alone, but around the middle of the second century BC this was replaced by a great temple with three cult rooms, laid out and elaborately decorated largely along Etruscan lines.[20] It was a Capitolium, dedicated to the Capitoline triad, Jupiter, Juno and Minerva, and as such was an evocative symbol of the power and authority of Rome.

The Augustan architect Vitruvius did not always find the result pleasing: 'the temples make an impression that reminds me of a man with a large, low broad head, standing with his legs wide apart'. However, he does expound the mathematical principles on which Etruscan-style temples were based, and also has a good deal of sage advice on the placing of temples in towns:

Those dedicated to deities who protect the city, and those dedicated to Jupiter, Juno and Minerva should be on the very highest point, commanding a view of the greater part of the city walls. The temple of Mercury should be near the forum or, like those of Isis and Serapis, in the market; those of Apollo and Bacchus near the theatre; that of Hercules at the circus, if there is no gymnasium; that of Mars outside the city, but near the military training ground; that of Venus outside the city near the harbour. The writings of the Etruscan *haruspices* [soothsayers] also say that the sanctuaries of Venus, Vulcan and Mars should be situated outside the city, so that young men and married women may not become accustomed to the pleasures of the flesh.[21]

There are many points of interest in this passage, not least the profusion of deities and traditions of different origins – Roman, Italic, Greek, Egyptian and Etruscan. Of the Egyptian gods Isis and Serapis and of other religions from the eastern part of the Mediterranean, we shall have more to say shortly. They were part of a huge pantheon which gradually took shape during the Republic. Asclepius is a case in point. Originating in Thessaly in Greece, he came into prominence as a healing god in the early fourth century BC. Epidaurus, in the Greek Argolid, became the major sanctuary, but others were soon founded, like that in Athens, built in 420 BC. Asclepius – Latinised to Aesculapius – came to Rome as the result of a plague in 293 BC. This was at the instigation of the Sibylline Books, the prophetic works housed in the temple of Jupiter on the capitol. It is said that the sacred snake, the incarnation of the god, chose the Tiber island in Rome as the site of the temple, which was dedicated on 1 January 291 BC.[22] No trace of the sanctuary remains, but the cult soon became immensely popular. This much is clear from terracottas depicting parts of the human body, often at life size, that were dedicated by the afflicted at healing sanctuaries. More than one hundred sanctuaries are known, the majority in western-central Italy, and while not all were presided over by Asclepius (for other deities like Diana at Nemi assumed curative powers), it is nevertheless clear that the inspiration for the idea stemmed ultimately from the temple in Rome itself.

Study of the terracottas is beginning to reveal the emergence of some specialised centres in healing. At Ponte di Nona, for example, a rural complex some fifteen kilometres to the east of Rome, the collections are dominated by feet and hands – precisely the parts of the body which are likely to suffer damage in the course of agricultural work. In the town of Veii, on the other hand, the terracottas from the Campetti sanctuary contain a huge proportion of male and female sexual organs. If not associated with some form of fertility cult, these may well hint at a high incidence of sexually transmitted diseases, of a sort that might well be picked up in an urban brothel.[23]

Asclepius (or Aesculapius) was to become an important deity in many parts of the Empire, not least because the worshipper had a more personal relationship with the god than was the case with most of the 'official' cults. However, the vogue for dedicating terracottas somewhat mysteriously comes to an end about the time of the collapse of the Republic. Just what happened at the sanctuaries is still largely unclear; but they can nevertheless be seen as part of a much wider process that spread temples and shrines everywhere. As one scholar remarked, writing of the pastoral scenes shown on the walls of the House of Livia on the Palatine in Rome: 'one can hardly see the landscape for shrines or statues'; or another: 'one could hardly take a step out of doors without meeting a little shrine, a sacred enclosure, an image, a sacred stone or a sacred tree'.[24] Some of the sanctuaries were truly vast, resembling examples in the Greek world, such as the remarkable terraced temple of Athena at Lindos on Rhodes.[25] In Italy these are matched by the great temple complexes of Latium, which include a theatre, imposing porticoes and terraces, and fine staircases. A comparatively modest example

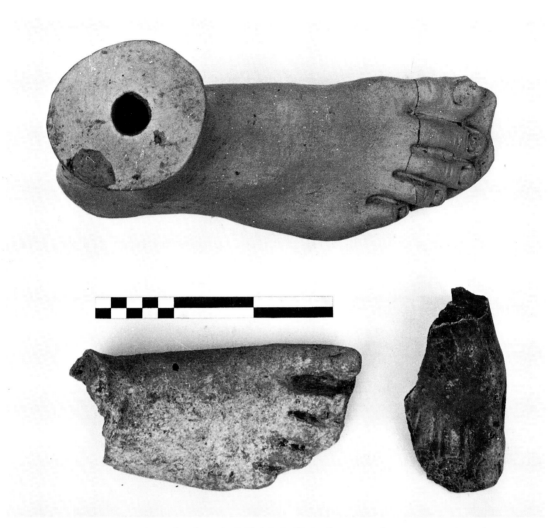

Votive terracotta feet, dedicated by sufferers to the deity who presided over the sanctuary at Ponte di Nona, to the east of Rome.

is to be found at Gabii, built in the second century BC, less than twenty kilometres to the east of Rome. Very much grander is the huge terraced sanctuary of Fortuna Primigenia at Praeneste (modern Palestrina), where construction work seems to have begun in the second half of the second century BC; or the temple of Hercules Victor at Tivoli, of around 50 BC.[26]

These great sanctuaries, to which could be added examples outside Latium, like the temple of Jupiter Anxur, perched high on a hill at Terracina, represent the pinnacle of Republican religious building. At a comparatively ordinary town like Pompeii (which probably had a population of about 20,000 when it was wiped out in AD 79), the scale of building was impressive but, nevertheless, more modest. We know of only nine major temples, two of them dating back to the town's beginnings. Three others belong to the pre-Imperial era: the lofty Capitolium, the official cult centre of the colony established in 80 BC, which towered suitably over the forum; and the temples

of Jupiter Meilichius and Venus. Venus was later to become the patron deity of the town. Traditional cults were also well established in Republican and early Imperial Ostia. Its special guardian was Vulcan, whose priest was appointed for life and who exercised authority in many aspects of the town's religious life. Castor and Pollux, for long associated with navigation, were

The mausoleum of C. Ennius Marsus, built outside the Benevento Gate, at Saepinum. It is a modest version of the large 'drum' tombs of Rome and elsewhere. His epitaph records both his public service as a magistrate in the town and his army service as military tribune and commander of engineers.

also particularly venerated, while other temples are known to Jupiter, Hercules and Liber Pater, an ancient Italian deity concerned with fertility.[27]

By Augustus' day, however, changes to Italy's traditional religious make-up were beginning to become apparent. Indeed, many believed that the awful conflicts and internal strife of the decades of the Republic were due to neglect of the old gods. As Horace wrote in his *Odes*, published about 23 BC: 'you will pay for the sins of your ancestors, Romans, until you repair the ruined temples of the gods, and the images begrimed in smoke'. Augustus was in fact doing precisely this; in 28 BC he wrote: 'I restored 82 temples of the gods in the city [of Rome], neglecting none that required restoration at that time.'[28] His aim was clear: by reinstating traditional values, the madness of the immediate past would be forgotten, and at the same time veneration of the Roman state gods not just in Rome but everywhere – hence the importance of the Capitolium – would bring a further degree of unity to war-torn Italy.

Augustus' religious buildings in Rome were indeed prolific. Although the plans of the temples were hardly innovative, the materials used in the superstructure were breaking fresh ground, for it was now that Carrara marble was used extensively for the first time, lending a symbolic whiteness to the temples. Apollo, with his solar associations, was for obvious reasons singled out, and a great temple, together with a library, was constructed for him on the Palatine, while a fine temple to Mars Ultor was built in his forum. *Ultor* means 'the avenger' and Mars was to avenge the murder of Augustus' adoptive father, Julius Caesar.

It is not altogether surprising that Augustus (whose name means 'reverend') came to be regarded as divine. Like all gods, he was *mundi servator*, saviour of the world, and as his great altar of peace – still to be seen, in reconstructed form, in Rome today – reminds us, he held the key to a secure and prosperous future.[29] Divine rulers had long been known in the east Mediterranean, not least Alexander the Great. Julius Caesar, probably aware that the Roman people needed a single ruler to lead them out of the murderous factions of the late Republic, laid stress on his own divine origins – his descent from Aeneas' son Iulus, and hence from Venus herself. It was no accident that in 46 BC he dedicated a temple in Rome to Venus Genetrix, Venus the Mother.

Augustus was altogether chary at declaring his own divinity: this would have been imprudent. But he did consecrate a temple to Caesar in 29 BC, henceforth calling himself *Divi filius*, Son of God, and *Augustus*, reverend. Suetonius says that Caesar was numbered amongst the state gods 'not only by public decree but also by popular belief', and it is easy to believe this of the average smallholder or craftsman, bound in by superstition and ritual and surrounded by peace and prosperity.[30] Indeed, the Neapolitans built a temple to Augustus and established games sacred to him while he was on the throne, a mark of how quickly the notion of a divine emperor spread in some areas; but, as Dio remarks, this was 'ostensibly because Augustus had restored the town ... but in reality it was because its inhabitants emulated Greek customs'.[31] For most Italians it was the *numen* or spirit of the emperor that became a focus for worship, rather than Augustus himself, and there was no doubt much cynicism about the quasi-divinity of a living person, particularly amongst the educated rich. It is best summed up by Seneca's biting satire about the emperor Claudius, who arrives in heaven to discover that he has been changed into a pumpkin rather than a god.[32] But a huge number of inscriptions to the *Numen Augusti*, the divine will of Augustus, are known, and the imperial cult, largely run by ex-slaves, very rapidly became established during the emperor's lifetime. When Augustus died in AD 14, his successor Tiberius felt obliged to build a temple to him, thereby setting a precedent which was to be followed by many of his successors down into the mid-second century.

Temples, normally coupling Rome with Augustus, soon appeared at many towns in Italy and elsewhere. They were generally placed in a prominent position, as at Ostia, where it was built at the south end of the forum. In combination with great capitolia, like the massive complex constructed in Vespasian's reign overlooking the forum at Brescia, in northern Italy, they symbolised the unity brought about by the new era. However, alongside the maintenance of the state gods and the emergence of divine emperors, there was also a significant advance in cults which had a decidedly more intimate and personal relationship between the deity and the worshipper. Sometimes known as the mystery religions, they derived from various parts of the east Mediterranean, including Egypt, Asia Minor and Persia.

Probably the most influential cult, until the official adoption of Christianity in AD 313, was that of Isis. She was an Egyptian goddess, who achieved huge popularity in the Hellenistic east from the fourth century BC. In Greece, together with other Egyptian deities, like Serapis and Harpocrates, she was soon absorbed into the state religion. Although she appeared in Greek areas of southern Italy from at least as early as the second century BC, most Romans remained suspicious of this oriental cult, associated as it was with the strange dynasty of the Ptolemies and, of course, Cleopatra. Once Augustus had annexed Egypt, however, matters began to change. The regular arrival of the Alexandrian grain fleet at Pozzuoli ensured contact and, once the emperor Caligula had built a temple to Isis and Serapis, dedicated in AD 38, in the Campus Martius in Rome, then the cult was given the stamp of official approval.[33]

The appeal of the worship of Isis is best understood by reading the delightful, if bawdy, story written by the North African Apuleius, entitled *The Golden Ass*. Published around the middle of the second century AD, it tells of the unfortunate Lucius, whose curiosity about the black arts results in his transformation into an ass. After various remarkable adventures, he is restored to human form by the goddess Isis and becomes a devotee, as no doubt was Apuleius. It is a movingly told story, and the followers of her cult must have revelled in the private communion, often through dreams, with their goddess. At Pompeii is one of the best-preserved temples, situated behind the great theatre and surrounded by high walls so that non-initiates were unable to peep in. Restored after the earthquake of AD 62 by one N. Popidius Celsinus (who, as the inscription makes clear, was only a boy of six at the time, an oblique way of saying that his father Numerius was really responsible), here is a temple on a podium, with a small *cella* containing the cult images; a small temple giving access to a reservoir for storing water from the Nile; an altar which, when found, still had the remains of the last sacrifice; and a hall for feasts and cells for the priests. Wall-paintings both from here and from Herculaneum show the white-robed priests performing the ceremonies, which down to this day retain a certain air of mystery and excitement.

The Roman taste for things Egyptian grew, as the obelisks, still to be seen in Rome today, remind us. Otho, briefly emperor in AD 69, was a devotee, as was Domitian, whose life was saved in the same year by, in Suetonius' words, 'the priests of that rather questionable order'.[34] At Ostia the cult did not make much headway until the second century, when the opening of Trajan's harbour exposed the city to many more visitors from the east. From then on, in company with the cult of Serapis, the religion rapidly gained ground, particularly in the Antonine period (AD 138–93). Popular, too, was the Asian Earth Mother, Cybele. First brought to Rome as early as 204 BC, she was a goddess of nature and fertility, associated in myth with a youthful lover, Attis. The cult of Attis had a reputation for orgiastic ceremonies, and at first Roman citizens were not allowed to have anything to do with it. But Claudius recognised Attis as one of the pantheon and it became increasingly popular. Amongst its less attractive features, also attested in the cult of Venus, was the *taurobolium*. Here, according to the Christian writer Prudentius (who was no doubt making capital), the priest had to descend into a pit and cover himself in the blood of a bull that was slain above him.

The appeal of this particular ritual is perhaps not easy to appreciate, but it is not difficult to understand why these personalised cults achieved such popularity. They offered a sense of experience and commitment that was lacking in the formal and often austere 'state religion'. This is not to suppose that the state religions lacked their devoted believers. For many Jupiter, Juno, Minerva and the rest of the pantheon were very real deities, who held promise of as much of an afterlife as did Christianity; countless dedications prove this. But there existed a certain staidness in these cults, which was rather in contrast with those of eastern origin. Bacchus, for example – the Greek god of wine, Dionysus – had a huge following. During the Republic there were attempts to suppress his worship, particularly after a crime-wave that accompanied the Dionysiac *orgia* in 186 BC.[35] But, as the paintings in the Villa of Mysteries at Pompeii and many burial sarcophagi with Dionysiac scenes show, the cult outlived these measures, and achieved respectability in Imperial times. The ceremonies, no doubt accompanied by liberal draughts

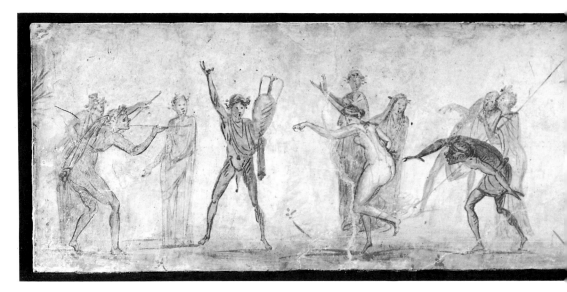

of wine, epitomise a rather materialistic, easy-going world, summed up by Petronius' Trimalchio, whose slave brings in a human skeleton, wrought in silver, to the dinner party:

> Man's life is but a span
> so let us live while we can.
> We'll all be like this when we're dead.[36]

A lively Bacchanalian dance, painted on the wall of a *columbarium* (chamber with burial chests) in the Villa Pamphili, Rome. *(British Museum)*

Despite the advance of the 'personal religions' duing the early Imperial period, the state cults nevertheless maintained their importance. We need not rehearse the long list of temples in Rome and elsewhere which testify to this, nor need we concern ourselves overly with the bents of individual emperors. Hadrian's Pantheon, a temple for all gods, aptly illustrates the spirit of the age. Not until the Severan emperors, a North African dynasty which ruled from AD 193 to 235, was there any decisive thrust in a new direction. The first Severan, Septimius, initiated a substantial building programme in Rome, partly to demonstrate his munificence. But it was his successors, Caracalla, the insane Elagabalus and Alexander, who built temples to eastern deities that included Isis, Serapis, Ba'al of Emesa and Sol Invictus. Elagabalus' excesses were notorious. Mixed bathing, previously banned, he made compulsory, and he attempted to elevate the Sun God, Sol Invictus, to the status of a supreme deity. He was murdered for his troubles, but sun-worship lived on. Aurelian (AD 270–5) built a great temple to the Sun on the edge of the Campus Martius, while Gallienus, emperor from AD 252 to 268, 'gave instructions for a statue to be made, larger than Nero's Colossus [which itself was 120 feet high], of himself in the guise of the Sun ... its construction had actually begun on such a scale that it seemed to be twice as large as the Colossus. Furthermore, he had intended to place it on the summit of the Esquiline [in Rome], with a spear in its hand so that a child

Sculpture from SS Giovanni e Paolo, Rome, showing Mithras slaying the primeval bull. The inscription reads: 'Alcimus, slave bailiff of Tiberius Claudius Livianus, gave this gift to the sun-god Mithras, in fulfilment of a vow.' *c.* AD 100. *(British Museum)*

could climb to the top inside the shaft.'[37] Significantly, when Constantine proclaimed the Christian Edict of Toleration, the sun-motif remained on his coins, and when in AD 321 the seventh day was proclaimed a day of rest, it was because it was Sun-day.

We shall examine the way in which Christianity emerged as the supreme religion in the following chapter; but we must here say something of another mystery cult which achieved prominence, namely Mithraism. Mithras was a Persian god, who, by slaying the primeval bull in his cave, released the blood from which life sprang. Consequently, Mithras was 'Lord of Light', 'Giver of Bliss' and 'Saviour from Death', to name but some of his titles. He came to stand for an upright and moral life, with the prospect of immortality beyond the grave. Devotees had to pass through seven sometimes very demanding stages of initiation, lending an exclusivity to the cult. Open only to men, it appealed particularly to soldiers, who found satisfaction in Mithraism's austere and rigorous code of conduct.

Although attested in Cilicia, in south-west Turkey, as early as the first

century BC, Mithraism would seem to have evolved in the form that we know it in Italy around AD 100. The cult may well have been something of an artificial creation, with eastern roots, but designed and adapted to meet the spirit and needs of the age. In Italy it soon became well established in some of larger and more cosmopolitan centres, like Rome, Ostia and Aquileia. Characteristically, the temples were either underground or in dark, low-lying situations, so as to reproduce the atmosphere of the cave in which Mithras killed the bull – the usual theme of the sculpture or painting behind the altar, a 'tauroctony'. In plan the temples were long and rectangular, with side aisles, normally consisting of raised benches where the worshippers could recline for sacred meals. The altar and tauroctony lay at one end, where Mithras was usually accompanied by his two torch-bearing companions, Cautes, symbol of light, and Cautopates, who represents darkness. The sun-god, Sol Invictus, is frequently associated with Mithras (as are other eastern deities like Serapis), and the god was commonly addressed as *Sol invictus Mithras*.

Many Mithraic temples are now known, including no fewer than fifteen at Ostia. The religion clearly thrived in this harbour town, athrong wth people of many nationalities, although none of the temples dates to before the mid-second century AD and the majority belong to the third, when Mithraism seems to have been at its height. However, in view of the commonly expressed view that Mithraism was a potential contender with Christianity for the title of the supreme religion, it is important to emphasise that the Ostian mithraea were small, the majority having space for no more than twenty to forty people. The cult was above all exclusive and very much the preserve of the well-to-do man.

Some finely preserved mithraea are known elsewhere in Italy. There is a magnificent painted example at S. Maria Capua Vetere in Campania, and ones no less interesting and important beneath the churches of S. Prisca and S. Clemente in Rome. At S. Prisca Mithras and the Sun are shown banqueting, while a procession of initiates of the fourth level, the lions (*Leones*), bring offerings. Such rites, including a form of communion meal, incensed Christians. That Mithras, born on 25 December, should appear to parody their own beliefs gave rise to outraged indignation: no wonder that the Edict of Toleration for Christianity of AD 313 was followed by the savage desecration of many of the mithraic sanctuaries.

Later we shall see how, in the fourth century AD, Christians by no means had it all their own way. In towns like late Roman Ostia, as well as in the countryside, the old gods continued to be venerated, rather as patron saints are in Italy today. The religious make-up of the Roman period comes down to us as a fascinating and complex web, reflecting both the enormous variety of beliefs within a vast empire, and the tolerant and eclectic manner with which the Romans came to regard most of them. Much we cannot hope to comprehend; but at least we can appreciate the complexity.

FURTHER READING

Amongst a copious number of general works are R. M. Ogilvie, *The Romans and their Gods* (1969); J. Ferguson, *The religions of the Roman empire* (1970); R. MacMullen, *Paganism in the Roman empire* (1981); and W. Warde-Fowler, *The Roman festivals of the period of the Republic* (1899), now largely superseded by H. H. Scullard, *Festivals and ceremonies of the Roman Republic* (1981). See also J. A. North, 'Conservatism and change in Roman religion,' *PBSR* 44 (1976), 1−12.

Samnite practices are well discussed by Salmon, Samnium and the Samnites (1967), while early cults in Latium are excellently covered in an exhibition catalogue, *Enea nel Lazio: archeologia e mito* (Rome 1981). Etruscan religion is profusely discussed, and L. Banti, *The Etruscan cities and their culture* (1973) and M. Cristofani, *The Etruscans. A new investigation* (1979) are two of many important works. For pre-Roman and Roman temples both in Rome and elsewhere, see (with references) A. Boëthius, *Etruscan and early Roman architecture* (1978), J. B. Ward-Perkins, *Roman Imperial architecture* (1981). E. Nash, *Topographical dictionary of ancient Rome* (2nd edn, 1968) is also very useful. For theatre-temples see particularly J. A. Hanson, *Roman theater-temples* (1959), and for Capitolia, I. M. Barton in *ANRW* 2, 12, 1, 259f., and M. Todd in Grew and Hobley (eds), *Roman urban topography in Britain and the western empire* (1985), 56f. For the Palestrina sanctuary, see F. Fasolo and G. Gullini, *Il santuario di Fortuna Primigenia a Palestrina* (1953).

There has been much recent discussion of votives: M. Fenelli in *Archeologia Classica* 27 (1975), 206−52; A-M. Comella, *Mélanges Ecole Française de Rome* 93 (1981), 717−803; T. W. Potter, *JBAA* 138 (1985), 23−47; J. Turfa in J. Swaddling (ed.), *Italian Iron Age artefacts in the British Museum* (1986).

For the imperial cult see S. Weinstock, *Divus Julius* (1971) and K. Hopkins, *Conquerors and slaves* (1978). There are very many books and articles on the eastern cults: see, *inter alia*, M. J. Vermaresen, *Mithras, the secret god* (1963), *idem, Cybele and Attis. The myth and the cult* (1977), R. E. Witt, *Isis in the Graeco-Roman world* (1971), M. J. Vermaresen and C. C. van Essen, *The excavations in the mithraeum of the church of Santa Prisca in Rome* (1965), M. J. Vermaresen, *The mithraeum at Santa Maria Capua Vetere* (1971).

Meiggs, *Roman Ostia* (1973) provides a splendid picture of the religious life of the town. Burial is not really covered here, but reference should be made to J. M. C. Toynbee, *Death and burial in the Roman world* (1971), and J. A. North's review article, 'These he cannot take', *JRS* 73 (1983), 169−74.

—9—

LATER ROMAN ITALY AND THE RISE OF CHRISTIANITY

T he fall and ruin of the world will soon take place, but it seems that nothing of the kind is to be feared as long as the city of Rome stands intact.

The sentiment is that of Lactantius, a Christian from North Africa, writing in the early years of the fourth century AD.[1] Born about AD 240, he had been privy to much of the turmoil and chaos of the third century. Between AD 235, when the last Severan, Alexander, was murdered, and the accession of Diocletian in AD 284, there were some twenty legitimate emperors, not to mention a host of co-regents and usurpers. Moreover, nearly every emperor – and usurper – met his end violently. Diocletian, who created a tetrarchy of four rulers, two in the eastern part of the Empire and two in the west, to some extent stopped the rot. He himself abdicated in AD 305 after a reign burdened by heavy fighting and drastic administrative reforms, and retired to his great palace at Split in Yugoslavia. He died there in 316, disillusioned by the civil wars that raged on after his abdication and that were only brought finally to an end by Constantine in 324. No wonder, therefore, that Lactantius should write in such pessimistic tones.

Yet there was always a pervasive view, echoed by Lactantius and many others, that Rome itself would always be sacrosanct; as the historian Ammianus Marcellinus, writing soon after AD 378, observed: 'as long as there are men, Rome will be victorious and will increase with lofty growth'.[2] When the city did eventually fall, sacked by Alaric's army of German Visigoths in AD 410, it seemed like the end of the world, a horror too awful to believe. Even though the city was no longer the centre of empire – after AD 300 Milan had become Italy's chief seat of administration, and the imperial court was frequently there during the fourth century – Rome still remained a symbolic capital of the world.

10 The magnificently situated early medieval town at Calcata in southern Etruria. From the late sixth century AD onwards many Roman settlements were abandoned in favour of places with strong natural defences.

192

11 S. Apollinare Nuovo at Ravenna, c. AD 490. Built by Theoderic, the mosaic shows his palace at the town of Ravenna, as well as a procession of saints.

12 The amphitheatre with its underground chambers at S. Maria Capua Vetere. Extensively restored in the second century AD, it rivalled the Colosseum in Rome in size and splendour.

Nevertheless, the reduction of Rome's political pre-eminence – and of that of Italy as a whole – had started long before. It is not really possible to pinpoint just when this began, for it was a long gradual process, but there can be little doubt that the reign of the first African emperor, Septimius Severus (AD 193–212), had decisive consequences for Italy. While Italians outnumbered all others in the Senate, Africans, and to a lesser extent people from the east and from Spain, came to occupy many of the more influential posts. Not the least of these were the procurators. These were powerful men who administered the emperor's holdings, the Privy Purse (*res privata*), particularly land. Successive emperors had built up their possessions and estates by means of purchase, inheritance and confiscation, so much so that Severus' predecessor, Pertinax, had to offer fiscal inducements to prevent some of the land going out of cultivation. Severus himself seized a great amount of property, particularly from rich landowners who were unwise enough to back the governor of Britain, Clodius Albinus, when he made his bid for imperial power. Severus thrashed Albinus' army near Lyon in AD 197 and there followed a notorious purge of the Senate, twenty-nine members of which were summarily executed.

The considerable revenue which accrued in this way was administered from a series of regional offices in various parts of Italy. These were run by the procurators, of whom no fewer than sixty per cent originated in Africa or the east, implying that here Severus was in part manipulating affairs in favour of people from his country of birth. In fact, some interpret the events of the period as a deliberate destruction of the old social order, although this is a view that is hardly without controversy.[3] Nevertheless, what is clear is that Severus took steps to secure his hold on Italy by drastically increasing the size of the standing army there. In Rome the famous Praetorian Guard, created by Augustus, was dismissed and replaced by a force twice the size, recruited from the loyal Illyrian legions; the *vigiles*, the firemen and policemen, were doubled; and the urban cohorts were tripled.[4] A new legion of 6,000 soldiers, the II Parthica, was also stationed in the hills outside Rome, at Albano, close by Domitian's palace at Castel Gandolfo (where the Pope now has his summer residence). In all probability the Ager Albanus was imperially owned, making this a very suitable site. There is still a good deal to be seen on the ground today, including the main gate of the fortress (the Porta Praetoria), long stretches of the defences, a reservoir and the amphitheatre, which could accommodate 15,000 spectators.

Altogether, the main military force in Italy was raised from about 11,500 to over 30,000 men. This gave Severus a field army that was immediately to hand, and must have had a profoundly deterrent effect upon any potential opposition. Moreover, he attempted to ensure the soldiers' loyalty by improving pay and conditions; promotion for ex-rankers was now easier and serving men were, for the first time, permitted to marry. When in AD 212 Severus' son, the emperor Caracalla, extended Roman citizenship to all free-born inhabitants of the Empire, it at a stroke removed one of the most divisive features of the Roman world and further reduced Italy's pre-eminence: even though tax exemptions remained, the country had in many ways become just another province.

Even so, the Severan era was not an unprosperous one for Italy. The historian Cassius Dio, who knew Severus well, wrote an obituary of him. He castigates his former emperor for a building programme which he regards as wasteful – and for his habit of putting his own name on buildings that he had only restored, 'as if he had erected them himself from his private funds'.[5] The list of buildings, renovated and new, is a long one, especially for Rome, where the emperor felt obliged to display his munificence. There was the famous arch in the Roman Forum, set up by the Senate and the People of Rome to Severus and his two sons 'on account of the restoration of the Republic and the extension of the Empire of the Roman people by their outstanding virtues at home and abroad'. Another arch was built to make an entrance to the Forum Boarium; there were new baths, and the palace, the Temple of Peace and the Pantheon were restored. Probably the most impressive building work, however, was the Septizodium, a three-tiered façade, one hundred metres or so long, at a corner of the Palatine Hill. Its name suggests that it held statues of the seven planetary deities, with at the centre the Sun, looking southwards – symbolically – towards Africa. The last remnants were demolished in 1588.

Severus also instigated the carving of a great map of Rome on 151 sheets of marble, placed on the wall of a hall by the Library of Peace. Many fragments still survive of this remarkable record of the layout of the ancient city which, whatever Severus' feelings were about Italy, symbolises the importance of Rome itself. Elsewhere in the peninsula the evidence for building activity is less conspicuous, although it should be said that proper archaeological investigation of later Roman levels in towns has tended to be neglected. Nevertheless, the inscriptions indicate that by this time private donations were beginning to decline,[6] and it is not easy to find many instances of either new or renovated buildings. One exception is Ostia, where there are many dedications to the emperor, as well as much new building. The grain warehouses were enlarged, reflecting Severus' interest in the corn supply,[7] the theatre was also increased in size and new baths were constructed. Elsewhere in Italy there is less evidence for building: baths at Lanuvium, near Velletri, and at Verona; the restoration of a theatre at Ferento; but on present indications – which may be misleading – not a great deal more.[8]

In Rome Severus' immediate successors to a considerable extent continued his building programme. Most notable are the vast baths of Severus' son Caracalla, constructed between AD 212 and 216. They cover an area of over twenty hectares, and remain one of the most impressive building achievements of the Roman world. Severus Alexander is also said to have constructed many smaller baths, as well as renovating those of Nero, and, as we saw in the previous chapter, the Severan dynasty was particularly

The theatre at Ostia (heavily restored). Originally built in the Augustan period, it was enlarged in the late second century, under Severus, and could hold 4000 people.

active in constructing monuments to the eastern gods like Isis, Serapis and Sol.

Whatever the political and social consequences of their reigns, the Severan emperors did at least confer added splendour upon the city of Rome and some other cities of Italy as well. But what of the countryside? Quite apart from the imperial holdings, which were considerably extended, we must envisage many of the great slave-run estates of the western-central part of Italy as largely extinct. On the other hand, the land became by no means depopulated. In the Ager Faliscus, for example, a thoroughly studied region some twenty-five kilometres to the north of Rome, there were about 163 sites in occupation during the second century, and 115 sites in the third century – a fall, but by no means an extreme one. Similarly, in the Ager Cosanus, while many of the villas near to the coast were abandoned by the Severan era, if not before, many of the inland farms of the Albenga Valley remained in occupation. Some smallholders certainly became more prosperous at this time, like the owner of a small estate at Crocicchie, on the Via Clodia, who added a bath-house with a pleasant mosaic, decorated with dolphins, in the early third century.[9]

Despite the evidence, therefore, both for the abandonment of many large villas and, as we saw earlier, for the importing on an enormous scale of goods and commodities – particularly from Africa – we must be careful not to paint too stark a picture of decline. Herodian, for instance, tells us that the Aquileia region, although badly hit by a plague in the late second century, was by AD 238 a major wine-growing area and teeming with farming communities.[10] Nor must we forget the hypothesis that many Italian vineyards had switched production to cheaper and poorer-quality wines for home consumption, transported in containers that in many cases may no longer survive.[11] Italy may have become more provincial under the Severans, but by no means poor. Indeed, by AD 211 the granaries in Rome were so full that there was a surplus equivalent to seven years' supply for the *annona* (the free hand-out to the urban poor and to the innumerable state-servants), as well as an olive-oil lake amounting to five years' supply.[12]

In AD 235 there began, however, the period of military and political turmoil and anarchy which so colours one's impression of the third century. We need not dwell either upon the movements of armies or upon vexed questions like the period's rampant inflation. The immediate issue is the effect that this state of affairs had upon Italy. Despite an exasperating lack of detailed evidence, one thing is immediately obvious: that expenditure on building, especially in the public realm, was drastically curtailed. Money was short and the situation hardly conducive to such expenditure. Not surprisingly, the construction and repair of town walls was an exception. Most striking are Aurelian's defences of Rome itself, begun in the early 270s. They took ten years to build, and extended for nineteen kilometres. Every 100 Roman feet (about 30 metres) there was a square tower, and there were eighteen main gates. That they survive so completely today is a comment upon their massive strength, serving as they did to turn the city into a defended stronghold.[13] Other work on town defences took place mainly in the north of Italy, where the Alpine passes were now corridors for campaigning armies. Gallienus (AD 253–68) fortified Verona as part of a defensive system that extended from Concordia, near modern Portogruaro in the Veneto, to Milan: the walls of Aosta and Como were strengthened; and at about the same time Aquileia and other cities in the north-east were walled.[14] Town walls, once built for reasons of civic pride and administrative ease, were now required to protect.

Too few excavations have taken place either in the towns or upon rural sites to enable us to picture how life may have changed in this period. This situation is being transformed, particularly in the north of Italy, where large trenches in towns like Milan, Verona and Genoa are beginning to pour forth a fund of precious new information.[15] Assimilating all this fresh data is a task for the years ahead, but there is already an impression that we should not exaggerate the effects of this 'age of crisis'. Some towns undoubtedly did go downhill. Ordona, for instance, the Apulian settlement that we last visited with Horace on his famous journey of 37 BC, was by the third century a poorish place. The civic buildings had been either abandoned or transformed, although whether through a lack of finance or the decay of once traditional responsibilities is open to question.[16] Increasingly, no-one wanted to serve as a town-councillor, or decurion, since the obligations were becoming ever more punitive. On the other hand, towns like Reggio di Calabria, Terracina, Pozzuoli, Capua, Gravisca, Luni, Imola, Verona and Oderzo – to name but a random selection for which there is evidence – do seem to have prospered during the third century. There was no real point in adding yet more public buildings and, to judge from items like the mosaics in the houses, much of the money was being poured into private ventures, a spirit that is readily understandable, given the uncertainties of the age; thus we should guard against characterising the period as one of total gloom and disaster. Even the countryside, where the population was certainly more vulnerable to the ravages of visiting armies, may well turn out – if current field-surveys are any guide – to have been more resilient to the disruptions than we might at first expect.[17]

Diocletian's accession in AD 284 brought some of these uncertainties to an end.[18] Like many of the third-century rulers, he was a social nobody; he was born near Split in Yugoslavia, ancient Illyria, and was elevated to power by a career in the army. Unlike most of his predecessors, however, he was a strong-willed, far-sighted and thoughtful man, with a pronounced puritan streak. Moreover, he had a gift for imaginative and carefully worked-out solutions for the infinity of problems that faced him; he has with justice been compared with Augustus himself.[19]

The campaigns that he, and his adoptive co-ruler, Maximian (who also came from Illyrian peasant stock), carried out on the Empire's frontiers need not detain us. There were skilful opponents to defeat, like the usurper Carausius, who seized Britain, or the martial ruler of the Persians, Narses; but in the end the job was done. What matters is that the Empire entered a period of relative calm, a climate in which cities and farms could once more begin to flourish. The measures that Diocletian enacted to bring this about are remarkable, both for their originality and, for the most part, their success. For instance, by AD 293 he had come to the conclusion that the most effective form of rule was a tetrarchy, with a senior and a junior emperor, known respectively as Augustus and Caesar, in both the east and the west of the Empire. Thus he was Augustus in the east, building himself a new capital at

Nicomedia in northern Turkey, while there was Maximian, aided by Constantius, in the west. Even though in the longer term this formula did not guarantee the legal succession that Diocletian devotedly wanted, it nevertheless worked well enough, at any rate for a time.

Astonishingly, Diocletian did not visit Rome until AD 303, nearly twenty years after his accession. Even then he cut short the celebrations that were due to him, detesting what he saw as a debauched and frivolous way of life, and removed the court to Ravenna, a difficult winter's journey. This, in a few words, sums up his attitude towards Rome and Italy: the country's once privileged position was to be swept aside, and the power of the senate reduced almost to naught. This task he set about with vigour and, one suspects, a degree of relish. Italy had always been exempt from taxes but, with the exception of those who lived in Rome and its immediate environs, the country's citizens had now to pay up. Not surprisingly, this caused considerable rancour; but it was only a beginning.

There were also major administrative changes both in Italy and throughout the Empire. As a famous manuscript, now preserved at Verona, records, Italy was split into some sixteen provinces, forming one huge diocese; these included Sicily, Sardinia, Corsica and Raetia (the Alpine area in the north-east, which today encompasses parts of Switzerland and Austria). As a sop to the old order, each of these was governed by senators, bearing the archaic Roman title of *corrector*;[20] but over them was a vicar (*vicarius*), who was recruited not from senatorial families (who held that privilege by right of birth), but by members of the equestrian order, whose qualification was solely one of property. Given that many other senior officials were also not of senatorial descent, this meant that a quite new social order began to emerge, breaking with the traditions of the past. Increasingly there developed a civil service of salaried career officials which in time became huge, top heavy – and a terrible burden.

No less sweeping were changes to the army. Command was now in the hands of dukes (*duces*), who were totally independent of civil government, and might well wield military power spanning several provinces. They were based in massively defended fortresses, with enormously thick walls and high towers on which to mount artillery. More like medieval castles, they represent a radical departure from the lightly defended bases of early Imperial times. Moreover, the size of the army was drastically increased. At least fourteen new legions were raised, often by means of conscription, and the thirty-nine old legions restored to strength. Across the Empire more than half a million men were under arms.

With four rulers, each with his own court, many more than one imperial centre was required. Moreover, these needed to be within striking distance of the frontiers, where most of the fighting took place. To a certain extent, therefore, the courts became peripatetic, shifting when the need arose. For Italy this had the profoundest consequences. Rome, for nearly a thousand years the seat of government, now gave way to Milan as the country's pre-eminent city. Geographically this was a good choice. Milan (as its huge importance today shows) was strategically sited at the hub of both east–west and north–south communications. It is also favoured with good farmland – its Roman name, Mediolanum, is a Celtic expression for a place 'in the middle of a plain' – and it had grown steadily during the Roman period. Under Diocletian and the Tetrarchy, however, it rapidly expanded as it came more and more to assume the role of a capital city. It was provided with a new circuit of walls, as well as other essential amenities such as a palace, large baths and a circus – all of which underlines the significance of the rescue excavations which are increasingly part of the everyday scene in contemporary Milan.[21]

Despite the imperial favour that was bestowed upon Milan, Rome was not wholly neglected. In a symbolic sense, it was still the centre of the Empire, and Diocletian took trouble to pay it due homage. The Curia, or Senate House, rebuilt after a fire in AD 283, still stands in the Forum today, just as his vast baths, the counterpart of those of Caracalla, have also largely survived the passing of the centuries. Constructed between AD 298 and 306, their central block is now the church of S. Maria degli Angeli, on one side of the Piazza della Repubblica – 'like the Pantheon a building to be experienced not described';[22] the rest now forms the core of the National Museum of Antiquities.

Huge sums of money were needed to finance all these ventures, and to Diocletian's credit was a novel system for measuring and taxing the Empire's wealth. As a result, money flowed in to the treasuries, aided of course by the fact that most Italians were now liable for taxation. However, the problem of inflation remained, leading eventually to Diocletian's famous – if unsuccessful – price freeze. The Edict, promulgated in AD 301, was an attack upon 'profiteers who . . . extort prices for merchandise not fourfold, not eightfold, but so great that human speech cannot describe it'.[23] Published throughout the Empire, it attempted to fix prices both for goods and for labour. Thus we read how the best Italian wines should cost not more than 30 *denarii* per pint, ordinary wine 8 *denarii*, British beer 4 *denarii*, and Egyptian beer a mere 2 *denarii*. By way of comparison, wages for an ordinary farmhand, including his maintenance, should be no more than 25 *denarii* a day.

For many reasons, the Price Edict did not really work. Despite monetary reform,[24] put in hand after the Tetrarchy had been established, no real stability in the currency was achieved – a situation that was not significantly to change until Constantine started to issue the gold *solidus* from about AD 308. Moreover, it is clear from our ancient sources that society was becoming ever more divided between the *honestiores*, members of the senatorial and equestrian classes, municipal officers and soldiers of all ranks, and the *humiliores*, the working people.

The distinction had begun to emerge after the extension of Roman citizenship to all free-born inhabitants of the Empire in AD 212, but became increasingly pronounced as time went on. Although trades were very largely hereditary, a man who married a miller's daughter was himself obliged to work in that industry, underlining how an element of compulsion entered into the structure of society. Similarly town-councillors, decurions, were now bound to their duties by law, an unpaid task that became ever more exacting, what with the maintenance of streets, roads and public buildings, the provision of festivals and the supply of food and water. Peasant farmers, too, became steadily more circumscribed in what they could and could not do. Legislation tied them to the land and, when bad harvests or other misfortune threw them into debt, they were more and more forced to work for the great landowners as *coloni*, or tenants. As the fourth century wore on, so the distinction between these serf-like tenants and slaves became ever more blurred.

This bleak picture is not one that can be easily corroborated by the much more anonymous evidence of archaeology; but it does provide a context for the enormous rise in popularity of the supreme religion of individual salvation, Christianity. We need not dwell upon the features that encouraged the spread of Christianity during earlier centuries; its very universality, a personal cult open to all, master and slave, men and women, straightway marked it out as something special. By the time of Diocletian it is estimated that about one fifth of the Empire's inhabitants were Christians, living mainly in the east and in North Africa.[25]

What so infuriated those who upheld the old deities was 'the Christians' arrogant insistence that *no* gods had ever walked the earth until an obscure Jewish teacher who was executed in the reign of Tiberius'.[26] Moreover, they were more than prepared to die for their beliefs. The Christians were well familiar with persecution; but the greatest and most notorious pogrom was launched against them on 23 February AD 303. The details are horrific, and many were brutally put to death; but within a couple of years the momentum had gone, and by AD 306 it was on the wane. Meanwhile, Diocletian had abdicated in total disillusion, taking himself off to his great fortress-palace at Split in Yugoslavia. The stage was thus free for another remarkable figure of late antiquity, Flavius Valerius Constantinus – Constantine the Great. The son of the Caesar Constantius Chlorus, he was proclaimed Augustus by the troops upon the death of his father at York in England on 25 June 306. The inevitable struggle for power ensued, culminating in Constantine's invasion of Italy in AD 312 and the great battle of the Mulvian Bridge, on the northern side of Rome. His opponent was Maxentius, son of Maximian, who had been elevated to Caesar of Italy by the Senate at Rome in 306. Constantine won a great victory, and Maxentius was thrown over the bridge into the Tiber and drowned. The event is commemorated by a four-way, brick-faced arch, now a farmhouse, at Malborghetto on the Via Flaminia, six kilometres from Rome,[27] as well as by a frieze on the Arch of Constantine in Rome.

Constantine was to go on to bring the whole Empire once again under a single ruler, a task that took a further twelve years. It was a remarkable, if not a lasting, achievement. However, he is remembered particularly for two other actions of immense and permanent significance. One was his decision to create a 'New Rome' of Constantinople (modern Istanbul, ancient Byzantium). While it was declared marginally lower in rank, this further underlined the declining pre-eminence of the former capital. Indeed, many of Rome's characteristics were duplicated in Constantinople. There was a senate, seven hills and even a free handout of corn to the poor – diverting most of the Alexandrian grain supply away from Italy. The other was his startling declaration of AD 313, the Edict of Milan (also known as the Edict of Toleration). This was an astonishing *volte-face* on the policies of a decade earlier which, by extending toleration to all Christians, ushered in the new world of late antiquity.[28]

The reasons behind Constantine's religious transformation, whether it was purely inspirational or more pragmatic, have been much debated;[29] but more important for our purposes is to measure the practical consequences for Italy. What is immediately striking is the enormous amount of ecclesiastical building, both in Rome and in other major centres like Aquileia. Aquileia's mosaics are justly well known and we know that a cathedral with two main halls, measuring some 20 × 37 metres, was completed by AD 319. It replaced a house church – the commonest Christian centre of worship before the Edict – emphasising how the Church had built up a well-organised regional structure long before AD 313.

Huge sums of money were of course required, but with imperial approval and patronage, funds poured in. Moreover, to be a Christian opened the way to high-ranking political jobs and great social status – and considerable financial benefit. Consequently many of society's upper crust found it well worth their while to be 'converted'; as the affluent aristocrat Agorius Praetextatus is later said to have remarked: 'Make me Bishop of Rome and I'll be a Christian tomorrow'.[30] Indeed, despite the 'New Rome' of Constantinople, Constantine took great care to see that Rome itself was well endowed with monuments, both ecclesiastical and secular. There was his famous arch, built close by the Colosseum to commemorate his victory over Maxentius; his baths, now covered by the Palazzo Rospigliosi on the Quirinal Hill; and two mausolea, one of which is today the beautiful church of S. Costanza, where his daughter Constantia was buried about AD 350. Here he was following in the footsteps of Maxentius, who, in the course of his six years of rule in Rome, had begun a huge basilica, constructed an imperial residence, a mausoleum and a circus by the Via Appia, and restored the Temple of Venus and Rome. Maxentius was the last pagan emperor of Rome and Constantine the first Christian ruler; thus it is fitting that Constantine should have initiated the building of churches which began the great ecclesiastical legacy that is one of Rome's major glories today.

Two features are immediately apparent. One is the complete breakaway from traditional temple architecture by the adoption of the basilican hall as a standard plan for churches. For it was the great judgement halls, *basilicae*, of the imperial palaces (and, to a lesser extent, the civilian basilicas) that were

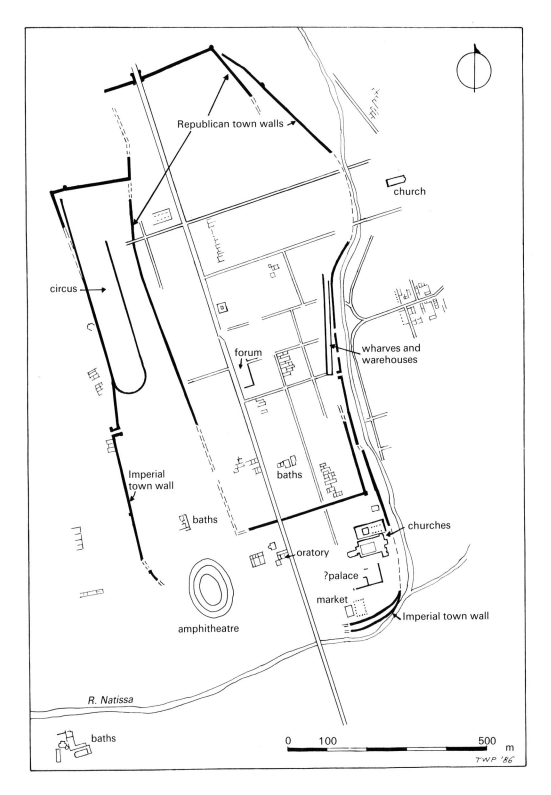

Republican town walls

church

circus

forum

wharves and
warehouses

Imperial
town wall

baths

baths

oratory

churches

?palace

market

Imperial town wall

amphitheatre

R. Natissa

baths

0   100   500
                                m

TWP '86

Above The arch dedicated in AD 23 to the dead Drusus and Germanicus, at Spoleto. Beside it is visible one column of a temple later converted into a Christian church (S. Ansano), demonstrating an unusual continuity from paganism to Christianity.

Left Plan of the Roman town at Aquileia. This became a major Christian ecclesiastical centre.

chosen as an architectural model for the churches, a conscious rejection of temples, with their specific association with the pagan gods of old. The other was in the siting of the new cathedrals. It seemed neither politic nor appropriate to place them within the monumental centre and in most cases much more peripheral locations were chosen. Rome's cathedral was established at St John Lateran on the east side of the city, in an area where there was an imperial palace. Begun in AD 313, its nave measured no less than 100 × 53 metres and it was capable of holding a congregation of about three thousand. Similarly vast was St Peter's, constructed between AD 319 and 322 on the site of what is thought to have been a martyrium for the Saint. Shrines to the martyrs had, of course, to be placed outside the city walls, in accordance with the ancient laws that prohibited burial within the urban

confines. This is why later on cemetery churches like S. Paolo fuori le Mura –
St Paul outside the walls – were built far from the main inhabited areas, a
matter that was additionally aided by the fact that much of the 'green belt'
around Rome was owned by the emperor by this time.

Constantine's investments on behalf of the Church are thought to have
brought in the considerable annual income of some 400 pounds of gold, a
sum that was used to pay for building, for charity and for the clergy
themselves.[31] He is also known to have constructed churches in Ostia,
Albano, Capua and Naples, and it is not difficult to imagine the hive of
activity in many towns in the wake of the Edict of Toleration as new and
overt centres of worship became established. Even so, it would be quite
wrong to suppose that Christianity swept the board overnight – far from it.
Pagan traditions were deeply entrenched in Italy, and remained so in many
areas. Ostia, for example, has yielded comparatively little evidence for
Christian worship, despite the huge area that has been excavated; and
Ammianus Marcellinus tells us of sacrifices in the temple of Castor and
Pollux when storms prevented the grain ships from entering port in AD
359.[32]

Slowly, however, the pagan temples fell into decline, lacking the rich
private benefactors to keep them in repair: The civic centres must
increasingly have become a sorry sight as pagan buildings were gradually –
or sometimes violently – spoliated for their gold and their materials.
Nevertheless, the building of new churches proceeded only slowly, another
hint of the strength of the pagan tradition. In Rome, for example, the original
S. Maria in Trastevere was constructed in the period AD 337 to 352 (possibly
over a still older third-century house church); but the main burst of
ecclesiastical foundations did not take place until after the mid-360s AD.[33]
The list of churches of the late fourth and first part of the fifth century AD is in
fact a long and impressive one, coupled moreover with a grandeur of design
and decoration that harks back to the splendours of the Imperial age. S. Paolo
fuori le Mura, for instance, had great columns, mosaics and a gilded ceiling,
together with a triumphal arch and an apse built into the eastern end; it was
started about AD 380 and completed by the turn of the century. Still later, but
just as splendid, is S. Maria Maggiore. Built between about AD 432 and 440,
it too had a triumphal arch and an apse which, together with its fine figured
mosaics, can be admired to this day.

There are many other beautiful and fascinating churches of this period in
Rome, emphasising how during the fifth century AD the seat of spiritual and
administrative authority came gradually to be vested there.[34] But during the
fourth century other cities in Italy also emerged as ecclesiastical centres.
Foremost amongst them was Milan, already the Imperial capital. Its huge
cathedral, later to be called S. Tecla, lay to the west of the present-day Gothic
duomo. It was probably built about AD 350 and excavation has shown that its
great basilican nave, flanked by pairs of aisles, was capable of holding a
congregation of about three thousand. But it was Ambrose, who became

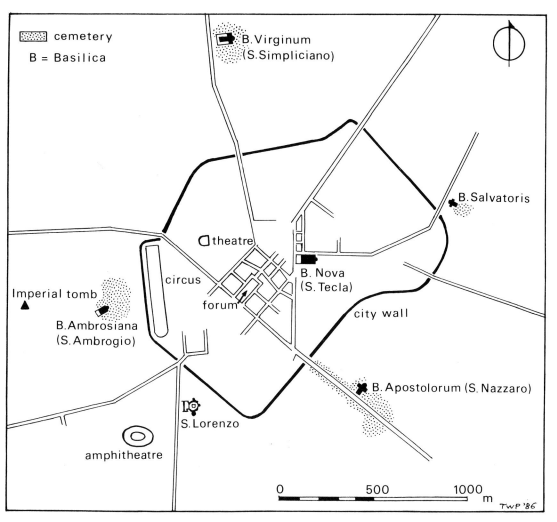

cemetery

B = Basilica

B. Virginum
(S. Simpliciano)

B. Salvatoris

theatre

circus

Imperial tomb

B. Nova
(S. Tecla)

forum

city wall

B. Ambrosiana
(S. Ambrogio)

B. Apostolorum (S. Nazzaro)

S. Lorenzo

amphitheatre

0   500   1000
m

TWP '86

Plan of Milan (Roman Mediolanum), *c.* AD 400, with its ring of extra-mural churches, many built by St Ambrose (Italian S. Ambrogio).

bishop there in AD 373, who was responsible for the Christian endowment of the city. Milan was ringed with churches which are magnificent both for their dimensions and for their inventive architecture. Some, like S. Lorenzo, still remain as centres of worship today. For Ausonius, describing twenty notable cities of the Roman world in the later fourth century, Milan was 'a fine town enlarged by its twin walls, with a circus for the enjoyment of the people, a theatre with its blocks of seats, temples, palaces, a rich mint, and a region famous for its bath of Hercules. It also has colonnades adorned with marbled statues.'[35]

The churches built by Ambrose were all outside the old walls and, like the extramural examples at Rome (and elsewhere), covered the graves of martyrs. Before long they became the focus of Christian cemeteries, in sharp contrast with the cathedrals within the town walls, where regulations prohibited burial. Many other towns, up and down the peninsula, followed suit. The list of known examples, already a fairly long one, will doubtless be extended as excavation proceeds; but it is clear that many elements of the plan of a basilican church were becoming standardised. There was usually a long nave, flanked by aisles and orientated with a semicircular apse to the east; quite often a deep porch; and frequently the embellishment of mosaic or fresco. Already by the late fourth century, church architects were looking towards the glories of the buildings of fifth-century Ravenna.[36]

Meanwhile, distant storm-clouds were gathering. Despite the efforts of Diocletian, Constantine and their successors, the situation on the Empire's frontiers remained uneasy. During the 370s nomads in southern Russia began to move, driving before them Germanic Visigoths and Ostrogoths. We need not dwell on the details of the chaotic events of the late fourth and early fifth centuries: it is sufficient for our purposes to recall, first, Alaric's siege of Milan in AD 401, then Radagaesus' invasion of Italy in 405 and finally Alaric's sack of Rome in 410. It was horrific news. As St Jerome, who was in Bethlehem, observed: 'when the brightest light on the whole earth was extinguished, when the Roman empire was deprived of its head, when . . . the whole world perished in one city, then I was dumb with silence'.[37]

The sack provoked much heart-searching. For St Augustine it was a testing of Christians by God, a theme developed at length in his *City of God*; for pagans the fault lay in the neglect of the old gods. However, the city soon recovered. Alaric had died in southern Italy on his way to sample the rich pickings of North Africa, and in Rome restoration and new building were soon put in hand. The nobility even paid for games in the Colosseum and, from about AD 430, there was something of a literary and cultural boom.

What then had been happening in the countryside during this period of traumatic change? The archaeological evidence will eventually here be of decisive importance; but already there are some important clues. To go back to the Diocletianic period at the turn of the third and fourth centuries, it is clear that the onset of more stable conditions encouraged settlement in the countryside. Villas like the fabulous Piazza Armerina in Sicily, with its magnificent mosaics, or Desenzano, a splendid rural retreat beside Lake Garda, show how the very rich found it well worth their while to invest in these costly mansions.[38] As their urban counterparts are correspondingly fine houses of fourth-century date in towns like Luni, near La Spezia, and Ostia. Elsewhere, long-abandoned villas like Posto in Campania were reoccupied, while field-survey suggests that many of the remoter farms of old foundation carried on much as before.

Some families were indeed staggeringly wealthy. Senators had an average income of about 120,000 gold *solidi* a year, about 1,600 pounds of gold; some earned as much as 4,000 pounds of gold. By way of comparison, a court official was paid about 1,000 gold *solidi*, a peasant just 5. And a single *solidus* was sufficient for a year's subsistence.[39] A hugely rich lady called Melania had estates all over Italy, and in Africa, Spain and even Britain. On one of her 'estates' (*massae*) near Rome there were sixty-two hamlets, each with about four hundred slaves – or so we are told. The statesman Symmachus, although a strong opponent of Christianity, nevertheless owned twelve villas in Italy alone, including sites in Apulia, Samnium and Sicily.[40]

Some private patronage is also recorded, particularly in areas where the rich estates lay, like Campania and Samnium. Thus, during the fourth century we hear of baths being restored at towns like Saepinum and Otricoli, repairs to the amphitheatre at Velletri and the meat-market at Isernia, while at Benevento an earthquake in AD 375 prompted calls for private contributions. Our informant, the affluent Symmachus, seems not to have paid up, however.[41] Governors seem also to have been active in the upkeep of streets, baths and other public monuments, so that for some regions at least life in towns was not wholly a picture of decay and decline.

Roads had a particular importance, since the economy was increasingly reverting to payment in kind. To take just one instance, stretches of the Via Appia were repaired under Diocletian, Maxentius, Constantine, Valentinian and Valens, and still provoked the admiration of Procopius in the sixth century AD. Road transport, as we know from Diocletian's Price Edict, was slow and expensive; but at all costs the communications network had to be kept open.

This picture of fourth-century Italy is, therefore, a rather rosier one than we might at first expect and, indeed, there is another side to the story. Whilst there were country estates that prospered, there were nevertheless many areas where cultivation did lapse. References to *agri deserti*, farmland no longer being worked, abound. Study of the Theodosian Code, a collection of laws published in AD 438, shows that in AD 395 more than half a million *iugera* of land lay abandoned in Italy's once highly prosperous region of Campania – about one tenth of the total area of farmland in that part of the peninsula. Indeed, Symmachus talks of food shortages in Rome in the late fourth century, so much so that pigs and cows had to be brought up from the south to feed the populace.

This is particularly interesting since the programme of field-survey to the north of Rome shows a substantial decline in the number of occupied sites in the course of the later third and fourth centuries. Archaeological evidence can rarely be invested with too much statistical precision, but it is broadly true to say that the estates being worked had fallen to about one third of the total of those existing in about AD 100. Some, of course, may well have grown at the expense of others; but the overall impression is of a much less populous landscape. From the early fourth century, however, there was one major new landowner, namely the Church. In the *Lives of the Popes*, compiled in the early sixth century AD and recording the biographies of bishops of Rome from AD 314, we read of the holdings of sixteen churches in the city. These include well over one hundred estates in Italy as well as a number abroad. No fewer than eighty-four are said to have been donated by Constantine, while others were given by wealthy individuals. Similarly, the

See of Ravenna owned property in the territories of Bologna, Urbino, Lucca, Imola and Gubbio, as well as in Sicily. However far-flung these estates, there is little doubt that the Church will have ensured their cultivation and thus their receipt of revenue.[42]

Ravenna was from AD 404 to become of prime importance. This low-lying city, then surrounded by marshes and tributaries of the River Po, had since Augustus' day been the naval base of one of Italy's two imperial fleets. Although nothing like as important as Aquileia, that huge city at the head of the Adriatic, Ravenna was nevertheless a sizeable and affluent place. When Alaric and his Visigoths laid siege to Milan, demonstrating its vulnerability, it seemed logical to move the imperial court to this far better protected spot, with its convenient communications both by land and by sea. Thus it was that, for more than three centuries, Ravenna was the capital city of Italy, whether for the western Roman emperors or, from AD 476, the Ostrogothic German kings, or, from AD 540, the Byzantine governor. Only in AD 751 did it finally fall to the Lombards and slip into obscurity.

Ravenna divides into two separate parts: the old town and the port of Classis, which lies some four kilometres to the south. Both are now situated in drab, flat farmland, distant from the sea; but in antiquity it was a fen-like environment bordering the Adriatic, where 'walls fall flat and waters stand, towers float and ships are seated': nature's laws turned topsy turvy.[43] To this day Ravenna is endowed with a breathtakingly fine range of ecclesiastical and secular monuments, spanning the fifth and sixth centuries. There are more than a dozen churches of this period and what is so fascinating is to trace the way in which they become ever more eastern in their design. San Vitale, completed in AD 546–8, with its mosaics of the Byzantine emperor

The church of S. Apollinare in Classe (ancient Classis, Ravenna's port), built in AD 535–49. The campanile (tower) dates to the late tenth century.

and empress, Justinian and Theodora, and its octagonal plan, would in many respects be equally at home in Constantinople as it is in north-east Italy — 'the one truly great building of the West in the sixth century'.[44] Similarly unmistakable is the city's grandeur. There is the beautiful so-called mausoleum of Galla Placidia, sister of the emperor Honorius, with its brilliant, largely blue, wall and vault mosaics, dating to about AD 425; and the mosaic scenes of the city in the church of S. Apollinare Nuovo, of about AD 490. Here is depicted the port of Classis with its harbour, high town walls and rich houses; and the palace of the Ostrogothic king, Theoderic, resplendent with its monumental entrance (labelled *palatium*, 'palace'), columns and rich, heavy drapes.

With late Roman Ravenna, however, we have passed into a different world. The Eastern Empire apart, all around Italy the Roman provinces were breaking up into small kingdoms. Much of North Africa fell to the Vandals in AD 429–30 and in AD 455 Gaiseric and his Vandal army spent a fortnight systematically looting Rome. There was little that either the Eastern or the Western Empire could do about it. When in AD 476 the German Odoacer deposed the last western emperor, Romulus — sending him to live on an estate in Campania — it was formally to bring to a close the long saga of Italy's imperial history.

Even so, the classical way of life did not stop abruptly. Disruption there certainly was, but it was to be a very long time before the world of late antiquity gave way to one that we can describe as medieval. It is a fascinating story that we can only begin to understand, and it is properly the subject of our final chapter.

FURTHER READING

Standard works include A. H. M. Jones, *The later Roman empire 284–602* (1964) and his *The decline of the ancient world* (1966); A. R. Birley, *Septimius Severus, the African emperor* (1971); and R. MacMullen's works, *Constantine* (1969), *Roman government's response to crisis, AD 235–337* (1976), and *Christianizing the Roman empire AD 100–400* (1984). See also S. Williams, *Diocletian* (1985); and T. D. Barnes, *The new empire of Diocletian and Constantine* (1982); and on the third-century church, H. Chadwick in *The Roman West in the third century*, ed. A. King and M. Henig (1981), 5ff. For towns, architecture and the decline of patronage, see B. Ward-Perkins, *From classical antiquity to the Middle Ages* (1984); J. B. Ward-Perkins, *Roman Imperial architecture* (1981); and R. Krautheimer's *Early Christian and Byzantine architecture* (1981) and *Three Christian capitals* (1983). See also S. Johnson, *Late Roman fortifications* (1983). For the countryside, see C. R. Whittaker, 'Agri deserti', in M. Finley (ed.), *Studies in Roman property* (1976); T. W. Potter, *The changing landscape of south Etruria* (1979); and M. Gualtieri *et al.*, *Lo scavo di San Giovanni di Ruoti* (1983), and (for Sicily), R. J. A. Wilson, *Piazza Armerina* (1983). R. Meiggs, *Roman Ostia* (1973), 388ff., is particularly interesting on Christianity; see also A. Momigliano (ed.), *The conflict between paganism and Christianity* (1963).

AFTERMATH: FROM ROMAN TO MEDIEVAL

W hen states have weakened, they have tended to lose control of everything that keeps Italy together . . . When the state falls, Italy itself springs apart.[1]

Rome exercised control over Italy by reason of strong, centralised government. Roads linked every part of the peninsula with the capital; goods and produce from many parts of the Empire flooded the markets; and, despite the profound differences from one region to another, Italy was a unified country. During early medieval times – for our purposes from about AD 500 to 1000 – all this disintegrated, as one area after another reverted to semi- or total independence. It is a complex but fascinating story, hitherto largely the preserve of the historian, drawing upon his charters, registers and other written sources. Now archaeological evidence is beginning to make its own contribution, through the investigation both of sites and of the artefacts that they yield.

Historians generally characterise the period of Gothic rule – of Odoacer (AD 476–93) and Theoderic (AD 493–526) – as a time when these new rulers did much to sustain the fabric of the Roman state and its traditions. There had already been a long succession of high-placed German generals, like Stilicho, who had effectively ruled the Western Empire from AD 395 until 408. Thus, in some senses the German kings were not so much of a novelty. Odoacer demanded a third of the Italian estates for his people, but this does not appear to have created excessive resentment: Liberius, who handled the land settlement, was in fact praised for his work: 'You have enriched the countless hordes of Goths with a generous grant of lands, and yet the Romans have hardly felt it. The victors desire no more, and the conquered have felt no loss'.[2]

The Gothic kings preferred to hold court at Ravenna, where a large number of Goths no doubt settled. There were many more around Verona and Pavia, towns in which Theoderic built palaces, as well as in the mountainous regions of east-central Italy, Marche and Abruzzo. We know little archaeologically of this new settlement, but it is a fair guess to assume that the sites would have remained fairly Roman in appearance. Indeed, many of the towns seem to have carried on much as before. This is established by documentary evidence for Pavia (Roman Ticinum), and by excavation in Verona.[3] Here fourth-century houses with fine mosaics seem to gone out of use as late as about AD 600, while others were being built in the late fifth century. It is interesting that these apparently encroach upon one side of the forum, suggesting a certain lack of respect for the civic centre of the Roman city. Similarly, at Luni, in north-west Italy, archaeological investigation has demonstrated how the marble slabs that floored the forum were being stripped away about AD 400, eventually giving way to domestic housing.[4] Even so, in Rome the Gothic kings took trouble to restore some of the public monuments. Odoacer refurbished the Colosseum, while brick-stamps indicate that Theoderic carried out maintenance work both on the Palatine and in the Baths of Caracalla. However, this must be set against other, literary, evidence which pictures Rome at this time as a place of 'utter shabbiness': buildings looted for marble, lead and brass; sewers and aqueducts in disrepair; public granaries in a state of collapse. Moreover, the population was fast declining. Once a city of a million or more, by AD 450 it had dwindled to (at a rough guess) 450,000, and by AD 500 probably no more than 100,000. Continuity of urban life there may have been, but in terms of quality it was a pale shadow of its Imperial days.[5]

How was the populace of Rome, and Italy's other cities, supplied with food and other goods? In recent years a number of important deposits of late Roman date have been discovered which are beginning to cast some light on the question. A refuse dump dating to about AD 430–40, at the Schola Praeconum on the foot of the Palatine Hill in Rome, is one of these.[6] In it were amphorae which demonstrate the importing of oil from Tunisia, wine from Gaza in the east Mediterranean and even produce from Turkey. There were also lamps and red-slip tableware from North Africa. Long-distance trade, therefore, was being maintained, even though much of North Africa was now under the dominion of the Vandals. Another particularly interesting feature of the dump was an exceptional prevalence of pig bones – almost half the total of animal bones. We know from the Theodosian Code, published in AD 438, that guilds of pork suppliers organised the buying and transport to Rome of pigs from as far afield as southern Italy – of which more presently.[7] Clearly, pork was – as in earlier Imperial times – an important element in the diet. Moreover, every part of the carcass is represented, even nearly meatless bones (presumably for soup), and trotters and heads, for brawn and tasty cheek bath-chap.

Just one group of material cannot be regarded as necessarily represen-

The Porta Savoia at Susa in the Alps. These massive defences probably date to the fourth century AD. Many Roman towns invested in huge walls in the uncertain times of the late Roman period.

tative of Rome as a whole, but at least it provides some pointers. Other town sites are also beginning to yield groups of finds of this period. We have already referred to Luni, close by the famous Carrara marble quarries. The marble, used extensively in buildings, was widely exported in classical times, creating the main basis for the city's wealth (although it was also noted for its cheeses and timber). Around AD 400 quarrying of the marble ceased, reversing Luni's prosperity – aggravated, perhaps, by the silting up of the harbour. Even so, amphorae and table-ware from North Africa, as well as glass from Syria, still found their way to the site; whatever the scale of the trade, it did at least continue to participate in long-distance networks.[8] A similar picture is emerging from Naples. Despite a chequered history, this still largely Greek-speaking city nevertheless displayed a strong resilience to the changing times. Its walls were repaired about AD 440, and the Gothic legemony seems to have had little direct effect upon the lives of its inhabitants.[9] It, too, imported large quantities of goods, particularly olive-oil, from North Africa, as well as unguents from Asia Minor. Only towards AD 500 does there seem to be a change when imports from the Byzantine world of the east increase, at the expense of African produce – a comment perhaps on Naples' traditional links with the Greek world.

We must surely be prudent about generalising from these tiny samples, but it is satisfying that so consistent a picture, wholly unrecognised a decade or two ago, is beginning to emerge. Much more complicated to unravel is the situation in Italy's many and diverse rural areas. To the north of Rome, field-survey has shown that a significant number of villas do seem to remain in occupation in the fifth and sixth centuries. In the Ager Faliscus, for example, of ninety-two sites with second-century material, twenty-two were still apparently functioning two to three centuries later.[10] In the same area the small settlement of Aquaviva, situated in a totally exposed position astride the Via Flaminia, has yielded a great abundance of fifth- and early sixth-century imported pottery from North Africa: its inhabitants were clearly not deterred by the events of the times, and were evidently doing well.[11] Similarly, to the east of Rome a villa on the Via Gabina saw the construction of a substantial long building in the late Roman period: it may have been a church, although the excavators prefer to regard it as a granary. Very close nearby, at Ponte di Nona, farmers were certainly planting vineyards in the fifth century, cultivating what in much earlier times had been land belonging to a pagan sanctuary.[12]

Findings from the environs of Rome cannot be regarded as typical of anywhere but the territory of this great city; yet in regions like the Ager Cosanus and the Albenga Valley, some hundred kilometres or so north-west of Rome, the picture is not so different: many villas, particularly in the remoter areas up the valley, tend to remain in occupation into late antique times.[13] Unfortunately, neither here nor in most other parts of the peninsula have rural sites of the late Roman period seen much in the way of modern, scrupulous investigation. One splendid exception is a villa at San Giovanni di Ruoti, a villa located in a remote upland valley twenty-four kilometres to the north-west of Potenza, in Italy's southern region of Basilicata. Work on the site has yet to be completed, but already an important story has emerged. Originally built about AD 50, the first villa was abandoned in the early third century AD. After a gap of more than a century the site was then rehabilitated and inhabited down to about AD 425. The chronology is complicated, but what is clear is that around AD 475 a new and imposing complex was erected with, as its most impressive feature, a great hall with an apse at one end. It is tempting to regard this as a church, but the excavators, probably rightly, think of it as the great reception room of the *dominus* (master), who, in Gothic style, lived mainly on the upper floor. Some of his goods he imported from abroad, but interestingly most of his pottery was made more locally in southern Italy, perhaps reflecting a decline in the availability of the luxuries of earlier times. Nevertheless, he certainly prospered, and it is fascinating to discover that the middens were dominated by the bones of pigs – animals known, as we saw earlier, to have been imported to Rome from the south of Italy. Did the *dominus* set up a special contract with the guild of pork-handlers in Rome?[14]

The villa at San Giovanni di Ruoti seems to have been burnt down about AD 530, a date that broadly coincides with the beginning of the Gothic Wars. These were launched by the Byzantine Romans of the east in an attempt to regain control of Italy, and lasted from AD 535 until 554. It was a long and hard struggle. Rome, for example, was taken by the Byzantine army under Belisarius in 536 and was soon under siege by the Goths; the Goths regained it in 546, left it, and took it again in 549, only to lose it – for the last time – in 552. In AD 554 Narses' Byzantine army finally triumphed, and Italy was in his control. The devastating consequences of these wars are not hard to imagine. Dreadful famine became prevalent from as early as AD 538, and many senators fled to Constantinople, never to return.[15] But worse was to follow. In AD 568 Italy was invaded by the Lombards, a West Germanic people who had been based in the former Roman province of Pannonia, modern Hungary. Sweeping southwards, the Lombard army soon overran large parts of northern and central Italy. Settlement rapidly followed. Rome and Ravenna, together with large parts of the south, remained as Byzantine enclaves, while Lombards clustered thickly around towns like Milan, Brescia, Verona, Pavia and others in the Friuli region. Lombard duchies were also established by breakaway groups at Spoleto and Benevento, both towns that controlled major crossings of the Apennine Mountains. By about AD 600, however, the Byzantine regions had consolidated their position, and during the 620s Pavia emerged as the Lombard capital. Endowed with palaces, churches and even public baths, this now comparatively quiet university town was in early medieval times a place of great importance.[16]

Archaeological scrutiny of this momentous period is still at an early stage, but holds considerable promise. Eventually it should be possible to say a great deal about what happened in the towns and in the countryside, and how this, and other factors, affected long- and medium-distance trade. But already there are some pointers. One particularly interesting excavation is currently taking place at San Vincenzo al Volturno.[17] The site is highly isolated in the Abruzzi Mountains, a little under thirty kilometres from Cassino. Field-survey in this area, and in the adjoining Biferno Valley (a remote corridor draining eastwards into the Adriatic at Termoli), suggests that here the majority of the villas were abandoned around AD 400. They were replaced by what appear to be small villages; that at San Vincenzo had farm buildings, a hall and a church, founded in the early fifth century AD. In contrast to the villas it replaced, it imported little, which underlines how the trading networks increasingly began to bypass such places. By the mid-sixth

century, however, the village had been abandoned and its populace had moved to a nearby, more defensible site at Vacchereccia.[18] Whether this was the result of the insecurity of the times, or for some more mundane reason such as flooding, is debatable; but in the Biferno Valley, sixty kilometres to the east, a hilltop settlement also founded in the sixth century seems to have pronounced military overtones. Known as S. Maria in Città (or, less glamorously, as D 85), it was encircled by 600 metres of defences, partly in wood and partly in stone. Built up against these walls were the houses, and there was a small church. The excavators envisage a population of about fifty, sufficient both to farm and to provide a garrison in the event of trouble.[19]

San Vicenzo was eventually reoccupied by a community of monks, who built a very large and important Carolingian monastery, started in AD 703, but that is a separate story. What is important for our purposes is to stress that in this mountainous region the classical system of farming seems to have given way to a network of villages, some of which were fortified, at an early stage in the medieval period. This may well prove to be typical of these more

The strongly defended site of Spoleto, seen from the Via Flaminia. Its strategic position on the road made it an obvious centre for a Lombard duchy.

isolated upland regions, where life always has been rather different from that of the plains and other lowlands. By and large, mountain-dwellers had in the early medieval period to look very much to their own resources.

Abruzzo and Molise are by no means the only areas of Italy where new fortified centres began to emerge in the course of the sixth and early seventh centuries. Byzantine strategy was very much directed at the creation of *castra* (forts), supplemented by what one scholar has termed 'strategic hamlets' – a description that could well fit D 85.[20] Our literary sources enable us to compile quite a long list of towns which were provided with defences in this period; amongst them was Rome itself.[21] Many *castra* lay along important routes. One was the Via Amerina; once Spoleto, on the Via Flaminia, had fallen into Lombard hands, this became the principal line of communication between the Byzantine enclaves of Rome and Ravenna. There were garrisons at Nepi, Orte and Fano, to name but a few of the towns safeguarding this crucial road.[22] Indeed, to visit North Africa today, where the Byzantine fortresses at places like Sétif, Timgad and Tebessa are so much better preserved, is immediately to appreciate the point.[23]

There has been much discussion as to the reasons for these fortified *castra* (Italian *castelli*), rather nicely summed up as follows: 'in their enthusiasm to break away from the old image of the early middle ages as a period of continuous battles, historians and archaeologists run the risk of underestimating the importance of insecurity . . . and of failing to appreciate that military direction is a common . . . factor in settlement change.'[24] Exploration in southern Etruria serves to support this view. The region abounds in fortified medieval sites, many of them perched in spectacular fashion upon cliff-girt promontories, jutting out into deep ravines. Research has shown that the majority of these sites, as in many other parts of the peninsula, were first occupied quite late in the early Middle Ages – generally in the late ninth or tenth centuries. They belong to a phenomenon known in Italian as *incastellamento*, the building of a fortified centre, and were traditionally regarded as a response to the Arab raids of the ninth century. Certainly, some wall-building (including the Leonine Wall, constructed between AD 849 and 852 around St Peter's in Rome) were the outcome of Arab attacks; but recent research has shown that most *incastellamento* took place not for military but for political reasons – 'the growth of immunities and the devolution of public powers that marked the retreat of the state'.[25] Thus it was largely a private initiative by individual lords.

In the Ager Faliscus, however, a small region that begins some twenty kilometres to the north of Rome, the pattern is turning out to be rather different. This was frontier country between the Byzantine Duchy of Rome and the area occupied by the Lombards. It was also a battle zone. Thus, in AD 592–3 Pope Gregory the Great refers to hostilities in this area on no fewer than seven separate occasions.[26] It was, therefore, particularly interesting that field-survey should bring to light a large quantity of glazed pottery of a type known as Forum ware (from a major group from the Forum in Rome) on many of the *castelli*: for this is a ware that was certainly current in the eighth century AD, and may date back to as early as about AD 600.[27] In other words, the *castelli* of the Ager Faliscus could well demarcate the northern frontier of Byzantine Rome, and were created directly as the result of the Lombard incursions.

Only one site has been excavated on any scale, a promontory overlooking a major river crossing of the Via Amerina (the main Rome–Ravenna road), at Ponte Nepesino, just south of Nepi. This work demonstrated how the site was ringed with a stone wall, within which were a number of rectangular wooden houses. There was a certain amount of weaponry – spears and knives – amongst the finds, and study of the animal bones suggests that this was not a farming community but a garrison supplied from outside. Moreover, Forum-ware pots turned up in profusion, which, whatever its date (a hotly debated matter), must put the start of occupation well before the traditional *incastellamento* of the tenth century.[28]

It is fascinating to note that this frontier line of *castelli* in the Ager Faliscus is today perpetuated by the boundary between the provinces of Rome and Viterbo, a coincidence which may well not be accidental. But how did the *castelli* begin? Very often it was the local inhabitants who were forced to build the Byzantine strongholds,[29] and it is therefore interesting to see that the great majority of these frontier *castelli* lie in very close proximity to large late Roman villas. Could the populace have moved from one to the other? This is something that we cannot yet say, although an excavation is currently being planned which will attempt to resolve this question.

Closer to Rome the evidence, both archaeological and historical, reveals a different story. Here the classical estates seem largely to have remained in cultivation well into early medieval times. There are hints of the prevailing insecurity of the times – a curious Roman building at Le Mura di Santo Stefano, near Anguillara, was for instance ringed with a defensive ditch in late Roman times – but much of the land remained in cultivation. Moreover, this became increasingly necessary. By the early seventh century, if not before, the long distance trade that had for centuries supplied the city of Rome was in sharp decline. The Popes had taken over the traditional role of handouts to the urban poor – now largely concentrated in the bend of the Tiber and Trastevere[30] – and it was a question of finding supplies. Mohammed was born at Mecca about AD 570, and his followers were before long to sound the death-knell for large parts of the Roman world; the Byzantines came increasingly to care nothing for Italy, so that Constans II was the last Byzantine emperor to visit the peninsula in AD 663,[31] while trade, such as it was within the Mediterranean, was by now more a question of gift-exchange between aristocrats rather than large-scale supply.[32] All over Italy, from about AD 600, perspectives became ever more parochial.

Matters were further exacerbated by a series of environmental problems for which there were neither the resources, nor, indeed, the manpower, to resolve. We have already seen how the Roman state had the capacity and the direction to put in hand huge schemes of land reclamation and control. From as early as the late second century AD, however, the situation began to deteriorate. Valleys where once there had been farms and fertile land were beginning to silt up and flood – some Roman buildings are now buried by two or three metres of deposits – and there was similar deterioration along the coasts and in the plains: witness Ravenna, now totally land-locked. Even in Rome flooding provided a continual problem, so that in the late eighth century there had on one occasion to be a punt-service along the Via del Corso, supplying people who were stranded in their houses.[33]

There can be little doubt that in large part this situation was engendered by the inability of the authorities to cope: from mid-Imperial times onwards there was neither the money nor the manpower. But things may have been made still more difficult by a deterioration in the climate, bringing with it higher levels of rainfall and thus more run-off of silt from hillsides already denuded of woodland. This is very much a matter for conjecture, but the consequences, whatever the causes, are wholly clear on the ground today – as at Ravenna.

The Popes were eventually to encircle Rome with a great series of estates, the *domuscultae*, which were intended to supply food for the city's populace.[34] One of them, that of Capracorum, was founded by Pope Hadrian I in about AD 780, and its centre has been located and excavated. In some respects it resembles a large Roman villa, suggesting a certain continuity of tradition. These estates were not ultimately a success, however, and were largely swallowed up when the process of *incastellamento* began in earnest in the tenth century.[35]

But we are running ahead of ourselves and must go back to the Lombards, and the consequences of their invasion. It used to be an axiom that, in the main areas of Lombard settlement, the Romans were effectively wiped out, to be replaced entirely by Germans. Such a view does not really stand up to scrutiny. Examination of place-names, tell-tale indicators of ethnic origins, show for example a fairly even mix of Roman and Germanic names in areas like those around Verona and Brescia. Likewise, the great Lombard cemeteries contain many graves with artefacts that are at home in both 'cultures'. Much Lombard pottery, to take one instance, was made with techniques typical of late Roman potters.[36]

It is also claimed that the Lombards were, above all, responsible for initiating fourteen centuries of Italian disunity. Certainly they never succeeded in conquering the entire peninsula and thus imposing their rule over all Italy; but there is impressive evidence to show that town life in particular was maintained. Some northern towns, it is true, did dwindle away into obscurity and, eventually, abandonment during the early medieval period. At Luni, near Carrara, for example, excavation has traced this process with some precision. By about AD 600 this once rich city had largely stopped importing goods, apart from a few lathe-turned stone vessels, made with materials mined in the Alps. Around the same date modest wooden and dry-stone houses were being erected over the forum, confirming its disuse; there may also have been dense settlement around the cathedral, which lay on rather higher ground on the north-east side of the town. The citizens of Luni resisted the Lombards until about AD 640, when the town finally fell. By this time the drains and water supply had long since ceased to function, being replaced by cess-pits and wells.[37]

Luni remained the centre of an extensive diocese until around AD 1200, when it was removed to the town's medieval successor, Sarzana, a few kilometres to the north. It was then lost to view, covered in swamp, until the nineteenth century. By contrast, however, many Roman towns in northern and central Italy — probably about three-quarters — have survived as urban centres down to the present day. Indeed, very often basic features of the Roman layout, especially the streets, became fossilised in the medieval plan, a feature that is much less conspicuous in, say, English towns of Roman origin.

The point is readily made by aerial photographs of, to name but a few instances, Como, Aosta, Verona, Pavia and even (though less clearly) Florence. Similarly, at Lucca one can still today walk into Piazza di Mercato and recognise from its oval form and four entrances the shape of the Roman amphitheatre, which lies buried beneath.

Archaeology and documentary sources alike show that the Lombard period was by no means a distinguished one in architectural terms. At both Verona and Pavia scattered early medieval burials across the urban area demonstrate the disuse of some areas; monuments were spoliated for their stone, and some parts were turned into gardens. Indeed, work at sites like the Lombard centre at Castelseprio, south of Varese, or at Tuscania in central Italy, show that domestic housing in this period was more often than not of wood or poor-quality reused masonry.[38] But the important thing is that the Lombard period, whatever its implications for Italian unity, did ensure a considerable measure of urban continuity.

We can say much less about the countryside, although the indications are that the Lombards may have founded a considerable number of villages, thus finally extinguishing the Roman villa system. Similarly, in the south of the peninsula, where much of its early medieval history is a story of incessant and bitter warfare, farming came to be carried out largely from towns and villages. However, many of the Roman towns fared badly. Capua, for example — once a city with a claim to be second only to Rome itself within Italy — rapidly dwindled after being sacked by the Vandals in AD 456. Only its amphitheatre, now fortified, gave protection, and by the late ninth century its inhabitants had moved to nearby Casilinum, the Capua of today. Now there is just a village, S. Maria di Capua Vetere, still dominated by the great Roman amphitheatre, on the site of the ancient city.

We could with profit pursue these and other themes: the Frankish incursions and the triumph of Charlemagne; the Arab raids and their defeat at the Garigliano River in AD 915; the emergence of *incastellamento* and the new settlement landscape that resulted. But with these words we have brought Roman Italy firmly to a close. Italy had 'sprung apart' and was entering a new and decisively different world: one where archaeology has much to contribute but about a quite separate story. Perhaps as we look back over the many centuries that have concerned us, it is the sheer longevity of Roman Italy that is so amazing: a remarkable history, and, too, a remarkable archaeology; everywhere an astonishing range of standing monuments and so much more under the ground. The investigation of these remains has now been pursued for several centuries; but it is a sobering, if exciting, thought that it will need to carry on for a good many more centuries yet.

FURTHER READING

See generally C. Wickham, *Early Medieval Italy* (1981); A. H. M. Jones' summary in *The decline of the ancient world* (1966); and B. Ward-Perkins, *From classical antiquity to the Middle Ages* (1984). Also C. R. Whittaker, 'Late-Roman trade and traders', in P. Garnsey (ed.), *Trade in the ancient economy* (1983), 163ff. For the Ostrogoths and Lombards, D. A. Bullough in D. Talbot-Rice (ed.), *The Dark Ages* (1965); V. Bierbrauen, *Die Ostgotischen Grab- und Schatzfunde in Italien* (1975); G. P. Bognetti, *L'età longobarda* (4 vols, 1966–8); and I. Kiszely, *The anthropology of the Lombards* (1979). On the Byzantines, see T. S. Brown, *Gentlemen and officers* (1984). For towns see P-A. Février in M. W. Barley (ed.), *European Towns. Their archaeology and early history* (1977); D. A. Bullough, 'Social and economic structures and topography in the early medieval city', *Settimane di Studio, Spoleto* 21 (1973), 351–99, and also (on Pavia) in *PBSR* 34 (1966), 82–131; P. Llewellyn, *Rome in the Dark Ages* (1971); and (on Rome and Milan), R. Krautheimer, *Three Christian capitals* (1983), *Rome. Profile of a city 312 to 1308* (1980), and *Early Christian and Byzantine architecture* (1981). For the economy, see P. J. Jones in *Storia d'Italia* (vol. 2, pt 2, 1974); and R. Hodges and D. B. Whitehouse, *Mohammed, Charlemagne and the origins of Europe* (1983). Basic for *incastellamento* is P. Toubert, *Les structures du Latium médiéval* (1973). Environmental changes are discussed, *inter alia*, by C. Vita-Finzi, *The Mediterranean valleys* (1969); C. Delano-Smith, *Western Mediterranean Europe* (1979); and T. W. Potter in R. T. Rowley (ed.), *The evolution of marshland landscapes* (1981). Finally, much crucial new archaeological matter is published annually in *Archeologia Medievale* (1974ff).

Gazetteer of sites to visit

This gazetteer is intended as the briefest guide to some of the more accessible and interesting sites and, together with the map, should help to plot an itinerary. The list could very easily be extended, of course; it includes not just Roman sites, but also older places which have either featured in the main text (such as Metaponto and Marzabotto) or which are of first-rate importance (for example Tarquinia and Cerveteri). It should further be noted that museums are not normally mentioned unless located in a town with a very significant collection but no other archaeological features; most Italian sites and towns have their own museum, and they are usually full of fascinating material.

This handlist should be used in conjunction with detailed maps and guides. The best tourist maps are those published by the Touring Club Italiano, *Atlante stradale d'Italia* (scale 1: 200,000); they are available in three volumes, *Nord*, *Centro* and *Sud*, and have very detailed indexes and mark many of the ancient sites. Similarly excellent are the Touring Club Italiano guides, which cover the peninsula in twenty-one volumes. Also useful are the much briefer Blue Guides, of which there are three: *Northern Italy*, *Rome and environs* and *Southern Italy*. The best archaeological guides, however, are the copiously illustrated *Guide archeologiche Laterza*, each of which is written by an expert and is provided with full bibliographic references. Sicily and Sardinia apart, there are twelve: 1) Piemonte, Valdaosta, Liguria, Lombardia; 2) Emilia, Venezia; 3) Etruria; 4) Umbria, Marche; 5) Lazio; 6) Roma; 7) Dintorni di Roma; 8) Ostia; 9) Abruzzo, Molise; 10) Campania; 11) Pompeii; 12) Magna Grecia. English readers will also find very useful M. Guido, *Southern Italy: an archaeological guide* (1972); and R. F. Paget, *Central Italy: an archaeological guide* (1973).

A final word of warning: sites, and museums, are generally closed on Mondays!

Note: The number beside each site on the list refers to the map overleaf; where possible, the Roman name of the place is also listed, in parenthesis.

NORTH-WEST (NW)

7 Albenga *(Albium Ingaunum)*: excavations
1 Aosta *(Augusta Praetoria)*: arch, theatre, baths, etc.
5 Bene Vagienna *(Augusta Bagiennorum)*: theatre, basilica
8 Como *(Comum)*: gate
2 Ivrea *(Eporedia)*: amphitheatre
12 Luni *(Luna)*: forum, houses, amphitheatre
9 Milan *(Mediolanum)*: churches
3 Susa *(Segusium)*: arch, gate, walls amphitheatre
10 Tortona *(Dertona)*: tombs
4 Turin *(Augusta Taurinorum)*: gate, theatre
11 Velleia *(Veleia)*: forum, houses, baths, amphitheatre
6 Ventimiglia *(Albintimilium)*: theatre, excavations

NORTH-EAST (NE)

20 Altino *(Altinum)*: museum
18 Aquileia *(Aquileia)*: houses, forum, harbour, Christian basilica (mosaics)
27 Bologna *(Bononia)*: museum
13 Brescia *(Brixia)*: Capitoline temple
14 Desenzano del Garda *(?Decentianum)*: villa
23 Este *(Ateste)*: museum
25 Ferrara: museum
33 Fano *(Fanum Fortunae)*: arch
28 Marzabotto *(Misa)*: town of *c.* 500–400 BC
26 Modena *(Mutina)*: museum
22 Montegrotto Terme: baths, theatre
21 Padua *(Patavium)*: amphitheatre (traces)
24 Parma *(Colonia Iulia Augusta Parmensis)*: museum
19 Portogruaro (nearby) *(Concordia Sagittaria)*: Christian basilica
29 Ravenna *(Ravenna* and *Classis)*: churches
32 Rimini *(Ariminum)*: arch, bridge
30 Russi: villa
31 Sarsina *(Sarsina)*: mausolea
15 Sirmione *(Sirmio)*: 'Grotte di Catullo' villa
17 Trieste *(Tergestum)*: theatre
16 Verona *(Verona)*: amphitheatre, theatre, arches, etc.

WEST-CENTRAL (WC)

65 Alatri *(Alatrium)*: walls, gate of fourth century BC
57 Amelia *(Ameria)*: walls of fifth century BC
38 Arezzo *(Arretium)*: amphitheatre
44 Assisi *(Asisium)*: temple of Minerva
49 Bolsena *(Volsinii)*: Etruscan walls, forum, houses with frescos
48 Carseoli *(Carsulae)*: theatre, amphitheatre, forum
43 Chiusi *(Clusium)*: Etruscan tombs
63 Civitavecchia *(Centumcellae)*: baths (Terme Taurine)
40 Cortona *(Cortona)*: museum
53 Cosa *(Cosa)*: Roman town and nearby villas
60 Falerii Novi or S. Maria di Falleri *(Falerii Novi)*: walls, gate, forum
64 Ferentino *(Ferentinum)*: walls, gate, theatre, market
56 Ferento *(Ferentium)*: theatre, baths
35 Fiesole *(Faesulae)*: temple, theatre, baths
36 Florence *(Florentia)*: museum
66 Frosinone *(Frusino)*: amphitheatre (slight traces)
39 Furlo Gorge *(Intercisa)*: road tunnel of AD 76 or 77
62 Gravisca or Porto Clementino *(Graviscae)*: temple of Hera, Roman colony
41 Gubbio *(Iguvium)*: theatre
34 Lucca *(Luca)*: amphitheatre
47 Orvieto *(?Volsinii vetus)*: Etruscan cemetery and temple
42 Perugia *(Perusia)*: gateways
51 Roselle *(Rusellae)*: forum, houses, amphitheatre, etc.
50 Saturnia *(Aurinia)*: gate

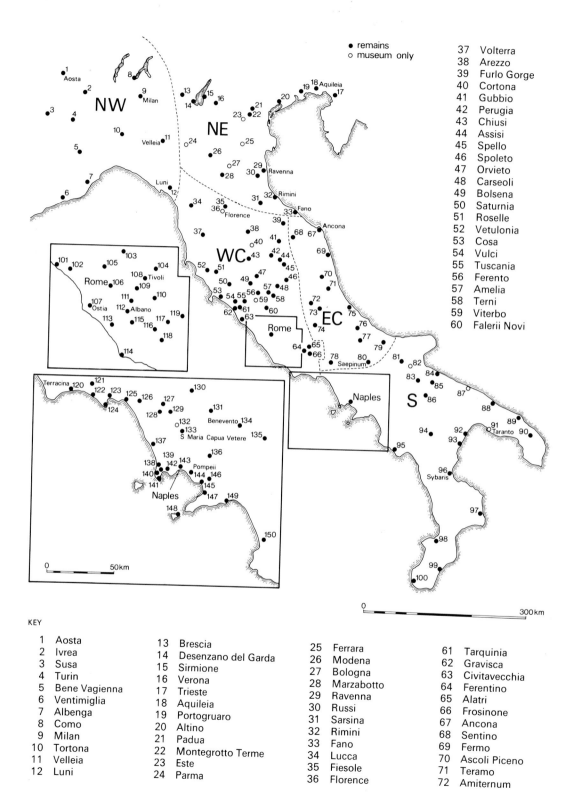

37	Volterra
38	Arezzo
39	Furlo Gorge
40	Cortona
41	Gubbio
42	Perugia
43	Chiusi
44	Assisi
45	Spello
46	Spoleto
47	Orvieto
48	Carseoli
49	Bolsena
50	Saturnia
51	Roselle
52	Vetulonia
53	Cosa
54	Vulci
55	Tuscania
56	Ferento
57	Amelia
58	Terni
59	Viterbo
60	Falerii Novi

● remains
○ museum only

KEY

1	Aosta
2	Ivrea
3	Susa
4	Turin
5	Bene Vagienna
6	Ventimiglia
7	Albenga
8	Como
9	Milan
10	Tortona
11	Velleia
12	Luni

13	Brescia
14	Desenzano del Garda
15	Sirmione
16	Verona
17	Trieste
18	Aquileia
19	Portogruaro
20	Altino
21	Padua
22	Montegrotto Terme
23	Este
24	Parma

25	Ferrara
26	Modena
27	Bologna
28	Marzabotto
29	Ravenna
30	Russi
31	Sarsina
32	Rimini
33	Fano
34	Lucca
35	Fiesole
36	Florence

61	Tarquinia
62	Gravisca
63	Civitavecchia
64	Ferentino
65	Alatri
66	Frosinone
67	Ancona
68	Sentino
69	Fermo
70	Ascoli Piceno
71	Teramo
72	Amiternum

73	S. Paolo di Peltuino	135	Mirabella Eclano
74	Alba Fucens	136	Nola
75	Chieti	137	Literno
76	Iuvanum	138	Cuma
77	Pietrabbondante	139	Baia
78	Cassino	140	Bacoli
79	Larino	141	Miseno
80	Saepinum	142	Pozzuoli
81	Lucera	143	Naples
82	Foggia	144	Ercolano
83	Ordona	145	Oplontis
84	Canne	146	Pompeii
85	Canosa di Puglia	147	Castellamare di Stabia
86	Venosa	148	Capri
87	Bari	149	Minori
88	Egnazia	150	Paestum
89	Brindisi		
90	Lecce		
91	Taranto		
92	Metaponto		
93	Policoro		
94	Grumento		
95	Velia		
96	Sibari		
97	Crotone		
98	Vibo Valentia		
99	Locri		
100	Reggio di Calabria		
101	Pyrgi		
102	Cerveteri		
103	Lucus Feroniae		
104	Licenza		
105	Veio		
106	Rome		
107	Ostia		
108	Tivoli		
109	Gabii		
110	Palestrina		
111	Frascati		
112	Albano		
113	Pratica di Mare		
114	Anzio		
115	Lanuvio		
116	Cori		
117	Segni		
118	Norma		
119	Anagni		
120	Terracina		
121	Fondi		
122	Sperlonga		
123	Formia		
124	Gaeta		
125	Minturno		
126	Sessa Aurunca		
127	Teano		
128	Francolise		
129	Calvi Vecchia		
130	Alife		
131	Telese		
132	Capua		
133	S. Maria di Capua Vetere		
134	Benevento		

45 Spello (*Hispellum*): gates, amphitheatre

46 Spoleto (*Spoletium*): theatre, arch

61 Tarquinia (*Tarquinia*): Etruscan tombs, fourth-century BC temple

58 Terni (*Interamna Nahars*): amphitheatre

55 Tuscania (*Tuscania*): baths, houses

52 Vetulonia (*Vetulonia*): Etruscan tombs, Roman houses

59 Viterbo: museum

37 Volterra (*Volaterrae*): theatre, Etruscan arch

54 Vulci (*Vulci*): Etruscan tombs, Roman houses, mithraeum

EAST CENTRAL (EC)

74 Alba Fucens, near Avezzano (*Alba Fucens*): excavated complex with forum, houses, amphitheatre, etc.

67 Ancona (*Ancona*): Arch of Trajan

72 Amiternum, S. Vittorino (*Amiternum*): Samnite settlement, theatre, amphitheatre

70 Ascoli Piceno (*Asculum Picenum*): gate

78 Cassino (*Casinum*): theatre, amphitheatre, tombs, etc.

75 Chieti (*Teate Marrucinorum*): 3 temples, theatre, baths, cistern

69 Fermo (*Firmum Picenum*): baths, pool

76 Iuvanum (*Iuvanum*): forum, theatre

79 Larino (*Larinum*): traces of amphitheatre

77 Pietrabbondante: Samnite sanctuary, theatre, temples

73 S. Paolo di Peltuino (*Peltuinum*): walls, theatre

80 Saepinum, near Altilia (*Saepinum*): extensive part of town – walls, forum, houses, gates, tombs, etc.

68 Sentino (*Sentinum*): walls, baths, house

71 Teramo (*Interamna Praetuttiorum*): theatre, amphitheatre

SOUTH (S)

87 Bari (*Barium*): museum

89 Brindisi (*Brundisium*): column at end of Via Appia by harbour

84 Canne (*Cannae*): settlement and site of Hannibal's victory in 216 BC

85 Canosa di Puglia (*Canusium*): arch and tombs

97 Crotone (*Croton*): Greek temple

88 Egnazia (*Gnathia*): gate, walls and forum

82 Foggia: museum

94 Grumento (*Grumentum*): aqueduct, theatre, baths, basilica

90 Lecce (*Lupiae*): theatre and amphitheatre; nearby traces of *Rudiae*

99 Locri (*Locri Epizephyrii*): Greek and Roman town: theatre, temples

81 Lucera (*Luceria*): amphitheatre

92 Metaponto (*Metapontum*): Greek temples, theatre

83 Ordona (*Herdonia*): forum, amphitheatre, market

93 Policoro (*Heraclea*): Greek town

100 Reggio di Calabria *(Rhegion)*: baths, Greek walls
96 Sibari *(Sybaris,* later *Thurii,* later *Copia)*: theatre
91 Taranto *(Tarentum)*: museum
95 Velia *(Elea)*: Greek town, fine gate, Roman baths, harbour
86 Venosa *(Venusia)*: amphitheatre, baths, early Christian remains
98 Vibo Valentia *(Hipponion)*: Greek defences

VICINITY OF ROME
112 Albano *(Albanum)*: amphitheatre, gate, walls, cistern, tombs
119 Anagni *(Agnania)*: walls
114 Anzio *(Antium)*: theatre, villa of Nero
102 Cerveteri *(Caere)*: acropolis, Etruscan cemetery
116 Cori *(Cora)*: fifth-century BC walls, Roman temples
111 Frascati: see Tusculum
109 Gabii *(Gabii)*: temple
113 Lavinium, Pratica di Mare *(Lavinium)*: altars (inside locked shed)
115 Lanuvio *(Lanuvium)*: walls, two temples, acropolis
104 Licenza: the so-called Villa of Horace
103 Lucus Feroniae *(Lucus Feroniae)*: town centre (forum, etc.), Villa of the Volusii
118 Norma *(Norba)*: walls of the fourth century BC, temples
107 Ostia *(Ostia)*: town and cemetery (Isola Sacra)
110 Palestrina *(Praeneste)*: temple of Fortuna Primigenia, forum, pre-Roman citadel of Castel S. Pietro
113 Pratica di Mare: see Lavinium
101 Pyrgi, Santa Severa *(Pyrgi)*: Etruscan temples, walls of *colonia*
106 Rome *(Roma)*
117 Segni *(Signia)*: walls, temple
108 Tivoli *(Tibur)*: temples, Hadrian's villa 6 kilometres distant
111 Tusculum, near Frascati *(Tusculum)*: theatre, forum, amphitheatre, Villa of Cicero
105 Veio *(Veii)*: Etruscan tombs, sanctuary

CAMPANIA AND THE NAPLES AREA
130 Alife *(Allifae)*: walls
139 Baia *(Baiae)*: temples, baths, etc.
140 Bacoli *(Bauli)*: theatre-nymphaeum, villa
134 Benevento *(Beneventum)*: arch of Trajan, theatre
129 Calvi Vecchia *(Cales)*: theatre, baths, etc.
148 Capri *(Capreae)*: Villa Jovis and other villas
132 Capua *(Casilinum)*: museum
147 Castellamare di Stabia *(Stabiae)*: villas
138 Cuma *(Cumae)*: viaduct, forum, theatre, amphitheatre, temples, the Sybil's cave; also nearby Lake Avernus
121 Fondi *(Fundi)*: walls
123 Formia *(Formiae)*: 'tomb of Cicero'
128 Francolise: San Rocco villa

124 Gaeta *(Caieta)*: mausoleum
144 Ercolano *(Herculaneum)*: Roman town
137 Literno *(Liternum)*: forum, theatre, temple
149 Minori: villa
125 Minturno (nearby) *(Minturnae)*: theatre, forum, aqueduct
135 Mirabella Eclano or Passo di Mirabella *(Aeclanum)*: houses, baths
141 Miseno, Capo di *(Misenum)*: theatre, baths
143 Naples *(Neapolis)*: catacombs, museum
136 Nola *(Nola)*: traces of amphitheatre
145 Oplontis: see Torre Annunziata
150 Paestum *(Paestum)*: Greek and Roman town
146 Pompeii: Roman town
142 Pozzuoli *(Puteoli)*: amphitheatre, temple, market, tombs
133 S. Maria di Capua Vetere *(Capua)*: amphitheatre, mithraeum, tombs
126 Sessa Aurunca *(Suessa Aurunca)*: theatre, baths, Ponte degli Aurunci (2.5 kilometres distant)
122 Sperlonga *(ad Speluncas)*: villa, Grotto of Tiberius
127 Teano *(Teanum Sidicinum)*: walls, theatre, amphitheatre
131 Telese *(Telesia)*: circus, amphitheatre, etc.
120 Terracina *(Tarracina Anxur)*: temple of Jupiter Anxur, Capitoline temple, etc.
145 Torre Annunziata *(Oplontis)*: villa (a second is under excavation)
148 Villa Jovis: see Capri

Notes

Introduction

1. D. H. Lawrence, *Etruscan Places* (1932), 49.
2. Cited in M. Bouchenaki, *Cités antiques d'Algérie* (1978), 9.
3. Barker 1985.
4. Cotton 1979; Cotton and Métraux 1985.
5. Carandini *et al.* 1985.
6. Carandini (ed.) 1985. See Oswyn Murray's review of the *Progetto Etruschi* in the *Times Literary Supplement*, 30 August 1985, 948–9.
7. See the papers in J. Bintliff (ed.), *European Social Evolution* (1984).
8. Some appreciation of this can be gleaned from successive conference proceedings, *Papers in Italian Archaeology* (Blake, Potter and Whitehouse 1978; Barker and Hodges 1981; Malone and Stoddart 1985).
9. Brown, F. E., 1980 is a highly readable account.
10. See the review by G. E. Rickman in *JRS* 71 (1981), 215–17; and the spirited reply in Carandini 1983.
11. Muckelroy 1980.
12. Frova *et al.* 1973, 1977; Ward-Perkins, B. 1978, 1981.

1 The land

1. Strabo 5, 1. See also Pliny, *Nat. Hist.* 3, 38–132.
2. Bullough 1968.
3. Pauli 1984.
4. Strabo 4, 6, 6.
5. Livy 21, 58, 3.
6. *CIL* IX, 2438; Corbier 1983.
7. Barker 1981.
8. Craven 1838, 259.
9. Pliny, *Nat. Hist.* 3, 38–132; Thomsen 1947.
10. Pliny, *Nat. Hist.* 5, 60.
11. Santoro 1978; Chilver 1941.
12. Pliny, *Nat. Hist.* 3, 5, 118.
13. Wheat: Polybius 2, 15, 1; millet: Spurr 1983.
14. Strabo 4, 6, 2; furniture: Pliny, *Nat. Hist.* 13, 29–31.
15. *Letters of the Younger Pliny* 1, 3.
16. Duncan-Jones 1982, 17f.
17. D. H. Lawrence, *Etruscan Places* (1932), 159.
18. Pliny, *Nat. Hist.* 3, 5, 53.
19. Cary 1949, 130–3.
20. Frederiksen 1984; D'Arms 1970.
21. Pliny, *Nat. Hist.* 3, 5, 60.
22. Suetonius, Tiberius 62; Ward-Perkins, J. B. 1981, 198–201.
23. Pliny, *Nat. Hist.* 3, 5, 42.
24. Strabo 6, 1f.
25. Boardman 1980, 171–2.
26. Strabo 6, 1, 13.
27. Rainey and Lerici 1967; *Not. Scav.* 1969, Supplement I; *Not. Scav.* 1970, Supplement III; *Not. Scav.* 1972, Supplement.
28. Strabo 6, 3, 5.
29. Horace, *Epodes* 3, 16; see also Bradford 1949.
30. Bradford and Williams-Hunt 1946; Bradford 1949, 1957.
31. Garnsey 1979, 4f.; carts, common twenty years ago, are now being largely replaced by motor *carrozzette*.
32. Bark 1932; Whitehouse 1979.

2 Romans, Etruscans, Greeks and Italians

1. Strabo 5, 3, 4.
2. Salmon 1982, 154; Pulgram 1958.
3. Momigliano 1963, 96f.; Pallottino 1979; also E. Gjerstad, *Legends and facts of early Roman history* (1962).
4. Gjerstad 1953–73 remains fundamental, but the interpretation

is questioned. Scullard 1981 is very up-to-date; see also Heurgon 1973; Ridgway and Ridgway 1979.
5. Colonna 1981; Scullard 1967, 1981; and, for the Forum, Coarelli 1983.
6. Gierow 1964, 1966 is fundamental. See Sestieri 1979 for the Osteria dell'Osa cemetery and its significance; also Cornell 1980 and Catalogue 1976.
7. Potter 1984.
8. Frederiksen 1984; Boardman 1980; Ridgway and Ridgway 1979.
9. Faliscans: L. Holland, *The Faliscans in prehistoric times* (1925); G. Giacomelli, *La lingua falisca* (1963). Grant (1980) and Cristofani (1979) are amongst many who summarise the Etruscan evidence. For the highly important Quattro Fontanili cemetery, see J. Close-Brooks in Ridgway and Ridgway 1979, 95f.
10. Pallottino 1975, 64f.
11. Cristofani 1979, 35.
12. Ridgway 1984; G. Buchner in Ridgway and Ridgway 1979, 129f. See also A. J. Graham in *Cambridge Ancient History* III (1982), 83f., and D. Ridgway in *Cahiers du Centre Jean Bérard* 1981, 45f.
13. Boardman 1980; Guzzo 1982; Frederiksen 1984, 55–116.
14. A. Blakeway, *JRS* 25 (1935), 129f.; full discussion is now in S. Steingräber, *Etruskische Wandmalerei* (Stuttgart and Zurich 1985).
15. See now, however, Pallottino 1981, 1984.
16. Livy 9, 13, 7; Salmon 1967, 77; Salmon 1982.
17. Oscan: Pulgram 1958; Salmon 1982.
18. Stabo 5, 4, 12.
19. Salmon 1967.
20. Salmon 1982.
21. Barker 1977.
22. Saepinum: La Regina 1980; Pietrabbondante: Salmon 1967, 137f.; La Regina 1980, 131f.; M. J. Strazzulla and B. di Marco, *Il santuario sannitico di Pietrabbondante* (1971).
23. Whitehouse, R. D. 1973.
24. Boardman 1980; Greco 1982; also Adamesteanu 1974, 129–86.
25. Salmon 1982, 19. Monte Sannace: Donvito 1982.
26. Mazzei 1984.
27. Strabo 5, 3, 1; for Hellenisation generally see the essays in Zanker 1976.
28. Poultney 1959.
29. Cianfarani 1970, 111f.
30. F. Ridgway in Ridgway and Ridgway 1979, 419f.; Barfield 1971; Peroni 1975.
31. Peroni 1975.
32. Diodorus Siculus 5, 39; see also Barfield 1971, 145f.
33. Spina: Uggeri and Uggeri 1974; Marzabotto: Mansuelli 1972, 1979.
34. Santoro 1978.

3 The rise of Rome

1. Livy 1, 1.
2. E.g. Hopkins 1978, 197f.
3. Propertius 4, 10, 29–30; Ward-Perkins, J. B. 1961.
4. Sherwin-White 1973.
5. Salmon 1969.
6. Via Appia: Castagnoli 1956; spread of Latin: Salmon 1982, 55f, 88f, 121f.
7. All these towns lie in south-west Italy; Thurii was a successor to Sybaris, Rhegion is present-day Reggio di Calabria.
8. Inscribed on his sarcophagus: H. Dessau, *Inscriptiones Latinae Selectae* I; see also Livy 10, 12f. and Salmon 1969.
9. Boëthius 1978, 130f.
10. For the First Punic War, Polybius Book 1.

11. Polybius 2, 24.
12. See further chapter 6.
13. Livy 22, 54.
14. Salmon 1969, 95f.
15. Virgil, *Aeneid* 6, 851–3. For the so-called 'just wars', see Harris 1979.
16. Appian, *Bellum Civile* 1, 7.
17. Coarelli 1977.
18. Brunt 1971, 121f.; see also Finley 1985, Chs. 2, 3 for slavery, and Finley 1980.
19. For the Gracchi, Appian, *Bellum Civile* 1, and Plutarch, *Tiberius and Gaius Gracchus*.
20. Dilke 1971, 92f. for centuriation stones; Jones, G. D. B. 1980 for the Tavoliere.
21. Keppie 1984, 51f.
22. Salmon 1969, 129f.; 1982, 132f. The figure of 120,000 is probably too high: Brunt 1971, 305.
23. Plutarch, *Pompeius* 2.
24. Sallust, *Cat.* 35; Rickman 1980.
25. *Res Gestae* 28; see Keppie 1983.
26. Crawford 1978, 193.
27. Tacitus, *Annals* 14, 26.
28. Duncan-Jones 1964, 1982.
29. Duncan-Jones 1982, 27; Pliny, *Letters* 7, 18, 2–4.
30. Cassius Dio 76, 17, 4.

29. Taranto: Keppie 1984a, 82f; Ivrea and the Salassi: Strabo 4, 6, 7.
30. Cf. Keppie 1984 for an excellent study of the development of the Roman army.
31. *Res Gestae* 28; Salmon 1969; Keppie 1983, 1984a.
32. Chilver 1941, Tozzi 1972.
33. Cicero, *Pro Sulla* 60–2; Keppie 1983, 101f.
34. Tacitus, *Annals* 14, 30.
35. For black-glaze ware see, most recently, Morel 1981.
36. Vitruvius 1, 4, 1.
37. Vitruvius 5, 1, 6; Keppie 1983, 154–5.
38. Duncan-Jones 1985, 29.
39. Richmond 1969; see also *Archeologia in Val d'Aosta* (Aosta 1982).
40. Ward-Perkins, J. B. 1981, 97f.; Ling 1985.
41. Blake, M. E. 1947, 1959; Blake, M. E. and Taylor Bishop 1973; Lugli 1957; Sear 1982, 69f.
42. Coarelli 1977.
43. Sherwin-White 1973, 165f.
44. Potter 1979.
45. Ruoff-Väänänen 1978.
46. Keppie (1983, 73f., 112f.) provides much detail on these and other projects.
47. D'Arms 1970, 79f.
48. Ward-Perkins, J. B. 1981, 45–96, 121–40, 415–40, provides the handiest summary.
49. Duncan-Jones 1982; Ward-Perkins, B. 1984.
50. Duncan-Jones 1982.
51. *CIL* XI, 5400; *CIL* XI, 3805; *CIL* X, 846 (Catalogue, *Pompeii* 79, no. 15 (1976).
52. Brunt 1971.
53. Hönle and Henze 1981.
54. Hanson 1959; Rawson 1985; Gros 1978.
55. Maiuri 1933; Ling 1984.
56. Rodriguez-Almeida 1981.
57. Ward-Perkins, J. B. 1981, 204f.
58. Bloch 1947; Helen 1975.
59. *Noctes Atticae* 15, 1, 1–3; Suetonius, *Nero* 38.
60. Ward-Perkins, J. B. 1981, 192.
61. Meiggs 1973, 244f.
62. *CIL* IV, 138.
63. On markets generally, De Ruyt 1983.
64. Ward-Perkins, J. B. 1981, 89–94.
65. For northern Etruria: Mansuelli 1979, 368f; for Bolsena: Gros 1981; for the Via Traiana Nova, W. V. Harris in *PBSR* 33 (1965), 113–33; for Vulci: Carandini (ed.) 1985.
66. Specialised works on the *cuatores* include G. Camodeca, 'Ricerche sui cuatores rei publicae,' *ANRW* II. 13 (1980), 453–534; and F. Jaques, *Les curateurs des cités dans l'Occident romain de Trajan à Gallien* (Paris 1984).
67. For Ostia see particularly Carandini 1983; see also Chapter 7.
68. Jones, A. H. M. 1964, 782f., 871.

4 Cities and urbanisation

1. Nissen 1883, 1902, and various works by Beloch (especially 1880) still remain basic. Beloch (1880, Ch. 1) lists 434 towns.
2. Particularly in the north of Italy: see for example Brogiolo 1983, 1984.
3. Aristotle, *Politics* 7, 1330b, 21f. For Hippodamus, see particularly Castagnoli 1972, 65–72.
4. Castagnoli 1972; Ward-Perkins, J. B. 1974; Boëthius 1978, 64f.
5. Very well illustrated by the site of Ficana (Catalogue 1980); see also Catalogue 1976 and Quilici 1977.
6. Cristofani 1979, 17f. contains a helpful discussion.
7. Marzabotto: Mansuelli 1972; 1979, 368f. Spina: Uggeri and Uggeri 1974.
8. For Rome, Nash 1968 and Coarelli 1980 provide convenient summaries; see also Scullard 1967, 267f.
9. Meiggs 1973, 20f.
10. Sherwin-White 1973.
11. Ardea is an example: Boëthius 1978, 103–4, and also in *Opuscula Romana* 4 (1962), 29f.
12. Harris 1971.
13. Appian, *Bellum Civile* 1, 7. Early Roman colonies are most usefully discussed by Salmon 1969, 1982.
14. Livy 6, 9, 4; Frederiksen and Ward-Perkins 1957, 89f.
15. Cf. Salmon 1969, 67f. for discussion of this point.
16. Alba Fucens: Mertens 1969, 1981; Cosa: Brown, F. E. 1980 and also in *MAAR* 20 (1950), and 26 (1960).
17. Brown, F. E. 1980, 15f.
18. Carandini *et al.* 1985; Carandini (ed.) 1985.
19. Sestieri 1967; Castagnoli 1972, 132. For the 'Comitium', E. Greco and D. Theodorescu, *Poseidonia-Paestum I, la 'curia'* (Rome, 1980).
20. Classical patronage is excellently dealt with in Ward-Perkins, B. 1984.
21. Crawford and Keppie 1984, 1985 for recent work and a survey of the site's history and topography.
22. Salmon 1969, 70f.
23. Livy 39, 22, 6; 40, 34, 2.
24. *Antichità Altoadriatiche* I, II, III (1972), IV (1973); Tavano 1984.
25. Frova 1973, 1977, usefully summarised in Siena *et al.* 1985.
26. Strabo 5, 2, 5; Pliny (*Nat. Hist.* 14, 8, 68) thought the wine was the best of Etruria.
27. Cf. Salmon 1969, 72 on the smallness of the land allocations to citizen colonists.
28. At Fabrateria Nova, modern La Civita near Falvaterra; Livy 41, 8, 8.

5 Villas, farms and the countryside

1. Hadrian's Villa: Aurigemma 1962; Grotta di Catullo: Ward-Perkins, J. B. 1981, 206f.; Villa Jovis: Maiuri 1956, 29–56; Oplontis: De Vos 1982, 250–4; C. Malandrino, *Oplontis* (1978), Jashemski 1979, 289f.
2. Strabo 5, 4, 8; see D'Arms 1970, McKay 1975, 114f.
3. De Vos 1982, 322–6.
4. The painting is widely illustrated: e.g. Rostovtzeff 1957, pl. VIII, McKay 1975, fig. 48.
5. Rostovtzeff 1957, 564f. (1st edn 1926, 503f.); Carrington 1931, 130.
6. *CIL* IV, 6867; Carrington 1931, 122.
7. Plutarch, *Tiberius Gracchus* 8; Gragnano: *Not. Scav.* 1923, 275–80; White 1970, 437f.
8. *Monumenti Antichi* 7 (1897), 398; White 1970, 422. It is also described by De Vos 1982, 242 (although the site is destroyed).
9. White 1970, 14f. Recent work in the vicinity of Pompeii is summarised in Kockel *et al.* 1985.

10. Appian, *Bellum Civile* 1, 7. Carandini 1973; Carandini and Settis 1979; Carandini *et al.* 1985; Rathbone 1983.

11. Toynbee, A. J. 1965; Brunt 1971, 269f.

12. Carandini 1973; Giardina and Schiavone 1981 contains many essays of particular relevance.

13. Garnsey 1979, 1981.

14. Bradford and Williams-Hunt 1946; Bradford 1949, 1957; Jones, G. D. B. 1980.

15. Dilke 1971; Bussi 1983.

16. Jones, G. D. B. 1980 describes the excavation of these traces.

17. P. Fraccaro was an early pioneer in this work (e.g. *Studi Etruschi* 13 (1939), 221f.). See now Tozzi 1972, 1974; Bussi 1983.

18. Schmiedt 1970; Barker 1985.

19. See, for example, Ashby 1927.

20. Potter 1979; Barker 1985.

21. Ward-Perkins, J. B. in Cotton 1979, 1.

22. Cotton 1979; Cotton and Métraux 1985.

23. Monte Forco: Jones, G. B. D. 1963, 147–58; Villa of the Volusii: Moretti and Moretti 1977 and now M. Taliaferro Boatwright *et al.*, *I Volusii Saturnini: una famiglia romana della prima età imperiale* (Bari 1982).

24. See King in Carandini *et al.* 1985 and, with a list of sites, in T. F. C. Blagg and A. C. King (eds.), *Military and civilian in Roman Britain* (1984), 201 (where he demonstrates a dietary preference in Italy for pig-meat, unlike northern Europe).

25. See Carandini (ed.) 1985; Fentress 1984; Attolini *et al.* 1982, 1983.

26. Carandini (ed.) 1985, 106f.

27. Carandini *et al.* 1985; the other villas are known as delle Colonne and della Provinca.

28. Jashemski 1979; MacDougall and Jashemski 1981.

29. Manacorda 1978. See also Rathbone 1981 and Paterson 1982, 148; also Purcell 1985.

30. Cotton 1979; Cotton and Métraux 1985.

31. See further Chapter 7.

32. Horace, *Carm.* 3, 5, 53–6; Tacitus, *Annals* 14, 27; Keppie 1984a, 82f.

33. Discussed especially in Arthur 1985.

34. Adamesteanu 1973.

35. Rossiter 1978.

36. Carter 1983, 1985.

37. Small 1977, especially 100–1.

38. Potter 1979.

39. Jones, G. D. B. 1963, 147–58.

40. Potter and Dunbabin 1979.

41. Potter 1979; Guzzo 1970.

42. Moretti and Moretti 1977.

43. Garnsey 1979, 1980; Duncan-Jones 1976, 15f.

44. A preliminary report on the Montarrente survey is published in *Archeologia Medievale* 11 (1984), 255f.

45. Attolini *et al.* 1982, 1983; Carandini (ed.) 1985.

46. Widrig 1980.

47. Barker, Lloyd and Webley 1978; Lloyd and Barker 1981.

48. Barker 1981; Gabba and Pasquinucci 1979.

49. Moeller 1976; Frayn 1984.

50. And thus implying that there was shared common land.

51. Dilke 1971; Bussi 1983.

52. Brunt 1971.

53. Bradford 1957; Jones, G. D. B. 1980 and forthcoming.

54. Strabo 5, 1, 12; Pliny, *Nat. Hist.* 18, 25.

55. Tozzi 1974.

56. Bussi 1983a.

57. Mansuelli 1962; Tabanelli 1980, 124f.

58. Velleia: Aurigemma 1940; Calvani 1984. The *alimenta*: Duncan-Jones 1964; 1982, 288f.

59. Tacitus, *Annals* 14, 27; Cicero, *de leg. agr.* 2, 28, 78.

6 Roads, aqueducts and canals

1. Procopius, *Gothic Wars* 5, 14, 9–11.

2. Sterpos 1970, 7.

3. Pliny, *Nat. Hist.* 3, 66; Chevallier 1976, 71–2.

4. Potter 1979, 79f.

5. Livy 9, 36, 1

6. Frederiksen and Ward-Perkins 1957, 73f. and 187f.

7. Castagnoli 1956; Horace, *Satires* 1, 5.

8. See Casson 1974.

9. For the high cost of land transport, as measured by Diocletian's Price Edict, see Duncan-Jones 1982, 366f.; but see K. Hopkins in P. Abrams and E. A. Wrigley (eds), *Towns in societies: essays in economic history* (1978), 35–77.

10. Diodorus 20, 36.

11. Livy 10, 47, 4.

12. Strabo 5, 3, 9.

13. Ashby and Fell 1921; Martinori 1929; Ballance 1951.

14. CIL xi, 6106; Procopius, *Gothic Wars* 2, 11, 10–14; Ashby and Fell 1921, 185–6.

15. Vitruvius 5, 1, 6–10; Ashby and Fell 1921, 189.

16. Frederiksen and Ward-Perkins 1957, 187f.

17. Livy 41, 27, 5.

18. Wiseman 1970; Chevallier 1976, 134f.

19. Livy 39, 2.

20. Chilver 1941.

21. Martial 1, 103, 9; Ward-Perkins, J. B. 1961.

22. Chevallier 1976, 131, based on the Antonine Itinerary.

23. Appian, *Civil War* 1, 3, 23.

24. Dessau, *Inscriptiones Latinae Selectae* 5801.

25. Sterpos 1970, 111.

26. Kent 1978, catalogue no. 255; Pflaum 1940 for the postal service *(cursus publicus).*

27. Potter 1979, 106–7.

28. *Res Gestae* 20, 5.

29. Ballance 1951, 86–8, 91–7.

30. Cassius Dio 53, 2; for the Alpine roads, Pauli 1984, 208f.

31. Guzzo 1970.

32. Potter 1979, 106.

33. Potter 1979, 107f.

34. Statius, *Silv.* 4, 3; Maiuri 1958, 102–5.

35. Chevallier 1976, 28f. and his very full bibliography; also Dilke 1985, 112f.

36. Dilke 1985, 112–14.

37. Castagnoli *et al.* 1968.

38. Strabo 5, 3, 8; Pliny, *Nat. Hist.* 36, 24.

39. Ward-Perkins, J. B. 1955.

40. Ward-Perkins, J. B. 1962; Judson and Kahane 1963.

41. Frederiksen and Ward-Perkins 1957, 123f.

42. Uggeri and Uggeri 1974.

43. Ashby 1935; Van Deman 1934.

44. Vitruvius 8, 6, 1–9; Aqua Alexandriana: Ward-Perkins and Kahane 1972; for siphons, Hodge 1983.

45. Ward-Perkins, J. B. 1955, 117; CIL x, 5807.

46. Sear 1982, 23 and 38f. for a convenient discussion of baths and their origin and development.

47. Dudley 1966; Earl 1968, 102; Suetonius, *Augustus* 28, 3.

48. Brown, F. E. 1980, 11, 64.

49. Serino: D'Arms 1970, 79f.; Venafro: Keppie 1983, 138; Lucus Feroniae: Jones 1962, 197f.

50. Frontinus, *De Aquis Urbis Romae*; Garbrecht *et al.* 1982.

51. Ward-Perkins, B. 1984, 12n.

52. Ph. Leveau and J-L. Paillet, *L'alimentation en eau de Caesarea et Maurétanie et l'aqueduc de Cherchel* (Paris); Pliny the Younger discusses blunders in aqueduct building (10, 37, 39).

53. See the excellent discussion in Ward-Perkins, B. 1984, 119f., and 121 for the numbers of baths.

54. Meiggs 1973, 44. On water-wheels in general see J. P. Oleson, *Greek and Roman mechanical water-lifting devices* (1984).

55. Procopius, *Gothic Wars* 1, 8, 45; Rutilius, *De reditu* 249–76. On baths generally, Heinz 1983.

56. Ward-Perkins, B. 1984, 128; Ashby 1935, 15f.

57. Gregory, *Ep.* 13, 3.

58. Forbes 1955; Potter 1981. Both contain detailed bibliographies.

59. Diogenes Laertius 8, 59–60.

60. Uggeri and Uggeri 1974.

61. Suetonius, *Claudius* 20, 1–2; 21, 6.

62. Strabo 5, 3, 8.

63. *Liber Pontificalis* (ed. Duchesne), I, 512, 513.
64. Alban Lake: Livy 5, 15, 12; Rieti: Cicero, *Att.* 4, 15, 5.
65. River Clanis: Livy 28, 46, 5.
66. Strabo 5, 1, 11.
67. F. Barnabei, *Not. Scav.* 1915, 137–44.
68. Suetonius, *Nero* 31.
69 Tacitus, *Annals* 1, 79.

7 The balance of trade

1. Finley 1973, 69.
2. Brunt 1971, 121f.
3. Carcopino 1941, 65.
4. Frontinus, *De aquis urbis Romae*, 116; Ashby 1935, 24–5.
5. Toynbee, A. J. 1965, II, 1f.; Brunt 1971, 269f.
6. Strabo 14, 5, 2; see also F. Coarelli *et al.*, *Delo e l'Italia* (1982), 150f.
7. Brunt 1971, 121f.
8. Potter 1979.
9. Bradford 1957, 156f.; Dilke 1971, 146f.
10. Manuals: see White 1970, 18–41; tools: White 1967; Carandini (ed.) 1985, 176f.
11. Varro 3, 2, 15.
12. Paterson 1982 and Purcell 1985 summarise much of the recent debate, with very full biliographies.
13. Apulia: Bradford 1957, Jones, G. D. B. 1980; Pompeii: Jashemski 1979; see also Rossiter 1978, 49f. and Purcell 1985, 7–8.
14. There is a huge bibliography, very usefully summarised by Paterson 1982. See also Sealey 1985, Peacock and Williams 1986, and also J. Riley in J. A. Lloyd (ed.), *Excavations at Sidi-Krebish (Benghazi)*, vol. II (1979), 91–467.
15. Dressel's two main publications, apart from *CIL* XV, were on Monte Testaccio (*Ann. dell'Instit. di Corrispondenza Archeologica* (1878), 118f.: see now Rodriguez-Almeida 1984) and on a deposit from Castro Pretorio, Rome (*Bull. della Comm. arch. com. di Roma* (1879), 36f and 143f.) See also Panella 1981 and her reports on Ostia in Carandini 1970, 1973.
16. E.g. Panella 1981 and Carandini and Settis 1979, pannello 39.
17. Lamboglia 1952.
18. Tchernia *et al.* 1978.
19. Morel 1981 is the most recent major publication, with a full bibliography.
20. Lequément and Liou 1975; Goudineau 1983, 80f.
21. Opimian: Pliny, *Nat. Hist.* 14, 55–7.
22. Duncan-Jones 1982, Ch. 2; but see Purcell 1985, 3–4 on the dangers of investing in vines.
23. Sealey 1985, 23f.
24. Frederiksen 1984, 72–3 discusses the whole question of gift exchange.
25. Tchernia 1983 gathers the evidence together.
26. Carandini and Settis 1979; Carandini 1980; Carandini *et al.* 1985.
27. Manacorda 1978; Paterson 1982, 148.
28. Cherchel: J. A. Riley in Benseddik and Potter, supplement of the *Bulletin d'Archéologie Algérienne*, forthcoming; Britain: Sealey 1985, *inter alia*, on imports into south-east England.
29. Tchernia 1983; Diodorus 5, 26, 3.
30. Tchernia 1983, 99.
31. Tchernia 1983, 95f.
32. Crawford 1969.
33. MacMullen 1970; Peacock 1982, 156f.
34. King 1983 is a succinct summary, with a good bibliography. For black-glaze see Morel 1981; and for this and other pottery, a series of articles by Morel, Pucci, Ricci and Pavolini in Giardina and Schiavone 1981, vol. II.
35. See the articles by Carandini and Morel in Giardina and Schiavone 1981, vol. II.
36. Henig 1983; Sealey 1985, 39f. for Dressel 2–4 amphorae.
37. Pucci 1973, 1981; Hopkins 1978; for other Italian centres, Kenrick 1978.
38. For Dressel 6 amphorae see Paterson 1982, 153f. Senatorial involvement in commerce is much discussed: see, *inter alia*, D'Arms 1980, 1981; Paterson 1982, 154f.
39. Pliny, *Nat. Hist.* 13, 29–31.
40. See Bailey 1976, 1980; Harris 1980. For the wreck in the Balearics, C. Domergue in *Mélanges de la Casa de Velazquez* II (1966), 5–40.
41. Price 1976, 1983; Petronius, *Satyricon* 50, 7. For the Portland Vase, D. E. L. Haynes, *The Portland Vase* (London 1975).
42. Ward-Perkins, J. B. 1980; 1980a; 1981, 43f.
43. Discussed at length by numerous authors in Giardina and Schiavone 1981, vol. II. See also Frank 1940; Cotton and Métraux 1985, 66f.; Cuomo di Caprio 1979.
44. Rickman 1980, 1980a. The word *annona* should not be confused with the *annona militaris*, the tax in kind first levied in Italy (and elsewhere) in the third century AD.
45 Tacitus, *Annals* 15, 18, 3.
46. For the harbours, Meiggs 1973, 54f. Whatever the city's status in the fourth century, there were still some splendid residences at Ostia: Meiggs 1973, 255f.
47. Meiggs 1973, 283f.
48. Rodriguez-Almeida 1984.
49. Rickman 1980.
50. D. Atkinson in *JRS* 4 (1914), 27–64.
51. Sealey 1985, 131f.
52. Hayes 1972.
53. Detailed reports in Carandini *et al.* 1968, 1970, 1973, 1977; see also Carandini 1983.
54. Cato, *Agr.* 57; Purcell 1985, 13.
55. Rathbone 1983.
56. Hopkins 1980.

8 Gods and their temples

1. Ogilvie 1969, 85.
2. Livy 44, 1, 2.
3. Ovid, *Letters from Pontus* 4, 2, 25f.; for the festivals, Warde-Fowler 1899, and now Scullard 1981.
4. Augustine, *City of God* 4, 26.
5. Virgil, *Georgics* 1, 388f.
6. *Res Gestae* 8.
7. *CIL* IX, 4672.
8. Poultney 1959.
9. Salmon 1967, 156f.
10. Blagg 1983, 1985 provide convenient summaries.
11. Strabo 5, 3, 12.
12. Livy 1, 45, 2.
13. Ovid, *Fasti* 3, 268–9.
14. Tilley 1947; Alfoldi 1965; Castagnoli 1972a, and especially *Enea nel Lazio* (Catalogue 1981).
15. See particularly Banti 1973, 206f.
16. Tacitus, *Annals* 11, 15.
17. Gjerstadt 1960, 168f.
18. Dionysius of Halicarnassus 4, 61.
19. See, *inter alia*, Macdonald 1982, 94–121.
20. Brown, F. E. 1980.
21. Vitruvius 1, 7.
22. Livy 10, 47.
23. Potter 1985.
24. Ferguson 1970, 67.
25. Dyggve 1960; Tomlinson 1976 for a general survey of Greek sanctuaries.
26. Boëthius 1978, 165f. provides a useful summary; see also Hanson 1959 and Almagro-Gorbea 1982.
27. Grant 1971 gives a very adequate summary of Pompeii; for Ostia, Meiggs 1973.
28. Horace, *Odes* 3, 6, 1; *Res Gestae* 20, 4.
29. See Propertius 4, 6, 36.
30. Suetonius, *Julius Caesar* 88.
31. Dio 55, 10.
32. Seneca, *Apocolocyntosis* (*The Pumpkinification of Claudius*).
33. See Ward-Perkins, J. B. 1981, 51 for an Iseum of *c.* 20 BC on the Palatine Hill in Rome.
34. Suetonius, *Otho* 12, *Domitian* 1.

35. *CIL* I, 196.
36. Petronius, *Sat.* 35.
37. Ferguson 1970, 53–4, citing *The Augustan History*, 18.

9 Later Roman Italy and the rise of Christianity

1. Lactantius, *Divinae Institutiones* 7, 25.
2. Ammianus Marcellinus 14, 6, 3.
3. Birley 1971, 290 discusses the question.
4. See Watson 1969, 16f. for these units.
5. Dio 76, 16, 1–4. For a full list of buildings see Ward-Perkins, J. B. 1981, 126f.
6. Duncan-Jones 1982, 356.
7. *The Augustan History*, *Sept. Sev.* 8, 5; Meiggs 1973, 80f.; Rickman 1980.
8. Lanuvium: *CIL* XIV, 2101; Verona: *CIL* V, 3342; P. Giannini, *Ferento* (1971).
9. Potter and Dunbabin 1979.
10. Herodian 8, 2, 3–5.
11. Purcell 1985.
12. *The Augustan History*, *Sept. Sev.* 8, 5; 18, 3; 23, 2.
13. Richmond 1930, Todd 1978.
14. Usefully summarised by Johnson 1983, 215f.
15. Cf. for example Mannoni and Poleggi 1977, Hudson and La Rocca Hudson 1985, amongst many recent publications.
16. For Ordona, see especially Mertens 1976, 1979. Horace's journey is discussed in Chapter 6.
17. Some scholars paint a more pessimistic picture: e.g. Williams 1985.
18. See Williams 1985, 36f. for a splendid impression of Diocletian's elevation to imperial power.
19. MacMullen 1976, 207.
20. This, however, applied only to the diocese of Italy. The number of provinces (known as districts) is not certain due to imperfections on the Verona manuscript, discussed, *inter alia*, by J. B. Bury in *JRS* 13 (1923), 127f., and by A. H. M. Jones in *JRS* 44 (1954), 21f.
21. Krautheimer 1983, 69–92, provides a useful summary.
22. Ward-Perkins, J. B. 1981, 421.
23. *De Pretiis*, cited in Tenney Frank 1940, 307f.
24. Helpfully discussed in Kent 1978, 44f.
25. Williams 1985, 168.
26. Williams 1985, 169.
27. Ashby 1927, 249. MacMullen's *Constantine* (1969) is a helpful introduction.
28. Brown, P. 1971.
29. MacMullen 1969, *inter alia*.
30. Jerome, *c. Joh. Hierosol.*, 8, cited by Jones, A. H. M. 1964, 151.
31. Jones, A. H. M 1964, 894f.
32. Ammianus Marcellinus 19, 10, 4. See Ward-Perkins B., 1984, 85f., for the gradual end of the pagan temples.
33. Krautheimer 1983, 93f.
34. Variously considered by Krautheimer (1980, 1981, 1983); the major corpus is Krautheimer *et. al.*, *Corpus Basilicarum Christianarum Romae* (5 vols, Vatican City 1937–7).
35. Ausonius, *Ordo urbium nobilium* 7.
36. Ward-Perkins, B. 1984, 52, provides a list of excavated or standing churches in Italy of this period, though it is inevitably far from complete. Most major towns became the seat of an episcopal see.
37. Jerome, *Comm. in Ezech.* 1, praef.
38. Wilson 1983; Ward-Perkins, J. B. 1981, 464–5.
39. Jones, A. H. M. 1964, 871; Brown, P. 1971, 34.
40. Jones, A. H. M. 1964, 782, 794.
41. Symmachus, *Ep.* 1, 3.
42. Jones, A. H. M. 1964, 784. The *Liber Pontificalis* is edited by L. Duchesne (Paris and Rome 1886).
43. Sidonius Apollinaris, *Ep.* 1, 5. Ravenna has a large bibliography and its own journal, *Felix Ravenna*; Krautheimer 1981, 192–8 is a convenient summary; also Cagiano de Azevedo 1977.
44. Krautheimer 1981, 248.

10 Aftermath: from Roman to medieval

1. Wickham 1981, 14.
2. Ennodius, *Ep.* 9, 23.
3. Pavia: Bullough 1966; Verona: Hudson and La Rocca Hudson 1985.
4. Luni: Ward-Perkins, B. 1978; 1981.
5. Brick-stamps: *CIL* XV, 1663–70. Krautheimer 1980, 65f. is a most useful summary; see also Cassiodorus, *Letters* 29 and, for the size of the population, Hodges and Whitehouse 1983, 51 and Krautheimer 1980, 65.
6. Whitehouse, D. B. *et al.* 1982; 1985.
7. Pharr 1952, *Theodosian Code* 14.3; 14.4; 14.7.
8. Ward-Perkins, B. 1978.
9. Walls: *CIL* X, 1485; Arthur 1985.
10. Potter 1979, 140.
11. Potter, *An archaeological survey of the central and southern Ager Faliscus* (forthcoming).
12 Widrig 1980, 129f.; Potter 1985.
13. Attolini *et al.* 1982, 1983.
14. Small 1980, 1985; Whitehouse 1981.
15. Procopius, *Wars* 6, 20; Wickham 1981, 27.
16. Bullough 1966.
17. Hodges *et al.* 1985.
18. Hodges *et al.* 1984.
19. Hodges *et al.* 1980.
20. Brown, T. S. 1978, 330.
21. Procopius, *Wars* 1, 14–21.
22. Bullough 1965.
23. Pringle, D., *The defence of Byzantine Africa*, BAR, International Series 99 (1981), is an excellent study.
24. Brown, T. S. 1978, 330; *idem* 1984, 39f.
25. Wickham 1985, 165. See also Wickham 1979, 76f.; *idem* 1981, 163f.; Toubert 1973.
26. Brown, T. S. 1978, 326.
27 Whitehouse, D. B. and Potter 1981; Whitehouse, D. B. *et al.* 1985.
28. Potter *et al.* 1984.
29. Brown, T. S. 1984, 45.
30. Krautheimer 1981, 109.
31. Llewellyn 1971, 157.
32. Hodges and Whitehouse (1983) discuss the new networks that emerged; see also Whittaker 1983.
33. Llewellyn 1971, 243.
34. Partner 1966.
35. Potter 1979, 152f. summarises Capracorum; a definitive report on the whole site is anticipated.
36. Hudson and La Rocca Hudson 1985.
37. Ward-Perkins, B. 1978; *idem* 1981.
38. Ward-Perkins, B. 1981, 97; Dabrowska *et al.* 1978–9; Potter 1979, 161f. and in *Archeologia Medievale* 7 (1980), 437.

Bibliography

Preference has been given in this bibliography to more recent books and articles in English, but inevitably a good many works in other languages, particularly Italian, have had to be listed. It has, of course, been necessary to omit many references of importance (they would take a book in themselves); but the titles that are cited should provide a sufficiency of leads.

There are a number of standard archaeological source books for individual sites and regions. Amongst them are the *Enciclopedia dell'Arte antica, classica e orientale* (1958–66 and supplements); the *Princeton Encyclopedia of classical sites* (ed. R. Stillwell, 1976); and, amongst many useful atlases, T. J. Cornell and J. Matthews, *Atlas of the Roman world* (1982) and R. J. A. Talbert (ed.), *Atlas of classical history* (1985). The ancient sources are generally available in the Loeb Classical Library, and, selectively, in the Penguin Classics.

Abbreviations

ANRW	*Aufstieg und Niedergang der römischen Welt*
BAR	British Archaeological Reports
CIL	*Corpus Inscriptionum Latinarum*
EAA	*Enciclopedia dell'Arte antica, classica e orientale*
JBAA	*Journal of the British Archaeological Association*
JRS	*Journal of Roman Studies*
MAAR	*Memoirs of the American Academy at Rome*
Not. Scav	*Notizie degli scavi di antichità*
PBSR	*Papers of the British School at Rome*

ADAMESTEANU, D. 1973. 'La suddivisione di terra di Metaponto', in M. Finley (ed.), *Problèmes de la terre en Grèce ancienne* (Paris), 49–61.

ADAMESTEANU, D. 1974. *La Basilicata antica* (Cava dei Tirreni).

ADMIRALTY HANDBOOKS 1944–5. *Italy*. British Naval Intelligence Division, 4 vols.

ALFOLDI, A. 1965. *Early Rome and the Latins* (Ann Arbor).

ALMAGRO-GORBEA, M. 1982. *El santuario de Juno en Gabii* (Rome).

ARTHUR, P. 1985. 'Naples: notes on the economy of a Dark Age city', in Malone and Stoddart 1985, vol. 4, 247–60.

ASHBY, T. 1927. *The Roman Campagna in classical times* (1970 reprint, Tonbridge).

ASHBY, T. 1935. *The aqueducts of ancient Rome* (Oxford).

ASHBY, T. and FELL, R. A. L. 1921. 'The Via Flaminia', *JRS* 11, 125–90.

ATTOLINI, I. *et al.* 1982, 1983. 'Ricognizione archeologica dell'Ager Cosanus e nella valle dell' Albegna', *Archeologia Medievale* 9, 365–86; 10, 439–65.

AURIGEMMA, S. 1940. *Velleia* (Rome).

AURIGEMMA, S. 1962. *Villa Adriana* (Rome).

BAILEY, D. M. 1976. 'Pottery lamps', in D. Strong and D. Brown (eds), *Roman Crafts* (London), 93–104.

BAILEY, D. M. 1980. *Catalogue of lamps in the British Museum.* II: *Roman lamps made in Italy* (London).

BALLANCE, M. H. 1951. 'The Roman bridges of the Via Flaminia', *PBSR* 19, 78–117.

BANTI, L. 1973. *The Etruscan cities and their culture* (London).

BARFIELD, L. H. 1971. *Northern Italy before Rome* (London).

BARK, L. G. 1932. 'Bee-hive dwellings in Apulia', *Antiquity* 6, 407–10.

BARKER, G. W. W. 1977. 'The archaeology of Samnite settlement in Molise', *Antiquity* 51, 20–4.

BARKER, G. W. W. 1981. *Landscape and society. Prehistoric central Italy* (London).

BARKER, G. W. W. 1985. 'Landscape archaeology in Italy', in Malone and Stoddart 1985, vol. 1, 1–20.

BARKER, G. W. W. and HODGES, R. (eds) 1981. *Archaeology and Italian society.* BAR S 102 (Oxford).

BARKER, G. W. W., LLOYD, J. and WEBLEY, D. 1978. 'A classical landscape in Molise', *PBSR* 46, 35–51.

BARTON, I. M. 1981. 'Capitoline temples in Italy and the empire', *ANRW* 2, 12, 1, 259–342.

BEARD, M. and CRAWFORD, M. H. 1984. *Rome in the late Republic* (London).

BELOCH, J. 1880. *Der italische Bund unter Roms Hegemonie* (Leipzig).

BENOIT, F. 1961. *L'épave du Grand Congloué à Marseilles.* Gallia supplement 14 (Paris).

BIANCHI BANDINELLI, R. and GIULIANO, A. 1973. *Etruschi e Italici prima del dominio di Roma* (Milan).

BIERBRAUEN, V. 1975. *Die ostgotischen Grab- und Schatzfunde in Italien* (Spoleto).

BIRLEY, A. R. 1971. *Septimius Severus. The African emperor* (London).

BLAGG, T. F. C. 1983. *Mysteries of Diana. The antiquities from Nemi in Nottingham Museum* (Nottingham).

BLAGG, T. F. C. 1985. 'Cult practice and its social context in the religious sanctuaries of Latium and southern Etruria', in Malone and Stoddart 1985, vol. 4, 33–50.

BLAKE, H. M. 1978. 'Medieval pottery: technical innovation or economic change?', in Blake, Potter and Whitehouse 1978, 435–73.

BLAKE, H. M., POTTER, T. W. and WHITEHOUSE, D. B. (eds) 1978. *Papers in Italian archaeology I: the Lancaster seminar.* BAR S 41 (Oxford).

BLAKE, M. E. 1947. *Ancient Roman construction in Italy from the prehistoric period to Augustus* (Washington).

BLAKE, M. E. 1959. *Roman construction in Italy from Tiberius through the Flavians* (Washington).

BLAKE, M. E. and TAYLOR BISHOP, D. 1973. *Roman construction in Italy from Nerva through the Antonines* (Philadelphia).

BLOCH, H. 1947. *I bolli laterizi e la storia dell'edilizia romana* (Rome).

BOARDMAN, J. 1980. *The Greeks overseas* (3rd edn, London).

BOERSMA, J. 1985. *Amoenissima civitas. Block V. ii at Ostia: description and analysis of its visible remains* (Assen).

BOËTHIUS, A. 1978. *Etruscan and early Roman architecture* (Harmondsworth).

BOGNETTI, G. P. 1966–8. *L'età longobarda*, 4 vols (Milan).

BRADFORD, J. S. P. 1949. '"Buried landscapes" in southern Italy', *Antiquity* 23, 58–72.

BRADFORD, J. S. P. 1957. *Ancient landscapes* (London).

BRADFORD, J. S. P. and WILLIAMS-HUNT, P. R. 1946. 'Siticulosa Apulia', *Antiquity* 20, 191–200.

BROGIOLO, G. P. 1983, 1984. *Notiziario.* Soprintendenza archeologica della Lombardia (Brescia).

BROUGHTON, T. R. S. 1960. *The magistrates of the Roman Republic* (New York).

BROWN, F. E. 1980. *Cosa: the making of a Roman town* (Ann Arbor).

BROWN, P. 1971. *The world of late antiquity* (London).

BROWN, T. S. 1978. 'Settlement and military policy in Byzantine Italy', in Blake, Potter and Whitehouse 1978, 323–38.

BROWN, T. S. 1984. *Gentlemen and officers. Imperial administration and aristocratic power in Byzantine Italy* (London).

BRUNT, P. A. 1971 *Italian manpower, 225 BC–AD 14* (Oxford).

BRUNT, P. A. 1971a *Social conflicts in the Roman Republic* (London).

BULLOUGH, D. A. 1965. 'La Via Flaminia nella storia dell'Umbria (600–1100)', in *Aspetti dell'Umbria dall'inizio del secolo VIII alla fine del secolo XI.* Atti del terzo Convegno di Studi Umbri (Perugia).

BULLOUGH, D. A. 1965a. 'The Ostrogothic and Lombard kingdoms', in D. Talbot Rice (ed.), *The Dark Ages* (London), 167–74.

BULLOUGH, D. A. 1966. 'Urban change in early medieval Italy: the example of Pavia', *PBSR* 34, 82–131.

BULLOUGH, D. A. 1968. *Italy and her invaders* (Nottingham).

BULLOUGH, D. A. 1973. 'Social and economic structure and topography in the early medieval city', *Settimane di Studio di Spoleto* 21, 351–99.

BUSSI, R. (ed.) 1983. *Misurare la terra: centuriazione e coloni nel mondo romano* (Modena).

BUSSI, R. (ed.) 1983a. *Misurare la terra: centuriazione e coloni nel mondo romano: il caso modenese* (Modena).

CAGIANO DE AZEVEDO, M. 1977. 'Northern Italy', in M. W. Barley (ed.), *European towns. Their archaeology and history* (London), 475–85.

CALLENDER, M. H. 1965. *Roman amphorae, with an index of stamps* (London).

CALVANI, M. M. 1984. *Lugagnano, Val d'Arda, Veleia* (Parma).

CARANDINI, A. 1973. 'Dibattito sull'edizione italiana della "Storia economica del mondo antico" di F. Heichelheim', *Dialoghi di Archeologia* 7, 312–29.

CARANDINI, A. 1980. 'Il vigneto e la villa del fondo di Settefinestre nel Cosano: un caso di produzione agricola per il mercato transmarino', in D'Arms and Kopff 1980, 1–10.

CARANDINI, A. 1983. 'Pottery and the African economy', in Garnsey et al. 1983, 145–62.

CARANDINI, A. and SETTIS, S. 1979. *Schiavi e padroni nell'Etruria romana. La villa di Settefinestre dallo scavo alla mostra* (Bari).

CARANDINI, A. (ed.) 1985. *La romanizzazione dell'Etruria: il territorio di Vulci* (Milan).

CARANDINI, A. et al. 1968, 1970, 1973, 1977. *Ostia I, II, III, IV.* Studi Miscellanei 13, 16, 21, 23.

CARANDINI, A. et al. 1985. *Settefinestre. Una villa schiavistica nell'Etruria romana,* 3 vols (Modena).

CARCOPINO, J. 1941 *Daily life in ancient Rome* (1973 reprint, Harmondsworth).

CARETTONI, G. et al. 1960. *La pianta marmorea di Roma antica* (Roma).

CARRINGTON, R. C. 1931. 'Studies in the Campanian villae rusticae', *JRS* 21, 110–30.

CARTER, J. C. 1983. *The territory of Metaponto* (University of Texas).

CARTER, J. C. et al. 1985. 'Population and agriculture: Magna Grecia in the fourth century BC', in Malone and Stoddart 1985, vol. 1, 281–312.

CARY, M. 1949. *The geographic background of Greek and Roman history* (Oxford).

CASSON, L. 1971. *Ships and seamanship in the ancient world* (Princeton).

CASSON, L. 1974. *Travel in the ancient world* (London).

CASTAGNOLI, F. 1956. *Via Appia* (Milan).

CASTAGNOLI, F. 1958. *Le ricerche sui resti della centuriazione* (Rome).

CASTAGNOLI, F. 1972. *Orthogonal planning in antiquity* (Cambridge, Mass.).

CASTAGNOLI, F. 1972a. *Lavinium I* (Rome).

CASTAGNOLI, F. et al. 1968. *La Via Aurelia* (Rome).

CATALOGUE 1976. *Civiltà del Lazio primitivo* (Rome).

CATALOGUE 1980. *Ficana* (Rome).

CATALOGUE 1981. *Enea nel Lazio: archeologia e mito* (Rome).

CHEVALLIER, R. 1976. *Roman roads* (London).

CHEVALLIER, R. 1980, 1983. *La romanisation de la Celtique du Pô* (2 vols, Paris).

CHILVER, G.E.F. 1941. *Cisalpine Gaul* (Oxford).

CIANFARANI, V. 1970. *Culture adriatiche d'Italia* (Rome).

COARELLI, F. 1977. 'Public buildings in Rome between the Second Punic War and Sulla', *PBSR* 45, 1–23.

COARELLI, F. 1980. *Roma* (Milan).

COARELLI, F. 1983. *Il foro romano, periodo arcaico* (Rome).

COARELLI, F. et al. 1974. *Etruscan cities* (London).

COLONNA, G. (ed.) 1981. *Gli Etruschi e Roma* (Rome).

CONGRESS 1970. *Studi sulla città antica.* Atti del Convegno sulla città etrusca e italica preromana (Bologna).

CORBIER, M. 1983. 'Fiscus and patrimonium: the Saepinum inscription and transhumance in the Abruzzi', *JRS* 73, 126–31.

CORNELL, T. J. 1980 'Rome and Latium vetus', *Journal of Hellenic Studies* 100, 71–89.

COTTON, M. A. 1979. *The late Republican villa at Posto, Francolise* (London).

COTTON, M. A. and MÉTRAUX G. 1985. *The San Rocco villa at Francolise* (London).

CRAWFORD, M. H. 1969. 'Coin hoards and the pattern of violence in the late Republic', *PBSR* 37, 76–81.

CRAWFORD, M. H. 1974. *Roman Republican coinage* (Cambridge).

CRAWFORD, M. H. 1978. *The Roman Republic* (Glasgow).

CRAWFORD, M. H., KEPPIE, L. J. F., et al. 1984, 1985. 'Excavations at Fregellae', *PBSR* 52, 21–35; 53, 72–96.

CRAVEN, K. 1838. *Excursions in the Abruzzi* (London).

CRISTOFANI, M. 1979. *The Etruscans. A new investigation* (London).

CUOMO DI CAPRIO, N. 1979. 'Pottery- and tile-kilns in south Italy and Sicily', in A. McWhirr (ed.), *Roman brick and tile.* BAR S 68, 73–96.

DABROWSKA, M. et al. 1978–9.'Castelseprio: scavi diagnostici 1962–1963', *Sibrium* 14, 4–138.

D'ARMS, J. H. 1970. *Romans on the Bay of Naples* (Cambridge, Mass.).

D'ARMS, J. H. 1980.'Republican senators' involvement in commerce in the late Republic: some Ciceronian evidence', in D'Arms and Kopff 1980, 77–90.

D'ARMS, J. H. 1981. *Commerce and social standing in ancient Rome.* (Cambridge, Mass.).

D'ARMS, J. H. and KOPFF, E. C. (eds) 1980. *The seaborne commerce of ancient Rome: Studies in archaeology and history. MAAR* 36 (Rome).

DELANO-SMITH, C. 1979. *Western Mediterranean Europe. A historical geography of Italy, Spain and southern France since the Neolithic* (London).

DE RUYT, C. 1983. *Macellum: marché alimentaire des romains* (Louvain).

DE VOS, A. and M. 1982. *Pompei, Ercolano, Stabia.* Guide archeologiche Laterza (Rome and Bari).

DILKE, O. A. W. 1971. *The Roman land surveyors* (Newton Abbot).

DILKE, O. A. W. 1985. *Greek and Roman maps* (London).

DONVITO, A. 1982. *Monte Sannace: archeologia e storia di peuceta* (Fasano di Puglia).

DUDLEY, D. R. 1966. *Urbs Roma: a source book of classical texts on the city and its monuments* (London).

DUNCAN-JONES, R. P. 1964. 'The purpose and organisation of the alimenta', *PBSR* 32, 123–46.

DUNCAN-JONES, R. P. 1976. 'Some configurations of landholdings in the Roman empire', in Finley 1976, 7–33.

DUNCAN-JONES, R. P. 1982. *The economy of the Roman empire* (2nd edn, Cambridge).'

DUNCAN-JONES, R. P. 1985. 'Who paid for public buildings in Roman cities?' in Grew and Hobley 1985, 28–33.

DYGGVE, E. 1960. *Le sanctuaire d'Athana Lindia et l'architecture lindiènne* (Berlin, Copenhagen).

DYSON, S. L. 1983. *The Roman villas of Buccino.* BAR S 187.

DYSON, S. L. 1985. 'The villa of Buccino and the consumer model of Roman rural development', in Malone and Stoddart 1985, vol. 4, 67–84.

EARL, D. C. 1968. *The age of Augustus* (London).

FASOLO, F. and GULLINI, G. 1953. *Il santuario di Fortuna Primigenia a Palestrina* (Rome).

FENELLI, M. 1975. 'Contributo per lo studio del votivo anatomico', *Archeologia Classica* 27, 206–52.

FENTRESS, L. 1984. 'Via Aurelia, Via Aemilia', *PBSR* 52, 72–6.

FERGUSON, J. 1970. *The religions of the Roman empire* (London).

FÉVRIER, P-A. 1977. 'Towns in the western Mediterranean', in M. W. Barley (ed.), *European towns. Their archaeology and early history* (London), 315–42.

FINLEY, M. I. 1980. *Ancient slavery and modern ideology* (London).

FINLEY, M. I. 1985. *The ancient economy* (2nd edn, London).

FINLEY, M. I. (ed.) 1976. *Studies in Roman property* (Cambridge).

FORBES, R. J. *Irrigation and drainage. Studies in ancient technology, 2* (Leiden).

FRANK, T. 1933. *Rome and Italy of the Republic. An economic survey of ancient Rome, 1* (Baltimore).

FRANK, T. 1940. *Rome and Italy of the empire. An economic survey of ancient Rome, 5* (Baltimore).

FRAYN, J. M. 1979. *Subsistence farming in Roman Italy* (London).

FRAYN, J. M. 1984. *Sheep-rearing and the wool trade in Italy during the Roman period* (Liverpool).

FREDERIKSEN, M. W. 1976. 'Changes in the pattern of settlement', in Zanker, P. (ed.), *Hellenismus in Mittelitalien* (Groningen), 341–55.

FREDERIKSEN, M. W. 1984. *Campania* (London).

FREDERIKSEN, M. W. and WARD-PERKINS, J. B. 1957. 'The ancient road-systems of the central and northern Ager Faliscus', *PBSR* 25, 67–203.

FROVA, A. (ed.) 1973, 1977. *Scavi di Luni* I, II (Rome).

GABBA, E. 1977. *Republican Rome, the army and the allies* (Oxford).

GABBA, E. and PASQUINUCCI, M. 1979. *Strutture agrarie e allevamento transhumante nell'Italia romana* (III–I a.c.) (Pisa).

GARBRECHT, G. *et al.* 1982. *Sextus Iulius Frontinus, curator aquarum. Wasserversorgung im antiken Rom* (Munich and Vienna).

GARNSEY, P. D. A. 1979. 'Where did Italian peasants live?', *Proc. Cambs. Philological Society* 25, 1–15.

GARNSEY, P. D. A. 1980. *Non slave labour in the Graeco-Roman world*. Cambridge Philological Society (Cambridge).

GARNSEY, P. D. A., HOPKINS, K. and WHITTAKER, C. R. (eds) 1983. *Trade in the ancient economy* (London).

GARZETTI, A. 1974. *From Tiberius to the Antonines* (London).

GIARDINA, A. and SCHIAVONE, A. (eds) 1981. *Società romana e produzione schiavistica. 1: L'Italia: insediamenti e forme economiche. 2: Merci, mercati e scambi nel Mediterraneo. 3: Modelli etici, diritto e transformazione sociali* (Rome and Bari).

GIEROW, P. G. 1964, 1966. *The Iron Age cultures of Latium*. Skrifter utgivna av Svenska Institutet i Rom, 2 vols.

GJERSTAD, E. 1953–73. *Early Rome*, I–VI. Skrifter utgivna av Svenska Institutet i Rom.

GOUDINEAU, C. 1983. 'Marseilles, Rome and Gaul from the third to the first century BC', in Garnsey *et al.* 1983, 76–86.

GRANT, M. 1971. *Cities of Vesuvius: Pompeii and Herculaneum* (London).

GRANT, M. 1980. *The Etruscans* (London).

GRECO, A. P. 1982. *I Lucani* (Milan).

GROS, P. 1978. *Architecture et societé à Rome et en Italie centre-méridionale*. Collection Latomus, 158 (Brussels).

GROS, P. 1981. *Bolsena. Guide des fouilles* (Rome).

GREW, F. and HOBLEY, B. (eds) 1985. *Roman urban topography in Britain and the western empire* (London).

GUALTIERI, M., SALVATORE, A. and SMALL, A.(eds) 1983. *Lo scavo di San Giovanni di Ruoti ed il perido tardoantico in Basilicata* (Bari).

GUZZO, P. G. 1970. 'Sacrofano – ponte romana in località Fontana Nuova', *Not. Scav.*, 330–44.

GUZZO, P. G. 1982. *Le città scomparse della Magna Grecia* (Rome).

HANSON, J. A. 1959. *Roman theater-temples* (Princeton).

HARDIE, C. 1965. 'The origin and plan of Roman Florence', *JRS* 55, 122–40.

HARRIS, W. V. 1971. *Rome in Etruria and Umbria* (Oxford).

HARRIS, W. V. 1979. *War and imperialism in Republican Rome 327–70 BC* (Oxford).

HARRIS, W. V. 1980. 'Roman terracotta lamps: the organisation of an industry', *JRS* 70, 126–45.

HAYES, J. W. 1972. *Late Roman pottery* (London); *Supplement* (1980).

HEINZ, W. 1983. *Römische Thermen* (Munich).

HELEN, T. 1975. *Organisation of Roman brick production in the first and second centuries AD. An interpretation of Roman brick stamps* (Helsinki).

HENIG, M. (ed.) 1983. *A handbook of Roman art* (Oxford).

HESNARD, A. 1980. 'Un dépôt augustéen d'amphores à La Longarina, Ostie', in D'Arms and Kopff 1980, 141–56.

HEURGON, J. 1973. *The rise of Rome to 264 BC* (London).

HÖNLE, A. and HENZE, A. 1981. *Römische Amphitheater und Stadien*. Antike Welt 4.

HODGE, A. T. 1983. 'Siphons in Roman aqueducts', *PBSR* 51, 174–221.

HODGES, R. *et al.* 1980. 'Excavations at D 85 (Santa Maria in Cività): an early medieval hilltop settlement in Molise', *PBSR* 48, 70–124.

HODGES, R. *et al.* 1984. 'Excavations at Vacchereccia (Rocchetta Nuova): a later Roman and early medieval settlement in the Volturno valley, Molise', *PBSR* 52, 148–96.

HODGES, R. *et al.* 1985. 'San Vincenzo al Volturno, the Kingdom of Benevento and the Carolingians', in Malone and Stoddard 1985, vol. 4, 261–86.

HODGES, R. and WHITEHOUSE, D. B. 1983. *Mohammed, Charlemagne and the origins of Europe* (London).

HOPKINS, K. 1978. *Conquerors and slaves* (Cambridge).

HOPKINS, K. 1980. 'Taxes and trade in the Roman empire (200 BC–AD 400)', *JRS* 70, 101–25.

HUDSON, P. and LA ROCCA HUDSON, C. 1985. 'Lombard immigration and its effect upon north Italian rural and urban settlement', in Malone and Stoddart 1985, 225–46.

JASHEMSKI, W. F. 1979. *The gardens of Pompeii, Herculaneum and the villas destroyed by Vesuvius* (New Rochelle).

JASHEMSKI, W. F. 1981. 'The Campanian peristyle gardens', in MacDougall and Jashemski 1980, 29–48.

JOHNSON, S. 1983. *Late Roman fortifications* (London).

JONES, A. H. M. 1964. *The later Roman empire, 284–602* (Oxford, 1973 reprint).

JONES, A. H. M. 1966. *The decline of the ancient world* (London).

JONES, A. H. M. 1970. *Augustus* (London).

JONES, A. H. M. 1974. *The Roman economy*, ed. P. A. Brunt (Oxford).

JONES, G. D. B. 1962, 1963. 'Capena and the Ager Capenas', *PBSR* 30, 116–208; 31, 100–58.

JONES, G. D. B. 1980. 'Il Tavoliere romano. L'agricoltura romana attraverso l'aerofotografia e lo scavo', *Archeologia Classica* 32, 85–100.

JONES, P. J. 1974. 'La storia economica: dallo caduta dell'Impero romano al secolo XIV', *Storia d'Italia*, vol. 2, pt 2, 1469–681.

JUDSON, S. and KAHANE, A. 1963. 'Underground drainage-ways in southern Etruria and northern Latium', *PBSR* 31, 74–99.

KAHANE, A., MURRAY-THREIPLAND, L. and WARD-PERKINS, J. B. 1968. 'The Ager Veientanus north and east of Veii', *PBSR* 36, 1–218.

KENRICK, P. 1978. 'Arretine pottery – a changing scene', in Blake, Potter and Whitehouse 1978, 237–42.

KENT, J. P. C. 1978. *Roman coins* (London).

KEPPIE, L. J. F. 1983. *Colonisation and veteran settlement in Italy, 47–14 BC* (London).

KEPPIE, L. J. F. 1984. *The making of the Roman army* (London).

KEPPIE, L. J. F. 1984a. 'Colonisation and veteran settlement in Italy in the first century AD, *PBSR* 52, 77–114.

KING, A. 1983. 'Pottery', in Henig 1983, 179–90.

KISZELY, I. 1979. *The anthropology of the Lombards*. BAR S 61 (Oxford).

KOCKEL, V. *et al.* 1985. 'Archäologische Funde und Forschungen in den Vesuvstädten I', *Jahrbuch des Deutschen Archäologischen Institut, Berlin. Archäologischer Anzeiger* (1985), 495–571.

KOLENDO, J. 1980. *L'agricoltura nell'Italia romana: tecniche agrarie e progresso economico dalla tarda repubblica al principato* (Rome).

KRAUTHEIMER, R. 1980. *Rome. Profile of a city, 312–1308* (Princeton).

KRAUTHEIMER, R. 1981. *Early Christian and Byzantine architecture* (3rd edn, Harmondsworth).

KRAUTHEIMER, R. 1983. *Three Christian capitals. Topography and politics* (University of California).

LAMBOGLIA, N. 1952. 'La nave romana di Albenga', *Rivista di Studi Liguri* 18, 131–236.

LA REGINA, A. *et al.* 1980. *Sannio, Pentri e Frentani dal VI al I sec. a.c.* (Rome).

LÉQUÉMENT, R. and LIOU, B. 1975. 'Les épaves de la côtes de Transalpine', *Cahiers Ligures de préhistoire et d'archéologie* 24, 76f.

LING, R. 1984. 'The Insula of the Menander at Pompeii: interim report', *Antiquaries Journal* 63, 34–57.

LING, R. 1985. 'The mechanics of the building trade', in Grew and Hobley 1985, 14–27.

LLEWELLYN, P. 1971. *Rome in the Dark Ages* (London).

LLOYD, J. and BARKER, G. W. W. 1981. 'Rural settlement in Roman Molise: problems of archaeological survey', in Barker and Hodges 1981, 289–304.

LUGLI, G. 1957. *La tecnica edilizia romana con particolare riguardo a Roma* (2 vols, Rome).

MACDONALD, W. L. 1982. *The architecture of the Roman empire* (New Haven).

MACDOUGALL, E. B. and JASHEMSKI, W. F. 1981. *Ancient Roman gardens* (Dumbarton Oaks).

MACMULLEN, R. 1969. *Constantine* (New York).

MACMULLEN, R. 1970. 'Market days in the Roman empire', *Phoenix* 24, 333–41.

MACMULLEN, R. 1976. *Roman government's response to crisis* (New Haven).

MACMULLEN, R. 1981. *Paganism in the Roman world* (New Haven).

MAIURI, A. 1933. *La casa del Menandro e il suo tesoro di argenteria* (Rome).

MAIURI, A. 1956. *Capri: storia e monumenti* (Rome).

MAIURI, A. 1958. *The Phlegraean Fields* (3rd edn, Rome).

MALONE, C. and STODDART, S. (eds) 1985. *Papers in Italian archaeology IV: the Cambridge Conference*. BAR S 246, 4 vols (Oxford).

MANACORDA, D. 1978. 'The Ager Cosanus and the production of amphorae of Sestius: new evidence and a reassessment', *JRS* 68, 122–31.

MANNONI, T. and POLEGGI, E. 1977. 'The condition and study of historic town centres in north Italy', in M. W. Barley (ed.), *European towns. Their archaeology and early history* (London), 219–41.

MANSUELLI, G. A. 1962. *La villa romana di Russi* (Faenza).

MANSUELLI, G. A. 1970. *Architettura e città* (Bologna).

MANSUELLI, G. A. 1972. 'Marzabotto, dix années de fouilles et de recherches', *Mélanges de l'école française de Rome* 84, 111–44.

MANSUELLI, G. A. 1979. 'The Etruscan city', in Ridgway and Ridgway 1979, 353–71.

MARTINORI, E. 1929. *Via Flaminia* (Rome).

MAZZEI, M. (ed.) 1984. *La Daunia antica* (Milan).

McKAY, A. G. 1975. *Houses, villas and palaces in the Roman world* (London).

MEIGGS, R. 1973. *Roman Ostia* (2nd edn, Oxford).

MERTENS, J. 1969. *Alba Fucens*. Belgian Academy, 2 vols (Rome).

MERTENS, J. 1976, 1979. *Ordona v, vi*. Belgian Academy (Rome).

MERTENS, J. 1981. *Alba Fucens*. Centre belge de recherches archéologiques en Italie (Brussels).

MILLAR, F. 1977. *The emperor in the Roman world, 31 BC–AD 337* (London).

MOELLER, W. O. 1976. *The wool trade of ancient Pompeii* (Leiden).

MOMIGLIANO, A. 1963. 'An interim report on the origins of Rome', *JRS* 53, 95–121.

MOMIGLIANO, A. (ed.) 1963. *The conflict between paganism and Christianity in the fourth century* (Oxford).

MOREL, J. P. 1981. *Céramique campanienne: les formes*. Ecole française de Rome.

MORETTI, M. and MORETTI, A. M. S. 1977. *La villa dei Volusii a Lucus Feroniae (Rome)*.

MUCKELROY, K. (ed.) 1980. *Archaeology under water* (London).

NASH, E. 1968. *Topographical dictionary of ancient Rome* (2nd edn, London).

NICOLET, CL. 1977. *Les structures de l'Italie romaine* (Paris).

NISSEN, H. 1883, 1902. *Italische Landeskunde* (Berlin).

OGILVIE, R. M. 1969. *The Romans and their gods* (London).

OGILVIE, R. M. 1976. *Early Rome and the Etruscans* (Glasgow).

PACKER, J. E. 1971. *The insulae of imperial Ostia*. MAAR 36.

PAINTER, K. S. (ed.) 1980. *Roman villas in Italy* (London).

PALLOTTINO, M. 1975. *The Etruscans* (London).

PALLOTTINO, M. 1979. 'The origins of Rome: a survey of recent discoveries and discussions', in Ridgway and Ridgway 1979, 197–219.

PALLOTTINO, M. 1981. *Genti e culturi dell'Italia preromana* (Roma).

PALLOTTINO, M. 1984. *Storia della prima Italia* (Milan).

PANELLA, C. 1981. 'La distribuzione e i mercati', in Giardina and Schiavone 1981, 55–80.

PARTNER, P. 1966. 'Notes on the lands of the Roman church in the Middle Ages', *PBSR* 34, 68–78.

PATERSON, J. J. 1982. 'Salvation from the sea: amphorae and trade in the Roman West', *JRS* 72, 146–57.

PAULI, L. 1984. *The Alps. Archaeology and early history* (London).

PEACOCK, D. P. S. 1977. 'Recent discoveries of Roman amphora kilns in Italy', *Antiquaries Journal* 57, 262–9.

PEACOCK, D. P. S. 1982. *Pottery in the Roman world* (Harlow).

PEACOCK, D. P. S. and WILLIAMS, D. F. 1986. *Amphorae and the Roman economy* (London).

PEKÁRY, T. 1968. *Untersuchungen zu den römischen Reichsstrassen* (Bonn).

PERCIVAL, J. 1976. *The Roman villa* (London).

PERONI, R. *et al.* 1975. *Studi sulla cronologia delle civiltà di Este e Golasecca* (Florence).

PFLAUM, H. G. 1940. *Le Cursus Publicus sous le Haut-Empire*.

PHARR, C. 1952. *The Theodosian Code* (Princeton).

PLATNER, S. B. and ASHBY, T. 1929. *A topographical dictionary of ancient Rome* (Oxford).

POPOLI E CIVILTÀ 1974–8. *Popoli e civiltà dell'Italia antica*, 7 vols (Rome).

POTTER, T. W. 1979. *The changing landscape of south Etruria* (London).

POTTER, T. W. 1981. 'Marshland and drainage in the classical world', in R. T. Rowley (ed.), *The evolution of marshland landscapes* (Oxford), 1–19.

POTTER, T. W. 1984. 'Social evolution in Iron Age & Roman Italy', in J. Bintliff (ed.), *European Social Evolution* (Bradford), 235–44.

POTTER, T. W. 1985. 'The Republican healing sanctuary at Ponte di Nona near Rome, and the classical tradition of votive medicine, *JBAA* 138, 23–47.

POTTER, T. W. and DUNBABIN, K. M. 'A Roman villa at Crocicchie, Via Clodia', *PBSR* 47, 19–26.

POTTER, T. W. *et al.* 1984. 'Il castello di Ponte Nepesino e il confine settentrionale del ducato di Roma', *Archeologia Medievale* 11, 63–147.

POULTNEY, J. W. 1959. *Bronze tablets of Iguvium.* American Philological Association.

PRICE, J. 1976. 'Glass', in D. Strong and D. Brown (eds), *Roman crafts* (London), 111–26.

PRICE, J. 1983. 'Glass', in Henig 1983, 205–19.

PUCCI, G. 1973. 'La produzione della ceramica arretina', *Dialoghi di Archeologia* 7, 255f.

PUCCI, G. 1981. 'La ceramica italica (terra sigillata)', in Giardina and Schiavone 1981, 99–122.

PULGRAM, E. 1958. *The tongues of Italy* (Cambridge, Mass.).

PURCELL, N. 1985. 'Wine and wealth in ancient Italy', *JRS* 75, 1–19.

QUILICI, L. 1977. *Roma primitiva e le origini della civiltà laziale* (Rome).

RAINEY, F. G. and LERICI, C. M. 1967. *The search for Sybaris.* Lerici Foundation, University Museum, Philadelphia.

RATHBONE, D. W. 1981. 'The development of agriculture in the "Ager Cosanus" during the Roman Republic: problems of evidence and interpretation', *JRS* 71, 10–23.

RATHBONE, D. W. 1983. 'The slave mode of production in Italy', *JRS* 73, 160–8.

RAWSON, E. 1985. 'Theatrical life in Republican Rome and Italy', *PBSR* 53, 97–113.

REICH, J. 1979. *Italy before Rome* (Oxford).

RICHMOND, I. A. 1930. *The city wall of Imperial Rome* (Oxford).

RICHMOND, I. A. 1969. 'Aosta', in P. Salway (ed.), *Roman archaeology and art* (London), 249–59.

RICKMAN, G. E. 1980. *The corn supply of ancient Rome* (Oxford).

RICKMAN, G. E. 1980a. 'The grain trade under the Roman empire', in D'Arms and Kopff 1980, 261–76.

RIDGWAY, D. 1984. *Alba della Magna Grecia* (Milan).

RIDGWAY, D. and RIDGWAY, F. (eds) 1979. *Italy before the Romans* (London).

RIECHE, A. 1978. *Das antike Italien aus der Luft* (Bergisch Gladbach).

RILEY, J. A. 1981. 'Italy and the eastern Mediterranean in the Hellenistic and early Roman periods: the evidence of coarse pottery', in Barker and Hodges 1981, 69–78.

RODRIGUEZ-ALMEIDA, E. 1981. *Forma urbis marmorea: aggiornamento generale,* 2 vols (Rome).

RODRIGUEZ-ALMEIDA, E. 1984. *Il Monte Testaccio* (Rome).

ROSSITER, J. J. 1978. *Roman farm buildings in Italy.* BAR S 52 (Oxford).

ROSTOVTZEFF, M. 1957. *The social and economic history of the Roman empire* (2nd edn, revised P. M. Fraser, Oxford).

RUOFF-VÄÄNÄNEN, E. 1978. *Studies on the Italian fora* (Wiesbaden).

SALMON, E. T. 1967. *Samnium and the Samnites* (Cambridge).

SALMON, E. T. 1969. *Roman colonisation under the Republic* (London).

SALMON, E. T. 1982. *The making of Roman Italy* (London).

SANTORE, P. (ed.) 1978. *I Galli e l'Italia* (Rome).

SCHMIEDT, G. 1970. *Atlante aerofotografico delle sedi umane in Italia* (Florence).

SCULLARD, H. H. 1967. *The Etruscan cities and Rome* (London).

SCULLARD, H. H. 1976. *From the Gracchi to Nero* (4th edn, London).

SCULLARD, H. H. 1981. *Festivals and ceremonies of the Roman Republic* (London).

SCULLARD, H. H. 1982. *History of the Roman world 753–146 BC* (5th edn, London).

SEALEY, P. R. 1985. *Amphoras from the 1970 excavations at Colchester, Sheepen.* BAR, British Series 142 (Oxford).

SEAR, F. 1982. *Roman architecture* (London).

SESTIERI, A. M. BIETTI 1979. *Ricerca su una comunità del Lazio protostorico* (Rome).

SESTIERI, P. C. 1967. *Paestum* (8th edn, Rome).

SHERWIN-WHITE, A. N. 1973. *The Roman citizenship* (2nd edn). Oxford).

SIENA, S. L. *et al.* 1985. *Luni: guida archeologica.* Centro di Studi Lunese (Sarzana).

SMALL, A. M. 1977. *Monte Irsi, southern Italy.* BAR S 20 (Oxford).

SMALL, A. M. 1978. 'The *villa rustica* of the Hellenistic period in south Italy', in Blake, Potter and Whitehouse 1978, 192–202.

SMALL, A. M. 1980. 'San Giovanni di Ruoti: some problems in the interpretation of the evidence', in Painter 1980, 91–110.

SMALL, A. M. 1985. 'The early villa at San Giovanni', in Malone and Stoddart 1985, 4, 165–78.

SPURR, S. 1983. 'The cultivation of millet in Roman Italy', *PBSR* 51, 1–15.

STERPOS, D. 1970. *The Roman road in Italy.* Quaderni di Autostrade, 17.

STOCKTON, D. 1979. *The Gracchi* (Oxford).

TAVANO, S. 1948. *Aquileia. Guida dei monumenti cristiani* (Udine).

TCHERNIA, A. 1983. 'Italian wine in Gaul at the end of the Republic', in Garnsey *et al.* 1983, 87–104.

TCHERNIA, A., POMEY, P. and HESNARD, A. 1978. *L'épave romaine de la Madrague de Giens.* Gallia Supplement 34 (Paris).

THOMSEN, R. 1947. *The Italic regions from Augustus to the Lombard invasions* (1966 reprint, Copenhagen).

TILLEY, B. 1947. *Vergil's Latium* (Oxford).

TODD, M. 1978. *The walls of Rome* (London).

TODD, M. 1985. 'Forum and Capitolium in the early empire', in Grew and Hobley 1985, 56–66.

TOMLINSON, R. A. 1976. *Greek sanctuaries* (London).

TOZZI, P. 1972. *Storia padana antica: il territorio fra Adda e Mincio* (Milan).

TOZZI, P. 1974. *Saggi di topografia storica* (Florence).

TOUBERT, P. 1973. *Les structures du Latium mediéval.* Bibliothèque des Ecoles françaises d'Athènes et de Rome 221.

TOYNBEE, A. J. 1965. *Hannibal's legacy,* 2 vols (Oxford).

TOYNBEE, J. M. C. 1971. *Death and burial in the Roman world* (London).

TOYNBEE, J. M. C. and WARD-PERKINS, J. B. 1956. *The shrine of St Peter and the Vatican excavations* (London).

TURFA, J. 1986. 'Anatomical votive terracottas from Etruscan and Italic sanctuaries', in J. Swaddling (ed.), *Italian Iron Age artefacts in the British Museum* (London), 205–13.

UGGERI, G. and UGGERI, P. 1974. 'Topografia e urbanistica di Spina', *Studi Etruschi* 42, 69–97.

VAN DEMAN, E. B. 1934. *The building of the Roman aqueducts* (Washington).

VERMARESEN, M. J. 1963. *Mithras, the secret god* (London).

VERMARESEN, M. J. 1971. *The mithraeum at S. Maria Capua Vetere* (Leiden).

VERMARESEN, M. J. 1977. *Cybele and Attis. The myth and the cult* (London).

VERMARESEN, M. J. and VAN ESSEN, C. C. 1965. *The excavation in the mithraeum of the church of S. Prisca in Rome* (Leiden).

VITA-FINZI, C. 1969. *The Mediterranean valleys* (Cambridge).

WALKER, D. S. 1967. *A geography of Italy* (2nd edn, London).

WARD-PERKINS, B. 1978. 'Luni: the decline and abandonment of a Roman town', in Blake, Potter and Whitehouse 1978, 313–21.

WARD-PERKINS, B. 1981. 'Two Byzantine houses at Luni', *PBSR* 49, 91–8.

WARD-PERKINS, B. 1984. *From classical antiquity to the Middle Ages. Urban public building in northern and central Italy, AD 300–850* (Oxford).

WARD-PERKINS, J. B. 1955. 'The aqueduct of Aspendos', *PBSR* 23, 115–23.

WARD-PERKINS, J. B. 1961. 'Veii. The historical topography of the ancient city', *PBSR* 29, 1–123.

WARD-PERKINS, J. B. 1962. 'Etruscan engineering: road-building, water-supply and drainage', in J. M. Renard (ed.), *Hommages à*

Albert Grenier, Collection Latomus 58, 1636–43.

WARD-PERKINS, J. B. 1970. 'From Republic to Empire: reflections on the early provincial architecture of the Roman west', JRS 60, 1–9.

WARD-PERKINS, J. B. 1974. Cities of ancient Greece and Italy: planning in classical antiquity (New York).

WARD-PERKINS, J. B. 1977. Roman architecture (New York).

WARD-PERKINS, J. B. 1980. 'The marble trade and its organisation: evidence from Nicomedia', in D'Arms and Kopff 1980, 325–35.

WARD-PERKINS, J. B. 1980a. 'Nocomedia and the marble trade', PBSR 48, 23–69.

WARD-PERKINS, J. B. 1981. Roman imperial architecture (Harmondsworth).

WARD-PERKINS, J. B. and KAHANE, A. 1972. 'The Via Gabina', PBSR 40, 91–126.

WARDE-FOWLER, W. 1899. The Roman festivals of the period of the Republic (London).

WATSON, G. R. 1969. The Roman soldier (London).

WEINSTOCK, S. 1971. Divus Julius (Oxford).

WHATMOUGH, J. 1937. The foundations of Roman Italy (London).

WHITE, K. D. 1967. Agricultural implements of the Roman world (Cambridge).

WHITE, K. D. 1970. Roman farming (London).

WHITEHOUSE, D. B. 1981. 'The Schola Praeconum and the food supply of Rome in the fifth century AD', in Barker and Hodges 1981, 191–6.

WHITEHOUSE, D. B. et al. 1982, 1985. 'The Schola Praeconum', I, II, PBSR 50, 53–101; 53, 163–210.

WHITEHOUSE, D. B. and POTTER, T. W. 1981. 'The Byzantine frontier in south Etruria', Antiquity 55, 206–10.

WHITEHOUSE, R. D. 1973. 'The earliest towns in peninsular Italy', in C. Renfrew (ed.), The explanation of culture change (London), 617–24.

WHITEHOUSE, R. D. 1979. 'Trulli in south-east Italy', Antiquity 53, 152.

WHITTAKER, C. R. 1976. 'Agri deserti', in Finley 1976, 137–65.

WHITTAKER, C. R. 1983. 'Late Roman trade and traders', in Garnsey et al. 1983, 163–80.

WICKHAM, C. J. 1979. 'Historical and topographical notes on early medieval south Etruria', PBSR 47, 66–95.

WICKHAM, C. J. 1981. Early medieval Italy. Central power and local society 400–1000 (London).

WIDRIG, W. M. 1980. 'Two sites on the ancient Via Gabina', in Painter 1980, 119–40.

WILLIAMS, S. 1985. Diocletian and the Roman recovery (London).

WILSON, R. J. A. 1983. Piazza Armerina (London).

WISEMAN, P. 1970. 'Roman Republican road building', PBSR 38, 122–52.

WITT, R. E. 1971. Isis in the Graeco-Roman world (London).

ZANKER, P. (ed.) 1976. Hellenismus in Mittelitalien (Groningen).

Photographic acknowledgements

The author and publishers gratefully acknowledge the following for providing illustrations:

British Museum half-title page, pp. 56, 78, 95 (bottom), 155, 159, 162, 164, 165, 167, 178, 188, 189, col. pl. 7

British School at Rome pp. 20, 78

G. P. Brogiolo (Soprintendenza all'Antichità di Lombardia) p. 11

Barri Jones pp. 102, 103

Simon Keay col. pl. 9

André Tchernia (Centre National de la Recherche Scientifique) p. 156

John Ward-Perkins (via British School at Rome) pp. 35, 46, 132

Roger Wilson pp. 25, 31, 55, 58, 82, 83, 122, 128, 137

All other photographs are the copyright of the author.

The maps were drawn by Stephen Crummy, all other line drawings are by the author.

INDEX

References in italic type are to pages with illustrations